FAT GUYS SHOULDN'T
BE DANCIN' *at Halftime*

FAT GUYS SHOULDN'T BE DANCIN' *at Halftime*

An IRREVERENT ROMP *Through* CHICAGO SPORTS

CHET COPPOCK

TRIUMPH
BOOKS

Triumph Books and colophon are registered trademarks of Random House, Inc.

Library of Congress Cataloging-in-Publication Data

Coppock, Chet, 1948–
    Fat guys shouldn't be dancin' at halftime : an irreverent romp through Chicago sports / Chet Coppock.
        p. cm.
    ISBN 978-1-60078-269-5
        1. Sports—Illinois—Chicago—History. 2. Sports spectators—Illinois—Chicago. 3. Chicago (Ill.)—Social life and customs. I. Title.
    GV584.5.C4C67 2009
    796.0977311—dc22
                                                                    2009025773

This book is available in quantity at special discounts for your group or organization. For further information, contact:

Triumph Books
542 South Dearborn Street
Suite 750
Chicago, Illinois 60605
(312) 939–3330
Fax (312) 663–3557
www.triumphbooks.com

Printed in U.S.A.
ISBN: 978-1-60078-269-5

Design and page production by Amy Flammang-Carter

Photos courtesy of the author unless otherwise indicated

CONTENTS

FOREWORD

Long before the annoying army of generic cable bobbleheads yukked their way through the nightly highlights like Top-40 DJs on crack, there was Chet Coppock. The self-proclaimed "Circus Barker of Sports," Chet was a showman through and through with an uncanny knack for knowing exactly what the people wanted. Whether it was the Super Bowl, the World Series, or the NBA Finals, he treated every "hallowed" event the same way…like pro wrestling. Chet flourished during the golden age of television, the ostentatious '80s. His full-length fur coat served as the AstroTurf of sports journalism.

Back then, news directors and general managers expected you to actually break stories. If you didn't have a camera at Halas Hall every day to get Mike Ditka roller-skating down the hallways or Walter Payton shooting birds out of trees, you were beaten. Leagues and franchises allowed more access to players. The controlled, sterilized news conferences and the propaganda-filled satellite handout feeds simply didn't exist. It was all about competition. Coppock's personal and sometimes petty wars with Johnny Morris and Tim Weigel played out weekly in the newspapers (remember newspapers?). He once told me, "Markie, if you don't love this job, it'll eat you alive." I've never forgotten that.

Just as the sounds of the '60s and '70s created the base for all music today, Chet's go-for-broke, tabloid approach to covering sports set the tone for modern-day media. It was a wild-and-wooly time. I still cringe with the memory of being the terrified passenger in Chester's vanity-plated, custom Cadillac as he raced to make a live-shot at the old Chicago Stadium…driving on the sidewalk!

When NBC decided "The Big Guy" was too much to deal with, he reinvented himself as the godfather of a new medium that seemed to be created especially for him: sports talk radio. His stream of consciousness (or unconsciousness) could fill a day's worth of programming. The way he pulled the listener into the tent and teed-up guests like they were the biggest box-office celebs of all time was amazing. So, curl up in a nice faux fur and give this pile of pulp-reality a read. If you don't love it, it'll eat you alive!

—Mark Giangreco

FOREWORD

To Carl Sandburg, Chicago was the "hog butcher for the world/tool maker/stacker of wheat/player with railroads and the nation's freight handler." But to Chicago sports fans, it is much more. It is the home of Da Bears, the Cubbies, the ChiSox, the Bulls, the Blackhawks, and a laundry list of some of the most memorable athletes in sports history—athletes who could take their place on the field and make any dues-paying Chicago fan feel good.

Unlike most other cities, Chicago is a place where millions upon millions—in the suburbs, the exurbs, throughout the Midwest—are rooted to and root for their teams and their heroes with a fanaticism that goes almost back to the time when Adam first heard the stampede of the apple salesman. Stories of their exploits have been told and retold over the dying embers of campfires for as long as such stories have been told—and are recycled by those who haven't fallen over under the weight of advancing age.

Who can ever forget, for instance, the linked names of Tinker, Evers, and Chance, three-quarters of the Cubbies' World Series–winning teams of 1907 and 1908? Or ChiSox heroes such as "Bullfrog" Bill Dietrich, "Fats" Fothergill, or Zeke "Banana Nose" Bonura? Or the Bears' "Monsters of the Midway?" Or any one of a thousand other sports heroes whose names echo down the long corridor of Chicago sports history?

Leave it to Chet Coppock, long the voice of Chicago sports, who now puts pen to paper to chronicle this story in his own unique way. He thus joins the ranks of Chicago sportswriters who have worn down a carload of pencils to the nubs writing about the city's sports scene. Even as many of those in the writing fraternity might be forced to mutter, "Forgive us our press passes" at his entry into the writing field, I can only say, "Welcome, Chet, it's great to have you." Here's to many more such efforts.

—Bert Sugar

PREFACE

Before we get rolling I've got to get this off my chest. Don't blame Conrad "Baby Madoff" Black and his hapless bride Lady Blackster for all the troubles the *Chicago Sun-Times* has been forced to endure. Keep in mind, I spent a full year as a Sunday columnist for the *Sun-Times* back in 1993. My majestic presence didn't exactly bust circulation records.

Anyway, you've heard this before, but in my case it's on the square. My old man gave me a great appreciation for newspaper writers, deadlines, and gin mills with 4:00 AM licenses. We never did talk much about the Cub Scouts or how to tie a square knot.

I've always stood in admiration of Grantland Rice, Ring Lardner, John Carmichael, Warren Brown, Mike Royko, David Nightengale, Jack Griffin, Ed Stone, David Condon, Bob Verdi, David Israel, Bert Randolph Sugar, Dick Young, Jim Murray, Rick Telander, David Haugh, Chris De Luca, Mark Gonzales, Phil Hersh, Lester Munson, John Jackson, Dave Van Dyck, and Paul Sullivan. Superb writers and reporters.

I hope this book doesn't irritate the scribes too much. I'm not here to invade or redefine. I just want to have some fun and poke some fun.

Yes, Jack Brickhouse will always be "The Voice of Chicago." I can only hope the Brick, wherever he may be, knows how much I love and miss him. I still think about his charm, drive, and personality virtually every day. And, Jack, your WGN sidekick Jack Rosenberg wanted me to mention that you were the greatest gin rummy pigeon he ever knew.

To the scribes and both Jacks, I offer a salute of complete respect.

This book, right, wrong, or swing-and-a-miss, belongs to all you guys—fellows who prowled the old Pink Poodle at Wrigley Field, the Bards Room at the Old Roman's Comiskey Park. It's done in tribute to those nails-tough writers who sat in that cramped prison cell of a football press box when the Bears called Cubs Park their home. It is written for those storytellers who occupied the old hockey press box on the west end of Chicago Stadium.

Guys, one and all, and many I have failed to mention, you're the main-eventers.

Now dim the house lights, raise the curtain, and please observe the No Smoking sign.

Let's see if this sucker is destined for greatness or the 10-cent bin.

—Chet Coppock
June 2009

ACKNOWLEDGMENTS

Personally, I would never have trusted me to write a book. Then again, over the years, my MasterCard bill has proven I shouldn't be trusted to do anything.

I owe a big shout-out to Mitch Rogatz, the front man at Triumph. The biggest salute I can give Mitch is to tell you he's every bit as classy as his father, the late Chicago sportscaster Bruce Roberts. Bruce was beyond a hero to me.

Don Gulbrandsen, my blocking back on this project, was the guy who kept me laughing when my word count reached 100,000. Hey, with ten more chapters, this book could have been the Old Testament.

Tyler and Lyndsey, my two wonderful kids, will understand the book for one reason. They know their old man is cockeyed...but basically harmless.

Suzy, thanks for enduring those nights when I felt brain-dead from exhaustion...and thanks for your steady stream of ideas.

My old man, Charlie Coppock, was a hustler, a businessman, and a friend to numerous Chicago sports figures. His love of sports had me gripped in a headlock by the time I was seven. Dad always told me, "It matters not who wins or loses but how the beer men did before the eighth inning."

This has been a labor of love. I absolutely plan to do a follow-up. Suggestions are welcome.

How about: *Is That You Out There, Sam Zell?*

FAT GUYS SHOULDN'T

BE DANCIN' *at Halftime*

GRIDIRON
Grumblings

1 *Chicago, table the addiction to the* 1985 CHICAGO BEARS

"Probably the most bizarre, outlandish request we got during the '85 season was when a women's magazine called and wanted to do a feature on William Perry and the possibility of male pregnancy."
—Kenny Valdiserri, former P.R. chief for the Bears

I know I'm going to break a few hearts with this pitch. Women, feel no shame in crying, but this is six, maybe eight years overdue. Chicago, the time has come to give up the "addiction" to the most raucous, outrageous, flamboyant, defiant collection of football rogues ever assembled under one tent, the mercurial Super Bowl XX Champion Bears.

Speaking of which, by XX standards, the Bears bumped off the New England Patriots 46–10 on an undercard that featured the French army beating Spain in the unforgettable Battle of Cerignola. It goes without saying that most of you know Cerignola began as a bitter dispute over Olympic drug testing and TV rights to *Friday Night SmackDown.*

No, you don't have to go cold turkey. This isn't Betty Ford Med Center for the rich and famous.

The next time the Bears advance to the NFC Championship Game, you may remind yourself that somehow, Michael McCaskey, the hunky president of the Bears, was chosen *Sporting News* NFL Executive of the Year in '85. Michael sneaked off with the hardware while Mike Ditka and Buddy Ryan beat each other up all the way to the Vince Lombardi Trophy.

McCaskey? NFL Executive of the Year? You talk about a hometown squeeze. That still rates as the biggest local fix since "Mooney" Giancana and his delightful throng of mob head-busters put Cook County in the John F. Kennedy column in November 1960, when JFK edged Richard Nixon.

Here's my game plan, and I expect full bipartisan support.

Henceforth, and forever, no Bears pass rusher will be compared to Richard Dent.

No left tackle will be mentioned in the same breath with Jimbo Covert until he competes in three Pro Bowls.

When the Bears come up with a three-and-out, no references will be made to Wilber Marshall's 52-yard run to the house off a fumble recovery against the

Mike Ditka was cool as a cucumber during his radio show the night before Super Bowl XX sealed the place of the 1985 Bears in history. (Coppock? Not so much.) On the left is former Bear and Ditka teammate Mike Pyle.

Los Angeles Rams in the NFC Championship Game victory that catapulted the Bears to New Orleans.

Are you getting in rhythm?

By law, Jeff Joniak, the Bears' hometown screamer, will not be permitted to shriek "Bob Babich, you are ridiculous."

Recollections of the banner year will cease—except on Fridays. A 20-minute window will be allowed for fans to recall the Bears creaming Dallas 44–0 during the '85 regular season. I do that only for sentimental reasons: I had the Bears and the over.

The misdirection play: The Honey Bears will be hauled out of storage while Staley, the Bears' hopeless mascot, will be instructed to begin walking west on Roosevelt Road until he reaches either Moline or Muscatine, Iowa.

We will put the lid on early season euphoria. No talking about "This is speedy Willie and I'm world-class…I like running, but I love to get the pass" when the Bears come surging out of the blocks 1–0.

Know what I mean? Go back to September 7, 2008. The Bears, led by Matt Forte's 123 rushing yards, clobbered the Indy Colts 29–13. By 11:00 that night, Forte was the second coming of Walter Payton.

It didn't matter that the Colts were pathetically banged up or that Peyton Manning had about three hours of practice time during the preseason, these 2008 Bears were a lock to go no worse than 14–2. The next morning, you couldn't ride a 151 bus or the Red Line without hearing that time-honored catch phrase, "These guys might be better than the '85 club."

These "Might Be Betters" closed the year 9-7, courtesy of two games with the Detroit Lions, Motown's most popular little league team. Anybody who knows football knows the '08 Bears backed their way out of the postseason.

Wait a minute. You thought the '70s were screwed up? It's Academy Awards time and I'm watching one of those inane red carpet warm-up shows. Up steps my hero, Mickey Rourke, Hollywood's answer to Lazarus. Naturally, some clown with syrup for brains starts chatting with the Mick. Does the "interviewer" ask about the energy he brought to *The Wrestler* or the tragedy of the Mick's character, Randy "The Ram" Robinson?

No. This psycho ward candidate asks O'Rourke who *designed* his suit. Just sensational, this guy would probably ask a group of welders if they prefer escargot to backgammon.

If I want you to drop the addiction, I guess I have to wean you off the '85 memories.

Here's the grinder: We will only deify Mike Ditka four days a week. Iron Mike's popularity continues to blow the charts from State and Madison to Benton Harbor, Michigan. Wasn't it just 12 years ago that Mike went through his dark "take this job and shove it" period as head coach of the New Orleans Saints?

Really, isn't something awry when Ditka's 1988 heart attack still gets more play than any current Bears defensive back? I was frankly knocked off the bar stool when Mike didn't win a Golden Globe in 2006 for his work opposite Will Ferrell in the romantic thriller *Kicking and Screaming*. Twenty-four years after his victory in the Super Bowl, Ditka still turns down no more than 300 speaking engagements a year.

Let's put it in these terms—Mike's so damn big in this town that if he were booked on six counts of arson, Richie Daley would personally hand-deliver bail money. Richie knows you can screw the folks in Bucktown, but you can't screw Ditka.

Mike can do no wrong because—and this, students, is the crux of the matter—our teams seldom know what day it is, let alone win anything of consequence. Throw out the "Jordan-Six" and Chicago's major sports franchises have won a grand total of four World Championships since 1961. Hawks—1. Bears—2. Ozzie Guillen—1.

You're right, those numbers correspond to Felix Pie's "can't-miss" career with Jim Hendry and the Cubs.

> *"More than any club in history, the '85 Bears coined the phrase 'sports marketing.'"*
> —Kenny Valdiserri

Kenny just nailed it. Prior to '85, the Bears' idea of a streamlined marketing blitz was lining up a bank or a wholesale furniture outlet to buy the back cover of its press guide. Do you see where I'm going? The '85 Bears were fuckin' delicious. But a generation and change has come and gone.

I love "Mongo," "Hamp," "Silky D," and the "Mamma's Boy Otis," but do we have to bring them up every time the Bears lead the Vikings 13–7 at halftime?

Saturday Night Live didn't debut Joe Mantegna's "Da Bears" routine three weeks ago. That bit got started in 1991.

Take note: It was our pal Michael Keller Ditka who said, "The past is for cowards." Mike reminds you his Chestnut Street restaurant kicks major-league tail. Mike reminds you he can be seen weekly—almost hourly—on ESPN during the autumn. Mike reminds you that he has set records for banquet turnouts and attendance at corporate golf outings.

Mike, answer this question: Aren't we all just too wrapped up in that one-year, snow-shower of football energy? I'm sorry, I withdraw the question. The answer is obvious.

2 Rally sons of NOTRE DAME: See the Fighting Irish come bursting out of the TUNNEL at historic N.D. STADIUM

> *"The only thing worse than a dead drunk Notre Dame fan is a dead drunk Notre Dame fan when we don't cover."*
> —Unnamed alumnus, class of '64

Notre Dame is an easy target for laughs—cheap laughs. The school would like to believe it invented football. And its alums on the wrong day can be a little too zealous, a little too arrogant, and just too darn full of Knute Rockne for their own good.

But here's why I love the Irish faithful. They put their money where their mouth is. Check the box office. Notre Dame has sold out 254 of its last 255 home games. The only swing-and-a-miss during this sold-out run was a Thanksgiving Day ballgame versus Air Force—not exactly Celine Dion at Caesar's Palace—back in 1974. So why didn't that game go clean? C'mon, too easy. The students were off-campus due to the holiday break.

Plus, three days before the end of any given season, they're already worried about who'll quarterback the team two years down the road.

> *"My first game at Note Dame, I was so nervous I threw up as I got set to run through the tunnel. It was a feeling of exhilaration... nervousness that I've never experience since."*
> —Aaron Taylor, Lombardi Award winner and consensus
> All-American defensive tackle at Notre Dame

Time out, A.T. I have to get the crowd warmed up for the main event.

A Saturday trip to watch Notre Dame is a full-blown "experience"—an experience that even people who think football is Neanderthal will find a way to love. It is not in the same league with childbirth but, damn, it has a flavor, a rush, a uniqueness all its own.

Pick a day in mid-October. The leaves are changing. The campus greenery is giving way to the colors of autumn, and the booze at roughly 5,000 tailgate parties could quench the thirst of the U.S. Marines.

You don't go to N.D. just to see the kickoff. You go to see the history, the tradition. Visit the Rockne Monument. I swear if you stare at the "Rock" for about 20 seconds, you get the impression he's daring you to blink. Naturally, you get photos with the Golden Dome and Touchdown Jesus in the background. Just walking the quad between the campus dorm rooms has its own special flavor.

Trust me. You won't find this kind of energy in Champaign-Urbana, East Lansing, or Raleigh, North Carolina.

Check out the Notre Dame band as it marches into N.D. Stadium. Visit the campus book shop. Count the scalpers.

Forget about the fact that Notre Dame finally won its first bowl game—beating Hawaii in the Hawaii Bowl—in December 2008 to end a 14-year swoon without a postseason victory. Tickets are golden. To get an N.D. ticket, you generally have to have a sister-in-law who works for this guy who's a friend of an auto parts dealer who sat with a CEO at a banquet where Lou Holtz was the keynote speaker. Alums beg to remain on the N.D. ticket list.

But back to the atmosphere. Most of all, the crème de la crème is watching the waves of blue-and-gold clad Notre Dame players surging out of the tunnel on to the emerald-green turf before the kickoff. It's breathtaking. If your grandfather was born in Ireland and you wouldn't dream of missing a St. Patrick's Day parade, it's even money that you'll break down crying.

It's not leaps and bounds better than the Bears running through that ugly inflated inner tube at Soldier Field—it's no contest. Side note: That inflated Bear should be given a one-way ticket to oblivion. Its appeal is nonexistent.

"The last time I ran through the tunnel, I was crying."
—Aaron Taylor, reflecting on his final home game as an N.D. player

Aaron is hardly unusual. Virtually ever N.D. player I've ever talked to about the tunnel gets weepy talking about the tunnel. The handful that don't are the kind of guys who think Dick Cheney was just a fabulous vice president.

The tunnel is the personification of the Notre Dame football experience. Its incremental value to N.D. just can't be measured. Sometimes I think it's half the reason NBC wouldn't dream of giving up its N.D. football package. I have no doubt it moves wealthy alums to dig deeper in their wallets to contribute to the school's massive endowment fund. (Contest time: Find a poor N.D. alum.)

I've seen the "tunnel" too many times and I still get the proverbial chills. The only thing comparable? Two great heavyweights with their handlers and hangers-on walking to ringside for a major heavyweight title fight. And let's get real. We haven't seen any big-time heavys go to war since Evander Holyfield was about 33 years old.

Experience the tunnel. Allow yourself to feel the vibes of N.D. Stadium, a ballpark Rockne helped design, a ballpark with the best sight lines in college football. Think about Paul Hornung, John Huarte, Tim Brown, and others who've grabbed the John W. Heisman Trophy while playing ball at N.D. Think about Frank Leahy, Ara "The Era of Ara" Parseghian, Dan Devine, and Lou Holtz—all Hall of Fame coaches.

The game itself may feel secondary. Sometimes it is. But give this one item high priority on your list: See the Irish running out of the tunnel.

"When we ran out of the tunnel…after touching the 'Play Like a Champion Today' sign at the bottom of our locker room, we knew we were playing big-time football."

—Aaron Taylor

3 *Attend a* NORTHWESTERN *football game. Please!*

Think about a gorgeous autumn Saturday. The leaves are changing and green has given way to red, gold, and various shades of yellow. Crisp air combines with a gorgeous blue sky.

God, am I a poet.

What have you got? A great day to rake the leaves? Fuuugggeeeddabout it. It's a great day to attend a Northwestern football game. Don't worry about a box-office crush. The Wildcats generally lead the Big 10 in two categories: empty seats and rival fans equaling or outnumbering the Northwestern faithful at Ryan Field.

You talk about box-office misery. This is so disgraceful it should qualify for the obituaries. N.U. closed its 2008 home schedule and recorded its ninth win—that's NINTH win—by knocking off downstate rival Illinois 27–10. The game drew a whopping 32,000 fans. You're right. Northwestern doesn't need new tackling dummies, a weight room, or shoulder pads. It needs John McDonough.

Thirty-two thou for a ballgame with Illinois, a successful bid for nine wins, and about 40 percent of the crowd was wearing orange. Northwestern is obviously taking journalism and the Kellogg School of Management much too seriously.

Years ago, a local TV buddy told me Northwestern's problem was basically simple. He said he was convinced that 75 percent of the people in the nine-county area didn't know where the school is. I'd have to bump that a step further. I'm convinced that 85 percent don't know or care if the school's in the western hemisphere.

So what's the problem? Northwestern really has no one to blame but itself. Ryan Field is a decent, if not a "new age," ballpark that's a quick drive from downtown Chicago or downtown Deerfield. The school has the Big 10 pedigree and its average alum wouldn't be caught dead driving anything less than a five-series BMW. You want more? "GO U Northwestern" is a rousing fight song.

Attendance is such a dirty word in Evanston that the Wildcats football press guide doesn't even carry a section about crowd counts over the years. Would you?

Conversely, look at Notre Dame. The Irish can't get five lines into a press release without telling you that their football team has filled N.D. Stadium 254 times over its last 255 games.

I know by now you just can't wait to read my favorite Northwestern memories.

1. This goes back a few days. I was in old Dyche Stadium—yes the joint was Dyche (as in "dike") before it was renamed Ryan Field (it's amazing what money can do)—way back in 1958 when a young and hugely charismatic Ara Paraseghian led Northwestern to a 55–24 victory over Michigan. The slaughter rule should have been put in play at halftime. After two quarters, Team Ara led the Maize and Blue by the outrageous score of 43–0.

2. This is really perverse. This tells you my mind is in the gutter. November 7, 1981: Michigan State roasted the Wildcats 61–14 before a crowd of around 16,000 people. It was the 'Cats' 33rd consecutive loss, which set a bundle of records for futility. But give those N.U. students their props. Late in the game they began marching north to south down the Northwestern side of the field chanting, "We're number one"…along with "we are the worst." For kicks, the kids also tore down the goal posts.

I have to mention this. Muddy Waters, the Michigan State coach, came up with one of the single most classless acts I've ever seen on any kind of playing surface. Deep in the fourth quarter with the Spartans just crushing N.U.'s rib cage, he dared to run a double reverse. A double reverse? Major violation of the coaching code. If N.U. coach Denny Green would have had access to a tire iron, I have no doubt he would have left Muddy face down in Lake Michigan.

So back to our original conversation: Who's to blame for Northwestern's lack of fan interest? How about Northwestern? The school has never done anything to really sell its product to the Chicago media or guys in Cicero and Naperville who might just want to see Ohio State or Michigan or Iowa face "purple pride."

N.U. lives in a league of elitism. Convinced that because Charlton Heston, noted actor and gun freak, attended their school, the world owes them a sellout. When the 'Cats do try to hustle their footballers, they generally come up with lifeless slogans like "Go Wild."

Go see a Northwestern football game. Remember, if you don't there's a hell of a chance that nobody else will either.

Timeout: Second guessers, we can't blame Northwestern's second-rate football status on an endless string of lousy field generals. In addition to Ara, the 'Cats were directed by the legendary Lynn "Pappy" Waldorf, who was selected conference coach of the year back in 1935. A con? Hell no—just one year later old Pap led Northwestern to a league title.

However, that achievement doesn't get headline treatment in Waldorf's bio. Pappy is best remembered for his brilliance with the California Golden Bears during the postwar years. But Pappy did carry a little bit of Northwestern in his back pocket out to Berkeley. His 1948, '49, and '50 clubs all got knocked off in the Rose Bowl.

That is just so Northwestern.

4 The great Chicago tradition: Boo a BEARS QUARTERBACK

> *"Fans around here boo quarterbacks because they've seen great running backs...Payton...Gale [Sayers] working with guys who couldn't give them any assistance."*
> —Tom Thayer, starting guard on the 1985 Bears

Tom is being much too generous. Every town has certain traditions. In New York, fans boo lousy plays on Broadway and the Triborough Bridge. Fans in Lincoln, Nebraska, boo the Cornhuskers for the obvious reason: What else is there to boo in Lincoln unless the Dairy Queen hikes the tab on banana splits 15 cents?

Ah, but in Chicago we have been booing quarterbacks since FDR was in plus-fours.

> *Who doesn't recall the brilliance of P.T. Willis, Will Furrer, Vince Evans, or the immortal Larry Rakestraw?*

If you're a Chicagoan and you have a little guy, you have to tell him the facts of life by the time he's three years old: 1. Never play head-to-head gin with a guy named Rocky; 2. Make the call: Cubs or White Sox—no in between; 3. Understand that some ethereal being placed quarterbacks in Chicago for one reason: to be jeered until their craniums burst.

Inner-city law should require all Bears fans to attend a game at Soldier Field just to boo a quarterback.

God, I've seen brutality—that's brutality over six decades. You think Rex Grossman was treated worse than dirt? Do you remember Bob Avellini? He got booed at the Burger King drive-through window. I honest to gosh believe that slo-mo Bob took the booing so personally—and with strong justification—that 24 years after his last game with the Bears, Robert still wishes he'd been blessed to be a Kansas City Chief, a Houston Oiler…hell, even a Winnipeg Blue Bomber.

Bob took it verbally and he took it physically. The Bears got burned by the Lions in Pontiac on Opening Day, September 12, 1982. By game's end, Bob looked worse than Joe Frazier after he lost to Ali in Manila. Avellini had at least seven face cuts. He looked like he'd been given a French kiss from a mountain lion, but he did get one break. It was a road game, so at least he didn't get booed.

Is that you out there Kordell "The Savior" Stewart, Zeke Bratkowski, Henry Burris, and Shane Matthews?

> *"Rusty played such lousy football he was afraid to get on board the team plane after the game."*
> —Kenny Valdiserri, longtime Bears P.R. man recalling one
> of Rusty Lisch's abysmal road performances during
> his one-year run with the Bears back in 1984

You think Lisch wasn't a water hazard? He closed his cameo in Halas blue and orange in '84 without a touchdown pass but, by gosh, he did have six interceptions. Those just scream Bears numbers. The kid's ears were like Silly Putty by season's end. What Johnathan Quinn was to the 21st century Bears, Lisch was to the mid-1980s Bears. I swear there were days I thought Dan Hampton might leave his teeth on the locker room floor.

Jim Harbaugh was just massacred. Mike Tomczak, a local kid, was fried. Following one effort that had 55,000 fans busting their lungs in anger, T-zak told me, "the fans can kiss my ass." Frankly, I thought Mike showed tremendous composure.

But no QB in Chicago history ever got roasted as badly as Bobby Douglass. Bobby was really a reality series that nobody ever got around to producing. He joined the Bears in '69 out of Kansas and immediately decided Rush Street was a helluva lot more fun than a playbook. Head Coach Jim Dooley once spent three nights at Bobby's Old Town crib prepping him for a ballgame with Detroit.

Now, here's a keeper. If Douglass had been a running back, a tight end, a weak-side linebacker, or a strong safety he would've been brilliant. He was a 230-pound physical freak. But George Halas refused to green-light Dooley to play Douglass anywhere but back of center.

The results? Bobby, surrounded by miserable talent, looked good about once every six games. Maybe.

You think this guy didn't carry the Bears? In 1972, playing a 14-game schedule, Bobby rushed for 968 yards, a QB record that stood up for 34 years until Michael Vick, playing 16 games, toppled Bobby's mark. The number two rusher on the '72 Bears, a lost soul named Jim Harrison, managed 622 yards.

Bobby also married a Playboy Playmate.

Douglass was invariably locked in a QB controversy with either Jack Concannon, Virgil Carter, Kent Nix, or Gary Huff. Whichever QB wasn't playing was the fans' flavor of the week. When Bobby was waived by Jim Finks one game into the 1975 season, he had to feel like he'd skipped out on Enron before the feds got wise.

Now, let's clear up a misconception. Don't buy this crap that the Bears haven't had a decent QB since Sid Luckman retired back in 1950. They have. Eddie Brown, a big, angular kid from San Francisco, was special. Before Halas screwed with his head, Brown was an All-Pro thee consecutive years beginning in 1954.

Have we all forgotten Jim McMahon? The sucker didn't need a coach. He could zip through game film in his sleep. His ability to break down defensive sets during the pre-snap was damn near as good as that of a Peyton Manning. If the Punky QB could've avoided the infirmary, he would have won multiple Super Bowls and earned a yellow Hall of Fame blazer from the folks in Canton.

My favorite Bears QB moment: Vince Evans actually did throw the ball in the stands in Pontiac against the Lions in 1981. The moment so inspired the Bears that they went on to get licked 45–17.

So all you young Jimmys and Joes: Rag on the old man. Get him to tap a scalper and go to Bears game. Life is incomplete until you've booed a hometown QB.

Jay will understand.

5 Visit pro football's answer to the Vatican: LAMBEAU FIELD

"We could never sell naming right to our stadium. It would be a mortal sin."

—Bob Harlan, Chairman Emeritus, the Green Bay Packers, and the nicest guy in the world

You talk about fast company. Bob's "plaque of honor" sits between statues of Curly Lambeau and Vince Lombardi in the Robert E. Harlan Plaza at the entrance to Lambeau Field.

Okay, before we begin the tour, I have to clear up a misconception. It drives me nuts when I hear people say that Gale Sayers' six-touchdown performance on December 12, 1965, against the 49ers was his greatest career achievement.

It wasn't.

Bump the clock to November 3, 1968. Gale rushed for 205 punishing yards at Lambeau to help lift the Bears over the Pack 13–10. That was the elixir. That was the essence of why Gale, the greatest open-field runner in NFL history, needed just 68 games to grab a ticket and a bust at the Pro Football Hall of Fame in Canton, Ohio.

Side note: One of the dumbest things I've ever heard was Hub Arkush, the ex-Bears color announcer and front man for *Pro Football Weekly*, telling me he thought Sayers was overrated. Yeah, so was Elvis Presley. So was Marlon Brando.

Things you don't know about Lambeau Field: In 1955–56, the Pack were on death's door. The franchise, playing out of old City Stadium—a glorified high-school ballpark—was on the respirator. Papa Bear George Halas spent a great deal of time, while the Pack was being readied for the mortuary, traveling to Titletown, pushing the city fathers to build a new stadium. The old man knew, in a changing climate, that the charm of this small-town franchise in the northland was invaluable.

So the old man goes out of his way to preserve football in Titletown. What was Halas' reward? The Pack knocked off the Bears 21–17 in the 1957 dedication game for the new stadium before a crowd that included Vice President Richard Nixon.

> *"George was very instrumental in helping us get our stadium built. We can never lose sight of that fact. George always put the league first."*
>
> —Bob Harlan

I still miss the old Northland Hotel in downtown Green Bay. You had to see the nondescript building where the Bears used to bunk before their annual appearance in Green Bay. The bar featured a husband-and-wife accordion team. Honest, so help me Mike Holmgren.

And plastered Packer fans had this delightful habit of banging the fire alarm at about 3:00 in the morning. Who needs the Grand Canyon, the Eiffel

Tower, or the Hancock Building? Witnessing beloved Bears player and coach Abe Gibron, carrying around 350 pounds, walking around at 3:00 AM in his underwear and screaming four-letter words about Packer-backers was kind of like seeing Niagara Falls for the first time. If you weren't overwhelmed, you should have been.

Here's your travel plan: Bring money! Friday, begin the journey to Lambeau with a stop in Kohler, Wisconsin, to play the fabulous Whistling Straits golf course. It's an Irish/Scottish links-style course on the edge of Lake Michigan. I could play the 8th hole forever—and usually do.

There's only one drawback. Get used to four, maybe five guys telling you before you tee off to keep your cart on the path. It finally dawned me on me why the rangers are so protective of their baby: They haven't got anything else to do besides wait for the next Friday fish fry.

Saturday, cruise to 1265 Lombardi Avenue. Pull into the parking lot at Lambeau Field. Notice the old '50s-style bungalow homes. They only enhance the Norman Rockwell perspective. Visit the Packers Hall of Fame. Feel the storied history of Johnny "Blood" McNally, Tony Canadeo, Bart Starr, Ray Nitschke, and Reggie White.

Oh yeah, when will the Brett Favre statue be built? Don't hold your breath. As long as Ted Thompson is general manager, Brett's out of the loop. It's sort of a minor personality clash…kind of like Benito Mussolini versus the human race.

Sunday—game day. You'll love the sight lines. It just amazes me that this most intimate NFL ballpark, which now seats 72,938 people with a bundle of luxury suites, opened 50-plus years ago with a capacity of—get this—32,000.

Over a half century, the Pack—thanks primarily to Bob Harlan—has grown its ballpark exponentially without losing ten cents' worth of warmth. You can still feel Bart over Kramer to beat Tom Landry and Dallas in '67 Ice Bowl. You can still feel the world wars between Bears coach Mike Ditka and his counterpart Forrest Gregg.

Lambeau Field is sacred. These guys have said no to concert requests by Bruce Springsteen.

> *"You'd be amazed how many couples stop at Lambeau for wedding pictures. Or how many tour groups arrive from Sweden."*
> —Rob Demovsky, *Green Bay Press Gazette*

The field is immaculate. If you're a regular at Soldier Field, you know that generally after mid-October the playing surface on the "Soldier" is glorified pig slop. That's due to the massive workload Chicago Park District flunkies are forced to carry.

Lambeau is convenience. A tremendous Sunday punch.

Bears fans should get combat pay just for walking from 18th Street and Michigan Avenue to get to Soldier Field. Soldier Field isn't about fun—it's the McCaskeys' Walmart-style cash cow.

6 *Visit the* GEORGE HALAS *bas-relief* SCULPTURE

"Without the old man we'd all be playing soccer."
—Former Cleveland Browns owner Art Modell,
at the wake for Chicago Bears owner George Stanley Halas

I have to admit this: I don't know what the devil "bas-relief" means. Or, what the hell basso-relievo means, although I hear it was all the rage in Rome around the 13th century…or, in other words, just a few years before the Bears determined that Bronko Nagurski might be a half-decent running back.

But I do know this: There is no sports figure in Chicago history more deserving of the "basso" treatment than the Papa Bear. And here's where I get ticked off.

Anybody who argues against this needs big-time help. If you build a statue, monument, bas relief tribute to Halas, it should be in a location so loaded with pedestrian traffic that at least 300,000 people per day get a chance to gaze at the likeness of the tough old Bohunk.

In case you missed it, Coach Halas was the visionary who took pro football out of the hick towns like Rock Island, Portsmouth, Canton, and Hammond and made it, without question, the most popular sport in America…at least this side of gambling.

But that's not the case. The Halas tribute is tucked away on the west side of Soldier Field beneath the renovated glass and concrete of the "new" Soldier Field.

You talk about a dead end. The Unknown Soldier became a main-eventer. Halas is in an alley on Damen, between Armitage and Fullerton. Coach may as well be a four-round prelim fighter from Dubuque. Papa Bear deserves Michigan Avenue or at least the outside of Soldier Field.

The ballclub—that's the ever-lovin' McCaskeys, if you're scoring at home—may as well have farmed their benefactor out to a genuinely secluded location. For example, I have no doubt Oslo, Norway, would've bid heavy to get a Halas bas.

(Question: Michael, Patrick, Ned, and other assorted McCaskey loafers, just what would you be doing to pay the freight these days if Grandpa hadn't left you a gold mine?)

Honest to gosh, no kidding, on any given Sunday—that phrase should really be laid to rest, along with Rush Limbaugh—if there are 60,000 fans in the house for a Bears game, no more than 2,200 will see the architectural genius that is the Halas bas master. And, in case you've missed it, Soldier Field isn't really on overload. The dump is dark roughly 335 days a year. Get it. This sucker isn't on display 24-7.

Jeez, the average cable-access channel gets more viewers by accident than the Halas Monument gets. And cable access never beat Vince Lombardi.

If your neighbor—the guy with four tix on the 32-yard line—says he's seen it, I say he's a liar.

Okay, so I'm a little prejudiced. The old man was my main man, my ultimate sports hero. When fans at Cubs Park booed him, I booed the fans. Shaking his gnarled hand was like gaining access to the Model T, World War I, bathtub gin, and flappers. The Halas "grip" was a reminder of the Coach guiding his "Monsters," his Bears, to a casual 73–0 victory over the Washington Redskins on December 8, 1940. If you truly know the NFL, if your range goes beyond Joe Buck—and God, I hope it does—you know that 73–love blitz ushered in the era of some gimmick offense called the "T-formation."

I also broke the story of the old man's death. About six months before Coach Halas passed away back in 1983, my Channel 5 producer, Jeff Davis, himself a superb author and football historian, suggested we run a check on the old man's health. That led me to call Sid Luckman, the Hall of Fame quarterback and George's favorite football son. Sir Sid confirmed what we suspected. Papa Bear wasn't going to last much longer. During my give-and-take with Sid, I exacted a promise from Luckman that he would call me the moment he learned of Halas's death.

Sid gave me his word, and he was a man of his word. Around 8:30 on Halloween night 1983, Sid called me from the coach's bedside to tell me Papa Bear was gone.

The wheels began to turn. I begged Sid to come down and do our 10:00 news to talk about the George's death. Sid agreed. Davis and I broke the story locally and nationally. We beat Howard Cosell and *Monday Night Football* by 28 minutes.

TIMEOUT! Lesson to be learned about the TV biz! Along with Mark Giangreco, our Channel 5 sports department—much to the chagrin of the news side—just owned the Halas story, wire to wire. No one in town covered the tragedy with more authority and class than we did.

Here's where it gets interesting. About three days after the old man's death, Channel 5's general manager, Monte Newman, walked down to my office to tell me he was so impressed by our coverage that he wanted to sign me to a "one-hundred year contract." That should have been the tip.

Runway clowns hustling softballs and bowling pins have more credibility than Monte Newman, as did the famed Spilotro Brothers. Fifteen days later, I was fired by Channel 5 and Newman. Honest to gosh. You can't make this stuff up.

If anybody was ever born to hustle used cars or busted vacuum cleaners, it was Monte Newman. When I see Tony Rezko or Tony Accardo, I see Monte Newman.

So, we have a nice happy ending coming up, no? NO. The Papa Bear's bas-relief sculpture is a remarkable visual, depicting the game from the era of Red Grange through the "Bronk," "Crunch" Butkus, "Sweetness" Payton, and "Galloping Gale," among others.

I'd like to tell you Mike Ditka gets big play. I'd love to tell you the old man has his arm around the tight end he coached and the "renegade" he brought back to Chicago to breathe life into an NFL embarrassment back in 1982. It would be so natural, so appropriate, so Halas.

No, it's so McCaskey. Ditka was omitted.

7 *Play* AUTOGRAPH *hound: Get a signed photo, helmet, or jersey from* RICHARD MARVIN BUTKUS

Keep this in mind before we open today's sermon: It broke my heart to watch Larry Holmes just chew up a nearly helpless Muhammad Ali in Las Vegas back in October 1980. I still see Holmes begging the referee to stop the fight. I still wonder why Angelo Dundee, Ali's corner man and an uncommonly decent man, waited so long to end the brutality. Ali does suffer from Parkinson's, but he is also a victim of "pugilistic syndrome." That's a polite way of saying that Ali's on what old-time boxing pundits call "Queer Street." The boxing world just loves to deny this inarguable fact. The cranium just isn't built to endure the punishment Muhammad endured versus Frazier in Madison Square Garden, or in Manilla, or the whipping he took from Holmes. Simply stated: Ali is punchy.

SO LET'S MOVE on from point A to point B. I don't want to shock anybody, but there are times when I ask myself this question: *Just why the hell did you do that?*

Go back to 1999. It's Dick Jauron's first forgettable year as head coach of the Bears. I got a call from the ballclub asking if I would be part of a panel—the phrase "blue ribbon" was never invoked—to select the greatest Bears of all time.

My choice at middle linebacker? William J. "Bill" George. A terrific player! George was beyond special, beyond brutal, a classic "coach on the field." He had a run of eight Pro Bowl appearances from 1955 to 1962. He virtually created the "modern" middle linebacker by dropping back in coverage, which led to the traditional 4-3-4 defense that is still the lifeblood of much of the NFL.

Side note: Bill was also my childhood hero. So, yeah, I voted with my heart. Okay, you want more? Bill is a member of the Pro Football Hall of Fame. The Bears retired his number 61 jersey.

George wasn't just wicked or ferocious. He made guys like Ray Nitschke, Sam Huff, and Mike Singletary look like Mahatma Gandhi. When a running back got wrapped up by Bill George, he got wrapped up by a CTA bus.

About four years later, I realized I'd fumbled—at the goal line. Why? Because I gave Bill the nod over a man who, inch for inch, pound for pound, was and is the greatest football player of all time: Richard Marvin Butkus.

> *"I begged Dick not to play that ballgame. I told him they're gonna go right after your knees. But he was a warrior. He knew he couldn't make the plays he wanted to make anymore but he was determined that if he was going out he was gonna take some people with him."*
> —Doug Buffone, former Bears linebacker, remembering the night before Butkus' career with the Chicago Bears came to a close

October 28, 1973, was the end of an era. Dick Butkus, just a shadow of the monster who had busted so many rib cages, played his final game versus the Kansas City Chiefs on *Monday Night Football*. The score? Who gives a damn.

No one will ever know the pain Butkus felt at that time. But we do know that his knees were virtually bone on bone, devoid of cartilage. His agility was gone. The gaps he could fill, his ability to drop back in coverage, were already gone—dumped in scrapbooks. Words like "devastating" and "overwhelming" could no longer be associated with Dick Butkus.

"Experience is great, but it doesn't help much when the guy you're facing is younger and stronger and bigger than you are."
—Doug Buffone

Butkus could deal with "physical pain." Hell, before his tour at Illinois, Butkus attended CVS High School just off the Calumet Skyway. CVS drew such a tough crowd that the crossing guards wore boxing gloves.

Dick evoked passion and rage. Call this a sign of the times. I was in the house at Northwestern in 1964 when the 'Cats played the Fighting Illini. I can't recall the final score. I just remember a terrific fight in the stands when an N.U. fan, who had to be half stiff or half nuts, screamed at the top of his lungs, "Butkus is a dumb Polack." I stopped counting punches thrown at around 36.

Sports Illustrated still wears the scarlet letter for a big-time cheap shot. *SI* just hung Butkus out to dry in a piece written during Dick's windup year at Champaign-Urbana that depicted him as a complete Neanderthal...or maybe the second phase of Darwin's theory of evolution. You talk about rotten. Butkus would've gotten a pass if he'd taken a contract out on the writer.

Dick Butkus is funny. His Miller Lite commercials remain advertising genius. Look at his movie work, his body of endorsements, his TV appearances. Butkus knows how to play the camera. Yes, he could have played the Ted Danson role in *Cheers*. He makes Jim Belushi look like an extra.

However, keep this in mind: Butkus is funny on his own terms.

Here's where Ali and Butkus mesh. What was Muhammad thinking about as Holmes, one of his old sparring partners, was taking endless pot shots at his jaw and rib cage? How badly was "Crunch" feeling the emotional pill—down the stretch—knowing that he was no longer the game's most dominant figure? Go back to boxing. Butkus was—to use the fight game's phrase for a guy who's lost it—"just an opponent." It had to kill him.

It shouldn't have ended this way. Scratch the Super Bowls. Butkus never even played on a playoff team.

This goes back a mere 44 years. I first saw Butkus with the Bears when he joined the club in Rensselaer, Indiana, back in '65. Butkus had just played in the long-gone College All-Star Game. He had the trademark crew cut and was wearing flip flops. His feet were huge. No surprise. Eventually, his teammates nicknamed him "Paddles."

We've played the Mat world together. Butkus was a "guest referee" and I was a ring announcer for Wrestlemania II. Don't ask about cash. Butkus made a bundle. I got enough to get my car out of the parking lot—barely.

Back to the Bears. Trust me, Butkus was so imposing, I think he scared half his teammates. The other half were too dumb to be scared.

I'm not big on the autograph game, but I am big on Dick Butkus. For about 100 bucks you can get your picture with him. Plus, "Crunch" will sign the photo: "Dick Butkus…HOF 1979."

I'm not hustling anything. I'm not saying your life is incomplete if you don't do this. Butkus has a plenty of dough. I'm saying it's kind of nifty to have a picture of yourself side-by-side with and signed by the greatest player the NFL ever produced.

There will never be another Butkus. They only made one. There are no plans to make another.

8 Enjoy the tropical breezes and white sands of CANTON, OHIO? Visit the PRO FOOTBALL HALL OF FAME

Let's get this straight: I'm not going to give you the virtual tour of the this 83,000-square-foot shrine to thigh pads, the old Chicago Cardinals, Art Rooney, the elegance of Sid Luckman, the toughness of Sam Huff, and the ballet-like agility of "TD" Tony Dorsett.

If we're doing the Hall of Fame, we're doing it on my terms.

Number one, upon arrival, we're going to bitch about Jimbo Covert not having a bust in the joint. Covert, absolutely raw power on the left side, should have picked up his gold blazer at least six years ago. His omission is criminal but typical of the morons who vote to determine hall inductees.

"Jim should be in. He was as good as anybody during his era. He was a quiet leader who did his job. Maybe his problem was he didn't blow his own horn. Maybe that's what you have to do."
—Mike Ditka, HOF Class of '89

The Hall of Fame is not about a twerp like Rich Eisen and the NFL Network. It's not about Chris Collinsworth whining about Ray Lewis failing to fill an A-gap to stop some guy running the ball for the St. Louis Rams. The hall is about people like the following 10 men—the 10 most influential men in the history of the game, Coppock-style:

1. **GEORGE STANLEY HALAS.** I don't know how the old man did it, but somehow he kept the league alive during the Depression.

2. **PETE ROZELLE.** The chain-smoking commissioner who guided the league through the turbulence of the '60s, made the McCaskeys filthy rich, and—hand in hand with Roone Arledge—created ABC *Monday Night Football.*

3. **RED GRANGE.** You talk about impact. Grange signed with the Bears in 1925, shortly after playing his final college game for Bob Zuppke at Illinois. On Thanksgiving Day 1925, he played his first game with the Bears and drew 36,000 people to Cubs Park for a bout with the Cardinals. The Bears had been used to drawing around 5,000 fans a date. A few days later, Grange filled the Polo Grounds—70,000 fans— for an appearance versus the New York Giants. The importance of that game can never be overstated. The Maras were already sick of football and on the verge of folding the franchise.

4. **ART MODELL, OWNER OF THE CLEVELAND BROWNS.** Art was the heavy fist behind the scenes who negotiated spectacular deals for the league with the TV networks.

5. **TEX SCHRAMM, SHOWMAN, PROMOTER, AND PRESIDENT OF THE DALLAS COWBOYS.** Gave the league T and A with the Dallas Cowboys Cheerleaders. Convinced the press from coast to coast that it was blasphemous to refer to his club as anything but "America's Team." Helped package the NFL-AFL merger.

6. **VINCE LOMBARDI, WHO COACHED THE GREEN BAY PACKERS TO FIVE NFL TITLES AND TWO SUPER BOWL CHAMPIONSHIPS.** The Pack, not the Baltimore Colts with Johnny Unitas, were network TV's first glamour team.

7. **GENE UPSHAW, HALL OF FAME GUARD WITH THE OAKLAND RAIDERS.** Fought toe-to-toe, jaw-to-jaw with the NFL over player salaries as the Emperor of the NFLPA. Long snappers earning a million bucks a year owe at least 82 percent of their cabbage to Gene Upshaw. Uppie had one failing: He pissed on retired players who sorely needed money and medical help. Once a guy retired, in Upshaw's world, he may as well have been hustling *Streetwise.*

8. **Joe Namath, the anti-hero.** Led the AFL Jets over Don Shula and the NFL Colts in Super Bowl III. In the process, Joe, with his long hair, Fu Manchu, chinchilla coat, and good old-fashioned western Pennsylvania charm, created a swarm of female pro football fans. I drank Red Label on the rocks because that's what Joe drank. No kidding.

9. **Howard Cosell, the most prolific sports broadcaster of all time.** Howard's ability to scene-set *MNF* was phenomenal. He could take the world's worst game and make it sound like *Gone with the Wind* or *Taxi Driver*. Howard and gambling—this was a new night for wise guys to flourish and suckers to plunge—made *Monday Night Football*.

10. **Paul Tagliabue.** He had just one job and he did it to perfection: Keep the NFL on the blueprints designed by George Halas and Pete Rozelle.

Okay, so you're going to Canton. The prices won't kill you. Admission is 18 bucks for adults, 12 dollars for children under 12. The exhibits are phenomenal. The interactive elements will satisfy any cyberspace freak.

Complaint time! The NFL has completely overlooked officials. Referees like Tommy Bell, Red "First Down" Cashion, my pal Jerry Markbreit, Cal Lepore, and Jim Tunney should at least be given the time of day.

Another Hall of Fame admission: Trust me, Jack Tatum, the superb Oakland Raider, a defining player, a prolific defensive back during the '70s, would have his blazer if he had just done one simple thing…offer up an apology to Daryl Stingley, the NFL, and America for his open-field shot on Daryl that left the poor guy in a wheelchair the final 30 years of his life.

I always check out the Al Davis bust and the Raiders displays for a couple of reasons. I love the Raiders mystique. You know, all that "Pride and Poise" nonsense. I know the Maverick doesn't win much anymore. It's a story when his club leads at halftime, but Al turned out three clubs that won Super Bowls and he saw something in John Madden that nobody else saw: a head coach.

Plus, here's the keeper: The Maverick's appearance at George Halas' funeral back in 1983 was priceless. Al arrived wearing his trademark three-quarter-length black leather jacket, walking side by side with Jimmy "The Greek" Snyder. The Greek, really a miserable son of a bitch, was the TV's first "recognized" football handicapper. Davis, an owner, The Greek, a gambler… they were the best of chums.

(I state once again for the record, your honor: Without gambling, TV numbers on the NFL would drop 30 percent by next Tuesday.)

You're in the "Hall." Let your imagination wander. Think about Bronko Nagurski in a head-on collision with Mean Joe Greene. Imagine O.J. Simpson in an open-field showdown against Mike Singletary. I hear, by the way, that lately O.J. has been unavailable to work autograph shows.

Think about ex-Packer Don Hutson. This guy was a gazelle, "The Alabama Antelope." Just stop and let this sink in. Don Hutson had 99 touch-down catches over 11 years in Titletown playing 10-, 11-, and 12-game schedules.

I may run for mayor of Green Bay. Think about Paul Hornung, No. 5 in Packers green and gold, scoring 176 points while playing a 12-game schedule back in 1960.

Rashied Davis won't score 176 points if he plays 26 years.

Plan to give the hall at least three hours. Spend a few bucks in the gift shop. It's about a five-hour drive from Chicago and, hey, who needs Puerto Vallarta in February when you can enjoy the creature comforts of Canton?

No, Curtis Enis and Anthony Thomas are not considered electable.

9 Remember the SOLDIER FIELD KNOCKOUT: Plank clobbers Tiles

"I knew I had to play like a maniac to survive. If you put fear into people, it shows up on tape."
—Douglas Walter Plank, former Bears defensive back

Doug Plank didn't really have to be a football player. If he'd added 15 pounds, he could have a been Shaun Michaels, "Nature Boy" Ric Flair, or if you're old school, "Nature Boy" Buddy Rogers, the consummate all-time, put-it-in-bold type wrestling heel.

Trust me, Vince McMahon could have done wonders with this kid from Greensburg, Pennsylvania, a working-man's, shot-and-a-beer town in western PA. (By the way, is there any town in Pennsylvania west of Harrisburg that isn't a working man's, shot-and-a-beer town? Just asking.)

Ever see the film *Wag the Dog* with Dustin Hoffman and Robert De Niro? It's beyond a keeper. If you have caught the flick, and you didn't bust out laughing at least a dozen times, then tell the guy in the black suit to flip the lid on the coffin—you're already in the next life.

There's this great scene where Hoffman, a Hollywood producer, having just offered up a mock State of the Union address to presidential staffers in the Oval Office, says to De Niro very matter-of-factly, "You know, I could have been president. It's really just a wardrobe change."

Same goes for Plank. He didn't have to snap on chin straps and wear football cleats. He could have been outfitted in baby blue trunks, taught to strut, billed himself as the "Blonde-Haired Assassin," and been a turnbuckle-lovin', over-the-top-rope, box-office kingpin.

Plank, with his boyish grin, blonde hair, and female fan appeal, would have been a classic "baby face." But by age eight, playing Pop Warner ball, Doug Plank's life revolved around football. He was an electric shock during an era when piling on and spearing and hitting a quarterback any damn place you felt like hitting him was still part of the action. In other words, as Mike Ditka would tell you, "Doug played ball before they put quarterbacks in dresses."

> "Once you get a reputation, before teams see you on tape, they
> know about you. It's a jungle. You attack them or they attack you."
> —Doug Plank

So we throw the switch back to October 6, 1980, at Soldier Field. The Bears dropkicked the Tampa Bay Bucs 23–0 on Monday Night Football. I don't know who quarterbacked the Bears (probably Bob Avellini), how many yards Walter gained, or if Tampa froze because the temperature was in the upper 50s. I remember Doug Plank and "the hit."

There has never been a more lethal blow delivered in that lakefront ballpark. Jack Dempsey's shot that floored Gene Tunney—the prelude to the famous long count—was a pat on the back by comparison.

Plank's blow was so violent, yet, in its own way so beautiful, you didn't know whether to cheer or hope that Tampa tight end Jimmy Giles, who'd absorbed the belt, wasn't going to spend six weeks in Northwestern Hospital—or just have the team bus take him to the nearest retirement community.

Giles ran a seam route, and Plank—who could zoom into high gear in a stride and a half—had about ten feet of space to reach fifth gear. Doug just devastated Jimmy with a knockout drop right below Giles' face mask that had to leave the poor bastard's sternum looking like the Rocky Mountains. Or a busted beer can.

I don't know how Giles sustained his breath. I don't know how he got up. Or why he wanted to get up.

I do remember Doug Williams, the Tampa Bay QB—a few years away from Super Bowl glory with Joe Gibbs and the Redskins—running down the field screaming bloody murder at Plank and the officials for one reason (and this'll knock you over): There was no flag thrown. The hit was legal! Completely on the square.

Now, TV timeout. I'm watching the Bears lick New Orleans in overtime in December 2008 and I see Roman Harper, a Saints DB, get yellowed for pass interference on Devin Hester during the extra period. The "contact" was so nondescript, so minimal, it wouldn't have affected the flight pattern of a moth. And this is in overtime…didn't some gridiron sage say about 80 years ago that deep in a ballgame, you let the players decide the issue?

But that's today's NFL. If the officials don't have a town hall meeting to walk off encroachment or throw a flag when they see the most minor of infractions, they get "dinged"—an NFL term—for failing on the job.

Plank didn't walk away clean. He got fined 10 grand, big-time cash to a guy who was making $90,000 that season. In other words, after taxes and the league penalty, Doug lost more than two games' salary.

Doug is now on the payroll of the New York Jets as an assistant coach. The Jets' head coach is Rex Ryan, the son of Buddy Ryan. Got the hook? Buddy's pet defense, the "46," got its title from Plank's jersey number. It's a fact—six degrees of separation and the kick-out block are remarkably similar.

Doug told me about a night his wife Nancy chastised him for playing "too rough." Nancy wanted to know why Plank couldn't be "like the other guys," so Doug figured next game maybe he'd ease up a little.

Nancy's grand scheme was about as successful as the Blagojevich administration.

The following Sunday, the Bears played a ball game with Denver and Plank "let up" on a ball carrier as he edged toward the sideline. The runner, Jon Keyworth, gave Plank a big-time belt. Naturally, as Plank shook out the cobwebs, he got the taunts from the Denver bench about being "such a tough guy."

Doug walked back to the huddle thinking, *I can't survive like this.* So on the next play he just put his head down, stormed the Denver point of attack, and left Paul Howard, a Broncos lineman, with a fractured sternum.

Why didn't we send Plank to find Osama bin Laden?

Plank made a bundle as Burger King franchisee. He's also done terrific work as an Arena Football League head coach in Phoenix and Atlanta. If I ran the NFL Network, I would've hired Doug three years ago. He's always been an A-list talker.

Intriguing guy? Keep in mind that while he went to three Rose Bowls during his time at Ohio State, he was never a starter for Woody Hayes. The Bears picked him in Round 12 of the 1975 draft. Plank was supposed to be the kind of guy who hangs around for about three-and-a-half weeks, plays the role of blocking dummy, and then gets advised to "See the coach and bring your playbook."

Instead, he became a Chicago folk hero. Walter Payton aside, it says here, there was no more popular Chicago Bears player in the late '70s than Doug Plank. Men wanted to hit like he hit. Girls wanted him in the back seat of a Pinto. Or a Lincoln Mark IV.

I DON'T WANT to get melancholy. But I have been witness to ultimate football tragedy. I was in old Tiger Stadium October 24, 1971, when Detroit receiver Chuck Hughes collapsed and died of a heart attack deep in the fourth quarter while running a route against the Bears. I saw the trainer and team physician frantically pounding his chest in an effort to save Hughes. I saw Chuck's arm drop off the stretcher as he was carried off the field.

I'll never forget the bad rap Dick Butkus picked up from the media in Detroit. Dick knew that Hughes was in serious trouble the moment Chuck went down. Butkus began waving frantically at the Lions bench to send in medical help. Naturally, there were dummies who thought Butkus was showboating because Hughes was prone.

Football is damn near barbaric, when you get right down to it. The sport is built on muscle, rage, and car-wreck collisions. The Bears never cared about how many cranial injuries Doug Plank sustained with his helmet-to-helmet approach to tackling. The club never held Monday meetings to say, "Gee, we better damn well do something about Doug so that his diet isn't Tylenol and smelling salts."

The ball club never spent three minutes wondering just why No. 46 couldn't remember so many first quarters. No, when the Bears decided Doug was no longer a fit, they just told him to get lost.

Pro football doesn't eat its young or old. It just tells them to get their personal stuff out of the locker room before the team gets there—no gold watch upon departure. And that's what Jim Finks and the Bears did to Doug early in 1982.

I've never seen a player, in any sport, take "the cut" with such grief. Nobody. Hey, there were still tight ends who needed to be educated. Busted up. Decapitated?

Doug Plank, a hitter? Was Bob Dylan a lyricist?

10 Break down HIGH SCHOOL FOOTBALL tape with TOM LEMMING

"I was gonna go to Western Illinois but I didn't have enough money for college. So I backpacked around Europe for a year after high school. I figured seeing the Kremlin and the pyramids was a pretty good education."

—Tom Lemming

Tom didn't mention that he was spending most evenings curled up in youth hostels for five bucks a night. He didn't mention that he while he's graduated from Motel 6s on the road, he loves the prices at off-the-main-drag Holiday Inns.

Let's get right to the point. Tom is without peer at what he does. He is the best prep football talent evaluator in America. Scouts.com and Rivals.com can scream all they want. Lemming is the Godfather in this business.

Tom moves in a hurry for obvious reasons. He speaks directly to 1,600 high school football players annually. It doesn't take our guy much time to figure out if a guy is a "player," a kid playing out of position, or a guy who should be thinking about working at his old man's appliance store. (Or maybe, a kid who's a cinch to get busted in a barroom brawl during his freshman year.) And he'll know a quarterback who can thrive in a zone running scheme.

Lemming tells you very candidly that he never looks at a kid's tape for more than five minutes. "College football coaches have the attention span of five-year-old," Lemming says. "I tell kids all the time, 'Put your great plays on the front end of the tape. It's all the coaches will remember.'"

Lemming can tell on a dime if a running back has the right kind of hips, if a receiver has the growth potential to eventually create better cuts coming out of the breaks. He doesn't have to be told that offensive linemen need a wide base, a big butt, big legs, long arms, and quick feet.

This is Coppock speaking. I'd love to scout. When I look at a college wide receiver, I always look for small ankles that support, strong but not overly developed calf muscles. It's kind of a Michael Jordan thing with me.

You talk about yarns, Tom has enough tales to fill up the United Center. Or the Jersey Meadowlands. Hollywood should do a movie on this guy. Ed Norton could play Lemming. I'll play Charlie Weis. Jon Voigt can play Urban Meyer.

Tom Lemming (left) chats with top recruit Noel Devine (center, now a West Virginia running back) and Deion Sanders before the 2007 U.S. Army All-American Bowl.

Lemming remembers scouting Alonzo Spellman, the ex-Bear, when he was playing ball at Cherry Hills High School in New Jersey, the same school that turned out Franco Harris. "Spellman was so strong, so cut, I thought he was already on steroids," Lemming says. "Or maybe he just naturally looked like a circus freak. In high school, he lifted weights like he was already an NFL player."

Lemming adds that Ohio State snuck Alonzo in the back door by, uh, shall we say, overlooking his grades. No big deal. No need to call the NCAA with your pulse racing. College football is like running a bookie joint. It's a dog-eat-dog world. Tom will tell you that Illinois and Michigan State and roughly 85 other schools are doing the same thing.

Time out for this Coppock recollection: The first time I saw Spellman without a shirt I thought he made a young Arnold Schwarzenegger look like a runway model with bulimia nervosa.

Lemming recalls driving to New Orleans and thinking at the eleventh hour to follow up on a tip to see an option quarterback named Brett Favre in Kiln,

Mississippi. Lemming says that Favre had the size to be a major-college quarterback, but he adds this little note: Favre's old man Irvin almost killed his career by making him run the option.

Lemming has stayed true to his roots. He began 30 years ago out of the trunk of his car. He interviewed every kid he was going to rate. Tom earned his recognition. It took him ages to see any kind of money. There just was no dough. Tom laughs about nights he slept in his car to save a few bucks. Or how he tried to park his car between trucks when he needed to grab some sleep because he figured the truckers would blackjack anybody who tried to smash his windshield.

He will drive 60,000 miles again this year across the continental U.S.A. Plus he has 22 kids he needs to do a meet-and-greet with in Hawaii.

Tom picked up a huge break in 1982 when *USA Today* selected him to name its High School All-America team. Lemming's been on the job ever since.

So why is Lemming so unique? He actually does talk face-to-face with all 1,600 kids on his hit list and their coaches…and any moms, dads, or truant officers who happen to be in the area.

He finds—and this is hardly surprising—that most 18- or 19-year-old kids will load up on "false cockiness" during their sessions. Hey, these guys are man-children. You're from Batesville, Mississippi, and suddenly you're on Lemming's list of the Top 100 prep football players in America, you know what happens? The gal at the drive-in just can't load you up with enough extra French fries. It can be an adjustment for a lot of young fellows who've never been more than 75 miles from home.

"Randy Moss is the greatest player I ever scouted," Tom says. "The coaching staff at Pittsburgh tipped me off to him when he was a sophomore in Rand, West Virginia."

Lemming adds, "Moss is the only player I've ever seen…well, maybe Herschel Walker is another…who could've gone right from high school to the NFL."

His quarterback was future NBA point guard and tattoo billboard Jason Williams. With all the time he spent flinging aerials and throwing no-look passes, I truly believe I understand why J-dub has the ugliest tattoos I've ever seen. He was too busy thinking about his next playing date to worry about some hillbilly tattoo "artist" making his chalk-white arms look like they'd been doused with buckets of blue ink.

Tom once motored down to Apopka High School in good old Apopka, Florida (who hasn't been to Apopka?) to look at tight end Warren Sapp.

Lemming knew that lovable Warren, just 6'1", was never going to be a receiver on the next level. What he saw was what Miami saw—a nose tackle.

If you ever run into Yankees centerfielder Johnny Damon, ask him about Warren Sapp. Warren nailed Johnny so badly one evening that Damon suffered his first athletic concussion. Maybe his last....

Tom isn't real big on cyberspace. He doesn't email. I don't think he's ever had time to learn. Actually, I think it flies in the face of his old-school approach. Lemming needs contact. Email is about as personal as a grump in blue on Wabash Avenue dishing out parking tickets.

Lemming still raves about Jeff George. Over the years, George, a quarterback out of Warren Central. H.S. in Indianapolis, has become truly mythical. Trust me. There isn't a year that goes by that some scout doesn't suggest that a guy from Little Rock or Nowhere, Iowa, doesn't have Jeff George–type skills.

Jeff was a 6'5", rifle-armed, quick-release passing machine. Recruiters didn't just drool when they saw him, they acted like teenage girls seeing the Beatles on the old *Ed Sullivan Show*. They went nuts. His spirals were so tight they could split a Life Saver. His vision was exceptional. He had John Elway–type talent. He was a better prospect coming out of high school than Dan Marino.

But there was a minor flaw. One NFL exec one gave me the ultimate Jeff George summation/obituary: "From the neck down, George was the greatest quarterback I've ever seen...from the neck up, he was the worst."

Lemming will tell you that Jeff never delivered, never spent NFL Februarys in Honolulu because "he was a spoiled kid."

Trust me, I'd bet half a hundred today that George could fall out of bed, throw on some sweats and, in a sleep-walk state, throw the ball better than Kyle Orton.

Jeff George is the biggest bust in NFL history.

Tom still wonders just how good Boo Boo Thompson out of Proviso West could have been. Lemming says he had Simeon Rice–type talent. There's no answer forthcoming. Boo Boo had injuries, arrests. He was a walking police blotter. He's currently in the joint preparing to face a murder charge. It goes with the territory. In case you missed it, NFL players generally aren't choir boys.

Big names, jocks, and actors gravitate to Lemming. It's April 2007 and I'm working Notre Dame's traditional "Blue-Gold" intersquad scrimmage in South Bend. Fifty thousand fans have turned out, primarily to see California Golden Boy Jimmy Clausen, a Lemming National Player of the Year selection. Tom walks in to our booth and introduces us to his pal Jim Caviezel. James, of course, was the man who brought so many people to tears in *The Passion of the Christ*, the controversial Mel Gibson film.

Our boy Tom ain't short on charisma. Russell Maryland, a Chicago kid out of Whitney Young, is just a world-class happy ending.

Russell, supercharged but way too heavy in high school, wanted to play at Notre Dame in the worst way. He had the grades and the boards. Notre Dame passed on Russell and missed a chance to tag-team him inside along the D-line with Chris Zorich.

As national signing day arrived—that's Tom Lemming's answer to Christmas, New Year's Day, and the Cubs with a series sweep over St. Louis—Maryland had one offer: Indiana State. However, Miami, with one scholarship left, sent a tender to Russell. He signed with the 'Canes, shagged weight, and eventually became the Dallas Cowboys' first pick in the 1991 draft—the first overall choice in round one. Three Super Bowl rings later, Russell moved on to the Oakland Raiders.

Our guy Tom Lemming hasn't vacationed in nine years. Who the hell has time for that? There's a "mike" linebacker in North Dakota who needs his attention.

Fifty-three years young, Lemming feeds CBS College Sports and does at least 200 radio interviews during a "slow year." His name is in print about once every 17 minutes.

Tom closed our most recent give-and-take in typical Lemming fashion. His buddy Mike Leach, the Texas Tech front man, is coming up to visit him. Lemming has promised to take Mike on the "Al Capone" tour of Chicago. You know, a little St. Valentine's Day massacre here, a little of the old Biograph here. Maybe they'll drift out to Elmwood Park where Tony "Big Tuna" Accardo's underboss Jackie "The Lackey" Cerone used to run a great joint called "Rocky's."

And they might break down some tape…but no more than five minutes a player. Don't have to. Don't need to.

11 *Visit the* COLLEGE FOOTBALL HALL OF FAME *in South Bend, Indiana*

Hey, Lee Corso, tell me how long Joe Paterno will coach. Lee responds with one of his classic tongue in cheek anecdotes: "Until Bobby Bowden dies."

Why not? They both want to end up No. 1 on the all-time-big-time college football wins list and—come on, get real—do you see either Bobby or Joe throwing on white belts and white shoes while they scout for "early birds" somewhere in Georgia? Me neither.

Don't ask me why, but Bobby and Joe are on my mind as I cruise down the Indiana Toll Road toward the College Football Hall of Fame. I'm thinking about Bobby holding court after he lost a No. 1 versus No. 2 game to Lou Holtz 31–24 at Notre Dame Stadium back in '93.

I remember Bobby saying late that afternoon, following the Florida State belly flop in which he'd learned "the biggest game on your schedule is the one you lose." This was back in the days when it really did feel like the only time Bowden got knocked off was when his field-goal kickers were, so it seemed, required by Florida law to boot wide right versus Miami with a game on the line. Bobby's 'Noles won 138 games and lost just 19 from 1987 through 2000. Still, in 2008 he seemed like a discount buy at $2.5 million a year for the good old boys in Tallahassee.

> *"Don't worry I'll pray for you."*
>
> —Joe Pa giving me the rib after I
> mentioned that my wife was Sicilian

Joe said that to me 16 years ago. He is still prowling the sideline in Happy Valley. My ex-wife is still collecting alimony.

So I go wheeling down St. Joseph's Street, by the statue of Knute Rockne, in the college football shrine. What do you want—a statue of Pop Warner, Barry Switzer, or Curtis Enis? This is South Bend. The "Hall" sits about three miles from the Golden Dome. It doesn't take Harvard intellect—hell, it doesn't take a certificate from American Truck Driving School—to recognize that these folks are playing toward anybody with the admission fee. However, they realize that Notre Dame fans do a heck of a lot to keep the doors in action.

My choice for the most unique exhibit in the Hall?

This is just me talking, and it helps that I was at the ballgame—one played in such icy, wet, subzero-windchill conditions that I felt I lost my thumbs, toes, and both my nostrils—but do you remember the 1979 Cotton Bowl in Dallas? It's the one that featured Notre Dame versus Bill Yeomans and the Houston Cougars. Sure you do. Joe Montana, in his windup game at N.D. led the Irish to a comeback so good—so *Rocky*, so *Rudy*—that the game was truly made for Hollywood. If Montana had never played a down for the 49ers, he could have made a living off that one New Year's Day.

Down 34–12 with a little more than seven minutes to play, Notre Dame rallied to win 35–34 thanks to Montana's brilliance and his ability to seize the moment by the jugular…but that's not really the take-home point.

Joe was fighting a horrific case of the flu. By halftime—and the legend just grows and grows—he was either: so sick he couldn't stand up; so sick he should have been in Parkland Hospital; or so sick a priest had been called to administer last rites. Actually, it was none of the above. Yes "Joe Comeback" was terribly ill, but the problem was that his body temperature had dipped dramatically beneath the norm of 98.6.

The Irish, desperate to keep the franchise on the dance floor, jammed hot chicken soup into his system at halftime and the rest is history. Joe threw a quick out to Kris Haines for the game-winner with nothing left on the clock. With various media people, Cotton Bowl officials, and probably Jerry "The Crasher" Berliant near the end zone, I'm guessing that only about 50 people in the stadium could see the catch—and you couldn't really see it on the tube. TV was still having its growing pains. There weren't 16 cameras in the Cotton Bowl and Suzy Kolber was nowhere to be found.

Tell me this isn't cool—the College Hall of Fame has the actual soup bowl and spoon that Montana sipped from during that halftime.

You can also check out Bear Bryant's fedora. The display depicting college football's greatest rivalries is tremendous. You can almost feel Earl Campbell glaring at Oklahoma or Woody Hayes yelling at anybody in maize and blue.

As you edge toward the Stadium Theater, you can see the familiar blue and orange of Illinois. It takes you a second, but you realize you are gazing at a jersey worn by Red Grange. The Hall says it might be worth in the low six figures. More important, it's like seeing Babe Ruth, Big Bill Tilden, bathtub gin, Warren G. Harding (was he a three-technique tackle?), and the Roaring '20s unfold before your eyes.

The Stadium Theater is a can't miss for two reasons: one, the statues illustrate crowds from the earliest days of organized football into the 1920s; and two, the raccoon coat emblematic of the era is a dandy.

For years I've worn a raccoon coat. Why? It produced great talkability and if Red Grange could wear one so could I. (Okay, an oversized ass and a great deal from York Furrier may have been more important to me than the fashion sense of the old red head.)

The theater doesn't preach college football; it celebrates college football. No deep bass voices talking about the single wing, the LSU Chinese Bandits, or the "Lonesome End." (Gotcha! The Lonesome End was Bill Carpenter, who played with Heisman winner Pete Dawkins on Army's unbeaten 1958 club. Carpenter later won the Distinguished Service Cross, the Army's second-most prestigious wartime honor.)

The theater's 11-minute flick, designed for kids and people with short attention spans—97 percent of Americans, if you include me—just lets the game speak for itself. Sideline and locker room dialogue from various head coaches and assistants is embedded within the film to give you the feeling that you are living a game from a perspective that Charlie Weis could never possibly give you…or want to give you.

The College Football Hall of Fame is just a hundred miles from downtown Chicago. It's four hours well spent, and while you're there you'll lose count of all the Chicago Bears enshrined in the Hall—it's a bundle.

12 The DANIMAL: The NFL at its BEST… or the NFL at its WORST?

You figure I should open this episode with a line about Dan Hampton and the Pro Football Hall of Fame? Please, your next door neighbor can probably recite half the speech Daniel gave during his induction in Canton back in 2002.

I submit that Dan Hampton may well be the greatest saxophone player in the history of Cabot, Arkansas.

> *"I always figured you played until you couldn't walk and then you just kept on playing anyway. I was willing to sell out… give everything up."*
>
> —Dan Hampton

That's Dan Hampton. I have never met an athlete—any game, any sport—who has the pain threshold that Hampton brought to the table.

He's had 14 knee surgeries over the years. Once he was cut-blocked so badly by Randall McDaniel, the former Minnesota Viking, that he could have been forgiven for crying. McDaniel wasn't some clown who just filled out the line of scrimmage. Randall was one of the greatest offensive guards of the modern era, a guy worthy of Hall of Fame consideration.

Anyway, there was this Vikings-Bears game back in the '80s when McDaniel

Coppock and The Danimal share the podium at a National Italian American Sports Hall of Fame event in 1992.

aimed his shoulder right at Hampton's knees. (I could name 100 guys who took dead aim on Dan's knees. They were good for 500 hundred points on the dartboard.) Hampton was left in unimaginable anguish. The Bears tried to get him an immediate surgery at Michigan State but discovered there would be a two-week wait.

So what does Hampton do? This is either the essence of courage or complete insanity. He kept on playing. In fact, he played beyond the scheduled surgery date. He played to a point where both his knees had to be cleaned up.

Keep in mind, the NFL doesn't want you to know about this kind of stuff. The league is too busy selling the United Way and personal seat licenses. The Bears, obviously, should have told Hampton to remain in street clothes, but they knew the obvious: Hamp would have told the club, "Go fuck yourself."

The league accepts no responsibility for ex-players who can't walk, or guys who have spaghetti for brains. The NFL would just love it if Mike Ditka would keep his yap shut about how many former NFL players are disabled and unable to afford proper medication. Guys left to rot, while the Bears and Jerry Angelo break down—play the role of scared little school girl—and give Brian Urlacher new money. After all, baby Brian—who's a light year past his prime—might pout.

Now let's take a different angle on this 280-pound former Arkansas All-American. A young Dan Hampton, fresh from the guidance of Lou Holtz and the Arkansas Razorbacks, was "adopted" by old-school heavyweights Dick Butkus and Ed O'Bradovich early in his stellar career with the Chicago Bears.

Butkus and O'B talked about their era, their game. About Doug Atkins, Bill George, "Fat" Freddie Williams…guys playing with fractured ribs, guys afraid to walk in to locker rooms and tell their teammates they couldn't answer the bell. If a teammate wasn't ready to have 140 ccs of blood drained from his knee the night before a ballgame, then they weren't buying in into the macho "culture" of Eddie and Dick.

Dan will tell you he was enamored, in awe, of both Dick and Ed. They were guys Hampton could understand. Stand-up guys who grew up without the frills. Both came out of working-class families. Both guys despised phonies. Both absorbed their injuries with a sense of pride.

Maybe "Hamp" was a willing listener for a different reason. This 280-pound hunk of muscle and agility didn't play any football during his final two years of grammar school and his first two years of high school. Why? It wasn't because Dan was learning five musical instruments. The poor guy fell out of a tree before his seventh-grade year. He was mangled. Both his hips were in body casts. His elbows and wrists were a mess. It would take nearly four years before Dan was physically ready to play ball again. He had to go stir crazy during the waiting period.

A young Dan Hampton, playing pee-wee football, was a running back. Hamp almost always had a size edge over the other kids. Throw in speed and natural athleticism and you had Led Zeppelin versus the house band at the bowling alley, or Mario Andretti, in a finely tuned Indy car, versus your mom's SUV. It's no surprise that Hamp had games where he rushed for 300 yards.

Christ, I didn't know there was enough time in a pee-wee game to rush for 300 yards.

Dan would eventually become his high school's first prep All-American.

Now, here is a big-time occurrence in the life of Dan Hampton. Arkansas wanted Dan as a tight end. Trash that, Jimmy Johnson, a Holtz assistant at the time, sized up Hamp and told the youngster he was going to play the defensive line.

Hampton's career with the Bears was just majestic. Along with Mike Ditka, "Mongo" McMichael, Mark Bortz, Jimbo Covert, Dave Duerson, Walter Payton, and a flock of others, the team became "Halas tough"

"We didn't just want to beat you, we wanted to hurt you."

—Hampton

Do you remember Tony Eason, the New England starting QB up against the Bears in Super Bowl XX? Tony wasn't just frightened, he was damn near shaking. Convicts turned prison bitches have looked more composed.

There was one thorn that perpetually stung the psyche of Dan Hampton. He couldn't accept Jim McMahon. Hamp didn't like Mac's approach, his unwillingness to play with pain that no average human being could ever endure.

In 1987, when Hampton appeared on my WMAQ radio show, he said he didn't give a damn if "McMahon or Mike Tomczak quarterbacked the Bears." Literal translation: Give the ball to T-zak. A short time later, at the old Halas Hall, Hamp says he called out Mac in front of his teammates. Jim told him, "I play this game to take care of my family." In Dan's world, that was basically unconditional surrender…Jimmy Mac wasn't buying the Hampton-Mongo-O'B-Butkus culture.

You tell me who's right. The jury is out. I love Hamp, but I couldn't do what he did. Mac and I have had our ups and downs, but he was a tough kid…just not tough enough to please the toughest one-man jury in the NFL empire.

In '82, Hampton just creamed John Hanna, the stud New England left guard. Just chewed him alive, shortly after *Sports Illustrated* had declared in a cover story that Hanna was the greatest offensive lineman of all time. You think Hanna wasn't a tough cookie? He made the NFL's team of the decade in both the '70s and '80s. Hampton reduced him to lemon meringue pie.

The Danimal retired after the Bears were knocked off by the Giants in the playoffs in January of '91. He needs both knees replaced. His ring finger on his right hand is still mangled from a run in with a face mask—and the face mask belonged to Walter Payton.

It could only happen to "The Danimal."

And here's the beauty of it all: Dan wouldn't change a thing. Nothing. It was his game, his culture…a culture Dan will take to his grave. Don't even try to tell him he should've taken a few Sundays off in the name of common sense.

Hamp ain't buyin' it.

13 *Don't ever forget* NO. 55

*"I had an offer to play for San Diego in the old AFL, and it paid
more money than the Bears were offering. But I told the Chargers,
'I was raised in cold weather, I need snow. I'm not gonna play in
some town with fuckin' palm trees.'"*

—Ex-Bears linebacker Doug Buffone,
talking about why he chose to sign with
the Chicago Bears over the Chargers

Here are two things I know about Doug Buffone. One, Tommy Lasorda
will tell you he was the greatest high school catcher he ever scouted. Two, during
a Caribbean cruise in '91 with Doug, our wives, and our friend Joe Antimuro,
Buffone, and I established a one-night record for eating flaming Baked Alaska
that will never be touched. We did have an edge. Due to turbulent weather,
about two-thirds of the passengers were in their rooms vomiting while dinner
was being served.

Trust me, the guys who belch red hots in the annual Nathan's International
July 4 hot dog eating contest would be upchucking if they saw what Doug and
I packed away. One maitre d' was so overcome by nausea he turned in his white
gloves and became a toll booth operator.

Doug joined the Bears in 1966, one year after the Sayers-Butkus draft. He
figured he was joining a dynasty in progress. He wound up on the losing side
of more games than any player who has ever worn the Halas colors. During the
Buffone era, the Bears figured 7–7 was a tremendous year.

That's no reflection on Doug. He was a brilliant football player. His biggest
playing issue was simple: He was surrounded by about 37 guys a year who
should have been bench warmers in the Canadian Football League.

A P.R. issue? Yeah. Doug lined up next to a guy named Dick Butkus. So if
he recorded 13 solo tackles and three sacks, he was still stuck in the overwhelming shadow that Dick cast across the gridiron. Lining up next to Butkus is like
standing next to Angelia Jolie. The guy with the spotlight is odds-on to miss you.

*"I signed with the Bears for $17,000 the first year with a $20,000
bonus. I was overwhelmed. Halas asked me what I wanted, and I
didn't know what to say. I called my old man after I signed and he*

*couldn't believe it. He thought I was stealing. My father was making
five-grand a year working in a coal mine."*

—Doug Buffone

So, you figure Doug is just another dumb jock locked in the past. You're dead wrong. He sees what I see—the NFL Network eventually putting the Super Bowl up as a pay-per-view event. Why not? The NFL's TV toy has to eventually flex its muscles and show the American public it has something besides a wooden Indian named Rich Eisen.

Do the math. $89.95 to buy an eight-hour Super Bowl package. Yes, Congress would stand on its hind legs and scream. But, a lobbyist here, some season tickets there, and the tabs would be covered. The door would be opened.

Every sports bar, hair salon, and bowling alley in America would have to have the Super Bowl. The game wouldn't do $25 million. It would probably do about $900 million. And gosh knows Michael McCaskey needs the bread.

Buffone will tell you without hesitation that he could play—make that thrive—in today's league. I couldn't agree more. The NFL Doug joined was still a six-month-a-year operation. Today with every team employing assistant special teams coaches (Just what the hell does an assistant special teams coach do—pump up footballs?), nutritionists, and weight rooms as big as the Aragon Ballroom, Buffone would be 250 ripped pounds of meaness with about 7 percent body fat.

Doug played at 230 pounds and he lived for halftimes for a very logical reason: He was dying to drag on a Marlboro. "Butkus and I used to have our cigarettes laid out," Doug joked. "Our coaches would be talking adjustments and we'd be going yeah, yeah, yeah." Hey, the Bears during the Doug Buffone era, all 14 years, weren't even worthy of a yeah, yeah, yeah.

You want the essence of Doug's 14 seasons at Cubs Park and Soldier Field?

This is just too classic. "We lost a game to the Lions one day, a close game," Buffone recalls. "So [head coach] Abe Gibron walks up to me afterward and says, 'Do you know we knocked 10 of their guys out of the game?' I said, 'What the hell does that mean? Detroit won the ballgame. The fuckin' league doesn't have parentheses that says, guess what, Chicago knocked out 10 players.'"

Buffone became an entrepreneur. He had investments in at least a half a dozen joints, including the old Nickel Bag on River Road in Schiller Park and The Bombay Bicycle Club on Division Street. Hell, he hooked up with Paul Anka to open a joint called Jubilation in Las Vegas. Doug still has a stake in

Gibson's, the Rush Street hot spot and biggest "see or be seen" restaurant between the two coasts.

"My first year in the league, I took greenies. We all did. They were passed out in the locker room. I was so full of energy I was still slamming the goal post when the game was over."

—Doug Buffone

I love Doug. In a way, I feel bad for him. Why? The guy is classically funny. His NFL pension could feed half the population of Rhode Island, but there's a big chunk of cinema noir.

Nobody wanted to win any more than Doug Buffone. Yes, he went to the playoffs with the Bears in '77 and '79. Both postseasons were one game, one loss, and on to the golf course.

Maybe Doug should have bought in to deals that could have sent him to George Allen in Washington or to Tom Landry in Dallas. He wouldn't give. He was a 110 percent Chicago guy.

Jeez, every year, Doug dreamed big and every year he had to look at a roster better suited to work as bouncers at the Admiral Theatre. Doug's battle cry could easily have been, "What have I done to deserve this collection of ham-and-eggers?"

To his credit, Doug knew when to leave. He was up against Tampa Bay in the "Big Sombrero" on the Gulf Coast late in his career. He put the shoulder into a young running back. The back went down. So did Doug. The pain was so acute, Doug thought he was permanently paralyzed. No movement. No feeling. He was fortunate to walk away. "I was lucky," Buffone will tell you. "That hit made me realize it was time to give up this fuckin' crap. I told Freddie Caito, our trainer, on the way to the sidelines, 'This is it. I'm out of here.'"

Buffone sees a league that will have a "$200 million salary cap within ten years…maybe more." He worries about the safety of today's players.

Me—Coppock—I worry about NFL violence, but I worry a little more about too many privileged running backs stepping out of bounds and linebackers failing to be the second man on a stop because, gee, they have to protect their non-guaranteed series of one-year deals. I'm not dissing players avoiding busted collar bones. I just want a dollar-for-dollar return on my season tickets.

Doug Buffone never had to apologize. He was what the game was meant to be. So he never made a Pro Bowl. When players vote, they usually don't campaign for guys on losing teams.

So what? Douglas John Buffone, out of Yatesville, Pennsylvania, is known for a lot of great things. He never stole a check. He played beyond his ability. He would have made one hell of a coach.

Buffone is a man. The NFL needs about 10 dozen more guys just like him.

14 Why do NFL COACHES have to dress like CHEERLEADERS FROM YALE?... plus other bonus RANDOM THOUGHTS

I don't want to offend anybody. It is just not my nature. But I have to get this off my chest: Any adult male, over the age of 42, who wears a Devin Hester jersey has, shall we say, some issues. Penis envy? A midlife crisis?

After a Hester jersey, what's next for a middle-aged guy with a 43-inch gut—nipple piercing? A Harley? A Michigan Avenue shrink?

You know this is fact, plain and simple: The NFL just isn't reaching out to its female audience the way it should. How long does America have to wait before the League starts hustling official Pittsburgh Steelers douche, or Seattle Seahawks tampons? Maybe the NFL can front a line of Roger Goodell thongs.

But, in the bigger picture, why does the league insist that all its coaches dress like mannequins? Why do coaches—these great, semi-great, and at times pathetic leaders of men—have to wear official NFL apparel on game days?

Sometimes, I think it's only a matter of time before Bill Belichick will show up on the New England sideline wearing a Tom Brady jersey. This is a cash business. Bad Bill, a guy who always looks like he had a great night's sleep on a bed of broken glass, could certainly increase revenues league-wide if he wore Tommy Boy's jersey. The possibilities are endless. "Scores" should pay a bundle to buy midfield naming rights.

I know the league makes a bundle on merchandise—far more scratch than Dick Cheney stole when he gave Halliburton its no-bid contract to have free rein in Iraq.

I also know this: I get tired of Lovie Smith, the original "Charisma Kid," and 12 of his assistants wearing sideline gear that tells me they either were dressed by Sports Authority or Michael McCaskey. Probably Michael—what else has he got to do?

One of these days, I'm going take a seven-day tour of Big Sandy, Texas,

Lovie's hometown. If, after a week of visiting with residents, I find that at least 67 percent of them are as dull as Lovie, I'm going to ask the White House to place the "Sandy" folks on Dexedrine…or maybe require them to drink three Red Bulls for breakfast.

THE NFL ONLY has two majors concerns. Neither involves anything as mundane as player safety.

One, announcers are forbidden to tell the audience that the Detroit Lions would be six-point dogs versus Western Michigan and two, this is the main event, if five or six seconds go by without a tight shot of a jersey or some shirtless drunk with a team logo painted on his chest, it's time to call a league meeting.

NFL running backs don't learn "cuts" or "kick-out blocks." They're human billboards. They're on board to convey messages to little Billy or Randolph in Albuquerque, New Mexico, that subliminally tell them their life is on a fast track to nowhere if they don't have an official Arizona Cardinals Polyfil 2 in 21 bubble jacket. Wait. That jacket's designed for babes.

Never mind. This is the NFL. Just pay by cash or credit card. American Express not accepted.

I know what you're saying. I get this all the time. Coppock is old school. Not true. I'm still mourning the demise of Notorious B.I.G. And I love Simon Cowell. Plus, Paula Abdul has a world class—made-to-order—rack.

Moving on, I want to make this clear to aspiring young broadcasters. Don't allow yourself to reach the age of 34. You want to know why? Get with it, pal. It scares the hell out of weak-kneed program directors because they have to deal with the reality that you know more than they do. I know, I've been there— too many times.

IS THAT YOU out there, George Halas? I miss the Papa Bear prowling Cubs Park in his dark suit with his trademark fedora. The old man always gave in to the elements in November and hauled out his grey, three-quarter-length overcoat. Halas looked like a coach. He didn't look like an advertisement for Sports Authority or Target.

Think about "The Coach." He was 68 years old back in 1963, when he won his last title as head coach of the Bears. Actually, a defense led by George, Atkins, O'Bradovich, and McCrae won the bundle.

The offense packed all the creativity of Megan Mawike, the WBBM sportscaster.

Megan, as anyone over nine years old knows, works at Channel 2 because of an insatiable desire to bust stories, a burning passion to be jockdom's answer to Mike Wallace, and razor-sharp interviewing skills. It also helps that she can hold a microphone.

Don't let anybody ever suggest to you that Channel 2 hired baby Megan because she's a smoking blonde with a reasonably well-done tush. Then again, I have heard reports that Megan recently walked into Wrigley Field and asked an usher, "Excuse me, could you tell me which team is the Cubs?"

Back to Halas: If he'd been coaching for director Francis Ford Coppola, there's no way on earth Francis would have allowed the old man to wear anything NFL-related. You think about Coppola, you think about *The Godfather*. Just imagine how your perspective on the film would have changed if during the initial scene, the Don, sitting in his study, was wearing a New York Jets nylon windbreaker while he told the "undertaker" he'd have the punks who took advantage of his daughter chewing cement.

Jeez, the whole script would have been given a rewrite.

I LOVE TITLETOWN. I love the cold weather. I'm grateful that I saw Lombardi coach on the "frozen tundra." The Arctic chill meant that St. Vincent trotted out his camel hair coat and his cap with the ear flaps.

Think about the "Ice Bowl" back in 1967—the Pack versus Dallas. 'Boys coach Tom Landry was dressed like a guy hiking through the Himalayan Mountains. If he'd worn the "official zip-hooded NFL parka" he might have died of frostbite before the coin toss.

Halas at the finish line. The Papa Bear and Packers Hall of Famer Paul Hornung had a love/hate affair.

"Halas used to love to call me a cocksucker," Paul told me. "It was his favorite word."

Paul doesn't realize how much truth there is to that comment.

Now I ask you, ladies and gentleman of the jury: How hard would you be laughing at a 68-year-old George Halas running down the sidelines in his "navy blue zip crew Bears jacket" calling referee Ron Gibbs "a cocksucker"? Better yet, how hard would Gibbs, a premiere official, be laughing?

Oh yeah, I loved watching Wes Welker make a "snow angel" in Foxboro while the Pats were toasting Arizona. It was funny. It was harmless.

Naturally, the NFL, nothing if not anal, fined Wes 10 grand.

15 From BRICK to JONIAK...Rating darn near six decades' worth of Chicago Bears PLAY-BY-PLAY MEN

"I remember the first time Kup and I flew to Los Angeles to work a Bears game. I had a lot of contacts in L.A., and I told him I'd be happy to help him with halftime guests. Kup said he thought he was fairly well set. So we get to the half and who comes marching in? Bob Hope, followed by Jayne Russell, the actress. I thought, this guy isn't bad. But I almost passed out when President Harry Truman walked into our booth and said, 'Where's Kup?'"

—Jack Brickhouse, long-time voice of the Bears,
talking about his sidekick, Irv Kupcinet

I don't want to get wrapped up in grading out color announcers. But I thought you might get a kick out of that tidbit Jack gave me a few years before he passed away.

Plus, it does get the silverware in place for our dinner discussion about those individuals, going back to 1952—Jack's first year as the Bears play-by-play man—to rate those individuals who've had the *honor* to handle the mic for the most storied franchise in the NFL.

Okay, one more bullpen session: I remember a call I got from Joe McConnell back in January 1977. I was doing 6 PM and 10 PM sports on WISH TV in Indianapolis and, frankly, having a ball. My return to Chicago was still four years away. Joe worked for WIBC radio in Indy. He was also the voice of the Minnesota Vikings.

Joe called and said he was wrestling with a decision. The Vikes, at the time, were head and shoulders, leaps and bounds, above the pack in the old NFC Central Division. Joe loved the gig and had no reason to think about a move.

But he'd just received a phone call from Bears' G.M. Jim Fink. Jim offered Joe the Bears job; McConnell asked me what I thought he should do.

Now, keep in mind, I'm the public-address announcer for the Bears at the time. I would have given no more than my left leg and my liver to have the same offer. So my answer to Joe was kind of blunt.

"You gotta be kidding," I told Joe Mac. "The Bears are Halas, Bronko,

Sayers, and Butkus. The Bears are the plum. Who the devil cares about the Vikings? Call Finks right now and tell him the next sound he hears is gonna be your car screeching into his driveway."

Did I influence Joe? Probably not. But he did take the job.

So roll up the sleeves, here we go—the official, unsanctioned, Chet Coppock Chicago Bears play-by-play ratings:

1. **WAYNE LARRIVEE, 1985–1998.** Talk about timing. Wayne-o's first club won Super Bowl XX. His cadence and natural rhythm were just unmatched. I still can't believe that the Bears didn't offer him the moon when he left to go to Green Bay. Frankly, if Al Michaels left NBC tomorrow, the network would be nuts if it didn't get a hold of Larrivee to work with Chris Collinsworth. A workaholic—during December, Wayne's been known to work two college basketball games on a Saturday before flying out to where the Packers are booked on Sunday. Grade: A+.

2. **JOE MCCONNELL, 1977–1984.** Had a dynamic—make that electrifying—bang-bang style of working a ballgame. He did something most guys just cannot do: He could take you out of the huddle, through the pre-snap, the snap, the initial contact, and into the tackle in a fashion that was effortless. Never missed a beat, classically solid. Grade: A

3. **JACK BRICKHOUSE, 1952–1976.** 24 years of play by play and, God, he had his share of lousy clubs. But his enthusiasm for the 1–13 Bears in 1969 was just as vibrant as his enthusiasm for the '63 Halas-coached champs. Yes, Jack and Kup would blow their share of names. Yes, they had their moments when somehow a holding penalty became a delay of game. But they understood drama, and they knew what today's play-by-play men don't know: The game is show biz. Jack, Kup, and their producer Jack Rosenberg knew halftime scores were not nearly as important as having nifty halftime guests. Jack's legendary "Hey-Hey" call just added to the fun. Grade: C+

4. **JEFF JONIAK, 2001–PRESENT.** Most people were shocked when he got the job. Think Appalachian State beating Michigan in 2007—it was that kind of upset. He has grown a little on the job, and his performance improved when Hub Arkush was bumped and Joniak could concentrate on dealing with Tom Thayer as his solo color man. Jeff just doesn't have enough impact. When you're the voice of the Bears for

eight years, you should be a major star. It just hasn't happened.
Grade: C-

5. **GARY BENDER, 1999–2000.** Fortunately, he was "the man" for just two seasons. A laborious, network-oriented guy who gave you the impression he'd just as soon be doing the San Francisco 49ers. His impact in Chicago was less than zero. Forget about the audience…Bender put his crew to sleep.
Grade: F

Feel free to send hate mail to: chetcoppock@gmail.com

16 *Tell* FITZ *to find a* FOOTBALL *factory*

*"Pat Fitzgerald is so deeply in love with Northwestern football,
I think he goes to bed at night wearing purple booties."*

—Chet Coppock

I wasn't waiting for the 2008 Alamo Bowl with sweaty palms and a rapid pulse. In fact, I'd flat-out forgotten that Northwestern was booked in San Antonio on the final Monday of the year to meet Chase Daniel and Missouri. But I did tune in to watch the 'Cats—heavy dogs—put on a decent performance (they covered) before losing to the Tigers 30–23 in overtime.

A few moments later, my mistake, I flipped over to Channel 2 to catch a late sports report. Megan Mawike, the local sports savant and female Howard Cosell, was just gushing about how proud N.U. should be that it wasn't blown out of the gym by the Tigers.

Great, nothing says alumni contributions quite like moral victories. If Megan says it, you can be at least 32 percent sure it's correct.

Are you old enough to recall the Rick Venturi era at Northwestern? Let me fill you in on this hunk of gridiron gold. Rick led the nation in two categories: moral victories and moral losses. Jeez, the poor guy went 1–31–1 during his three years of guiding N.U.'s student athletes. Rick was behind the wheel as Northwestern began its memorable journey toward the longest losing streak in major college football history. Please, no numbers. Let's show a minor degree of respect.

Anyway, two thoughts popped into my mind. One (I've maintained this for years. I know big-time college coaches are treated like royalty. I know drooling alums can hardly wait to give "their guy" solid-gold golf bags and the keys to, at worst, a high-end Lexus. Don't get me started on country clubs.): College football is a business. No more, no less…despite the protestations of Kirk Herbstreit.

Two: It's time for Pat Fitzgerald to get the heck out of Evanston.

This is beyond argument. Patrick is the greatest player/coach in Northwestern history. No one compares. Ara Parseghian never played at N.U. He just licked Notre Dame so many times that the Irish, having dropped four in a row to Ara, figured, at worst, it could take one loss off the ledger by adding Parseghian to the payroll. N.D. wound up adding a man so charismatic, so football savvy, that 35 years after Ara left the N.D. sideline, he ranks just below "Touchdown Jesus" on the all-time Irish list.

Back to Fitzy. This undersized linebacker, who just dripped with guts, won the Bednarik Award twice and the Bronko Nagurski Award twice. Plus, he was two-time Big 10 Defensive Player of the Year under his mentor, Gary Barnett. Fitzgerald just needed another three inches of height and 20 pounds of weight to be a six-time NFL Pro Bowler.

At the ripe old age of 33, Pat was inducted in to the College Football Hall of Fame.

Fitzgerald's manic sideline style clearly has a way of maximizing player talent. Watching Fitz on the prowl is to watch a guy who always seems about three plays ahead of the action.

Pat's only drawback? He treats press conferences like U.N. meetings. He'll talk about a game with Iowa in such direct, somber tones, you find yourself waiting for him to say, "And if Iowa City refuses to accept our proposal, we will seek U.N support in calling for an immediate ground assault."

That can be changed. We'll get Fitz a media coach. These days, they're a dime a dozen.

Patrick, get with it. You're too good for Northwestern. You can coach the school for the next 30 years and you'll never be connected with the phrase, "BCS Title Game."

Call your agent. Begin making plans. Think about a football factory, a school that slides in a dozen non-predictors ever year. You know, a joint like Michigan.

Prepare to tell N.U. that you love Sheridan Road and the access to the Lake Michigan shoreline, but you can't resist (choose one): Texas Tech, Texas, Oklahoma, or any school in the SEC with the exception of Vandy and, maybe, South Carolina. Tell N.U. you want your résumé to include a closing credit that reads: "Won National Championship."

Eventually, the NFL is going to come calling. Think about Lovie Smith making $4.5 million a year. All that just to say, "Kyle is our quarterback," or his Oscar winner, "Rex is our quarterback."

Pat, find a football school that doesn't just *think* it's going to play for the bundle, but *insists* upon playing for the bundle.

Frankly, you're too damn good for Northwestern. End of issue.

Postscript: So help me Otto Graham, I can't believe this. Our guy Fitz just inked a deal to stay on the job in Evanston through 2015. What does that tell us? C'mon, this is too easy. Nothing lasts forever, most notably college football contracts.

N.U. fans, enjoy "the kid" while you can. By 2011 Patrick's running a program with enough dough to choke Urban Meyer. You want a side dish? By 2014 Fitz won't be taking orders from an A.D.—he'll be playing country club golf with the owner of some NFL club he's running.

17 *30 years of* FOOTBALL FUTILITY: *The Coppock list of* BEARS DISAPPOINTMENTS

Frankly, I feel like I'm jobbing you on this round of gab. If we extended the list of Bad News Bears back to the 1960s, I could throw in guys like Larry Rakestraw and Frank Cornish.

Rakestraw, Class of 1964, really only had one problem. His spirals looked more like boomerangs. Or drunks falling out of Jilly's on Rush Street.

Cornish, Class of 1966, was a load before "load" became a chunk of pop culture. He generally played about 30 pounds overweight. His pass rush was roughly as thrilling watching Lee Trevino stand over a 6-inch putt.

So we're going to name the most disappointing Chicago Bears, absolute Monsters of the Midway, over the past 30 years. There is really just one ground rule. You have to understand a guy can be tremendous, he can have a great win-loss record, but you have the haunting feeling that his career in Halas colors was somehow either empty, incomplete, or "The Wreck of the Edmund Fitzgerald." When you write your book, you can set your own plan of attack.

First off, we have to have a chairman emeritus, a guy we can all look up to for inspiration. Since this is my ballpark, the award goes to Mike Hull, Class of 1968.

Hull was a slightly above average fullback out of USC. The Bears saw him as a "natural tight end," the ideal candidate to replace some guy named Mike Ditka. Honest to gosh, I have no memory—pro or con—of Hull making any contribution to the Bears. Christ, I have no memory of this guy going through a pre-game warm-up.

All right, cue the spotlight. Here we go. Please observe the No Smoking sign.

Welcome to the First Annual All-Coppock All-Bears All-Disappointment Gala and Boat Show:

1. **JIM MCMAHON, CLASS OF 1982.** I can hear the screaming already. How can I put the "Punky QB," a Super Bowl Champion, on a bum's rush list? Simple. McMahon was a fabulous quarterback. His ability to recognize and break down coverage made him a 1980s Peyton Manning.

   But Jim sadly left too many plays on the field. The Bears couldn't keep him healthy. By the end of '88 and after he'd clobbered the McCaskeys in a book authored by Bob Verdi, the Bears kissed him off to San Diego.

   A healthy McMahon, with a dozen good years in Chicago, would have gone to the Hall of Fame. Instead, Mac became a football drifter. Still likes to play golf in his bare feet. Don't ask me...

2. **ALONZO SPELLMAN, CLASS OF 1992.** 'Zo gets a partial mulligan because he was obviously haunted by demons that actually scared the hell out of Sigmund Freud. From the belly up, Spellman looked like he could knock out the Rock of Gibraltar in under 30 seconds.

   Alonzo either could not or just would not bring his "A" game. Just a tragic waste of talent.

3. **VINCE EVANS, CLASS OF 1977.** Good God, was he athletic. He had all the tools to be a sterling silver running back in a nickel offense or a slot receiver. Sadly, the Bears requested that he play quarterback. Vince could throw the ball through a brick wall. However, he never did quite master of the art of finding a wide receiver running a crossing route.

4. **WILLIE GAULT, CLASS OF 1983.** I hate to do this because I think the world of Willie. But has there ever been a wideout who left more plays on the field? His hands were made of corned beef hash. Gault was so wrapped up in dreams of becoming a leading man that he put football in the back seat. Chicks always give him a pass because of his pelvic thrust in the "Super Bowl Shuffle."

5. **STAN THOMAS, CLASS OF 1990.** I don't know how the devil he started at Texas. Blessed with terrible footwork and a complete inability to handle either an inside spin move or a bull rush. Other than that, as left tackles go, this guy was Anthony Munoz. His nickname should have been "False Start."

6. **KORDELL STEWART, CLASS OF 2003.** An unforgettable player. The Master of the John Shoop offense. Every time you booed Rex Grossman, you were booing the legacy of Kordell Stewart.

7. **RASHAAN SALAAM, CLASS OF 1995.** CIA still investigating how he rushed for 1,000 yards his rookie year. Treated footballs like unwelcome relatives in town from Sheboygan. Once left the crowd at Soldier Field breathless with indifference when he was running in the open field on the east side of the ballpark and just dropped the ball. Maybe, he got hit by a bug. Oh, yeah…mon liked hees ganja.

8. **CADE MCNOWN, CLASS OF 1999.** A complete louse. Even Bear apologist Jeff Joniak couldn't stand this guy. Had no interest in football except on paydays. One of the Bears' truly great first-round busts. Led UCLA in illegal use of handicap parking stickers.

9. **CHRIS ZORICH, CLASS OF 1991.** Ditka loved him. Dave Wannstedt thought he should have been a full-time fundraiser. Zorich just got too wrapped up in the "celebrity scene" for his own good. Chris also lacked the height to really be a big-time "presence."

10. **MIKE BROWN, CLASS OF 2000.** Just loaded with talent. Tremendous instincts. A bona fide playmaker. He would have been a poor man's Ronnie Lott if he could've avoided the injury bug. Years from now, old timers will talk about "Hall of Fame talent" when they talk about Mike Brown.

11. **MARC COLOMBO, CLASS OF 2002.** I'm not sure what the Bears did for Colombo besides try like crazy to get him healthy before they moved him to the Dallas Cowboys.

12. **TANK JOHNSON, CLASS OF 2004.** Impossibly immature, to the point of being a kindergartner. A 10-year-old in shoulder pads. Drove Jerry Angelo, the Bears G.M., nuts. A classic example of a guy with great ability who played when he felt like it. Great con man. Could convince you he was the pride and joy of the Eagle Scouts.

13. **EDDIE KENNISON, CLASS OF 2000.** I'll never forget this. When the Bears added E.K. to the roster, an NFL G.M. told me, "there's no way he'll be with that club more than a year." He was right.

14. **CURTIS ENIS, CLASS OF 1998.** Did have some creativity. Once did an

end zone "beach style" pose, lying on his side with his head propped on the palm of his hand after scoring a rare TD. Insiders tell me Enis never heard the phrase, "Act like you've been there."

15. **WILL FURRER, CLASS OF 1992.** That was Ditka's final year as Bears head coach. So, if you're looking for a scapegoat…

Honorable mention, Old Timers Division: Bobby Layne, Class of 1948. You talk about a disaster. The Bears traded this Hall of Fame pitcher to the long-gone New York Bulldogs. Trust me, if Layne had played for the Bears, you wouldn't hear all this garbage about the team not having a solid QB since Sid Luckman retired. Instead, you'd hear a much different refrain: The Bears haven't had a QB since Bobby Layne retired.

Applications pending:
Cedric Benson, Class of 2005
David Terrell, Class of 2001
Bob Avellini, Class of 1975

18 *Give your sweat glands a workout—attend* BEARS *training camp in* BOURBONNAIS

"20 years ago, training camp was far more physically demanding. Now it's an aerobics class."
—Dan Pompei, NFL writer, *Chicago Tribune*

Okay, let's cut right to the chase. I don't feel real well today. I'm home with my 43rd annual mid-winter virus. My situation hasn't been helped by watching Mr. T on DirectTV—cable is just so old school—hawking a cooking product that actually grills salmon in under 12 minutes. You need more? I've seen enough of Suzanne Somers to declare her facial mission a success. Her lips are now every bit as large as Tina Turner's or Mick Jagger's.

Roughly 50 years ago, Newton Minow, Chairman of the U.S. Federal Communications Commission, came up with a great line about the tube. Basically, Newton said TV "was a vast wasteland." I wonder what the hell he'd say in 2009 if he got a look at Jillian Barberie flaunting her knockers on *Extreme Dating*. I don't want to suggest that *Extreme Dating* is helpless, but it makes Jerry Springer look like Walter Cronkite.

Now I feel better. Let's talk football. There are guys in my business who just live to stand on the sidelines watching the Bears prepare for another year of excuses. Count me out. I just don't get a kick out of the preseason, workouts or games. I've been screaming "18 and 2" since about 1983. The NFL doesn't need more Curt Menefee, it needs an 18-game regular-season schedule with a 50-man game-day roster limit.

That being said, I have to confess...there was a time. When I was just a young brat, my old man used to take me to Rensselaer, Indiana, every year to see the Bears go through the grind. And it wasn't just a grind. The old guys were handed a summertime prison sentence.

Think about this: NFL teams played six exhibition games until 1978. George Halas figured he was giving his guys a day off if they only wore helmets, shoulder pads, and shorts in 94-degree weather during an afternoon workout following preseason games in exotic cities like Memphis and Akron, Ohio.

But, gosh, I loved those trips to Rensselaer. I stood on the sidelines and watched Doug Atkins, Bill George, and Mike Ditka, all future Hall of Famers. I was just spellbound when I met a young Harlon Hill in 1957. Harlon is the most overlooked, underrated Bear in club history. "The Indian" was years ahead of his time. A legitimate physical freak. A 6'3" wide out who ran the 40 in about 4.3.

Harlon's résumé includes a "Rookie of the Year" selection and an "NFL MVP Award" along with three All-Pro selections. Hill really only had three great seasons due to injuries. But as pro football 2009 began, he was still the Bears all-time leader in 100-yard receiving games and second in career receiving yards. No, he never caught a pass from Sid Luckman.

And, hello, Harlon played 12-game schedules.

Hill also played when defensive backs had free tickets to mug wide receivers. The "clothesline" was part of the action. The league's sales pitch should have been, "No one gets out of here without a lifetime of physical hell."

What was Harlon Hill? Randy Moss before Randy Moss. Did I mention that in 1955 Harlon averaged a mere 25 yards a catch?

The summertime gospel? Listen to John Jurkovich, ESPN-1000 radio stalwart and the pride and joy of Calumet City: "If you're going to hit a running back when you're scrimmaging, the rule is to 'stay up.' No coach wants to lose a back in August." Jurko knows the game. He was a grinder of a defensive tackle with Miami, Green Bay, Jacksonville, and the Cleveland Browns.

Okay, so you're headed down I-57 to Bourbonnais, often referred to as the "Florence, Italy" of the Midwest. Here's the first bit of advice. Go at night.

Why bother to stand in blazing-hot 3:00 PM sunshine?

Check out T.J. Donlin's. You can't miss it. It's right across from the Dairy Queen, a longtime hot bed of Bourbonnais culture. At least once a summer, Alex Brown can be expected to buy the house a round during "last call" at Donlin's.

Call this a rarity. The McCaskeys have far too many fumbles, offside penalties, and genuine screw-ups to outline in detail. But props are in order on training camp.

The Lake Forest "George Halas early retirement" club got it right when they moved the team from Platteville to Bourbonnais for the summertime frolics.

> "The camp is kid friendly. Free. Great access. Close proximity.
> For three weeks, it's an interactive NFL museum for Bears fans.
> Autographs. Pictures. Conversation…then it ends and some
> players convert back into robotic prima donnas at Halas Hall."
> —David Haugh, football columnist, *Chicago Tribune*

Naturally, in this post-MTV era, the Bears have a bundle of promotions designed to enhance the "training camp" experience. Fan-friendly translation: Let's get the old man conditioned to dig into his pocket to buy more of our licensed NFL merchandise.

Training Camp 2008 was highlighted by the chance to "Run with Staley" the team's impossibly stupid mascot. My play would have been, "Throw darts at Staley." Or for UFC fans, "Put the sleeper hold on Staley."

Okay, so much for the grumpy old man routine.

I don't dislike training camp. I just miss the "World War II" days when a 9-on-7 scrimmage left guys with bloody knuckles. And maybe two loose teeth.

Anyway, Olivet Nazarene is a snap to reach. Your kids will gawk in amazement when they see Matt Forte or Jay Cutler. Hopefully, you'll land a workout with "live" contact.

If you don't, so what?

Let your wife check out Peanut Tillman's "abs" or Devin Hester's ass while you ask yourself, "What does Bob Babich really do?" Babich carries the title "Defensive Coordinator." But, during the winter of 2009, his level of influence at Halas Hall wasn't just slashed, it was left in a bin with torn sweat socks.

You need more info? Log on to chicagobears.com…and tell 'em Coppock sent you.

19 The BLOOD-AND-GUTS North Shore Football Classic: NEW TRIER VS. EVANSTON

This just amazes me. You think football players haven't grown in leaps and bounds over the years? Check this out: The 1985 World Champion Chicago Bears O-line averaged 265 pounds from tackle to tackle. In 2008, New Trier High School's offensive line—these are just 17- and 18-year-old kids—averaged 280 from tackle to tackle.

We're talking new age, baby. Current New Trier coach Matt Irvin likes to go no-huddle, run the spread, and toss in the "Hawkeye" from time to time.

That's just slightly different from the offense we ran when I attended N.T. Our coach, Walt Aschenbach, was one of roughly three guys left on this continent who still ran the single wing. It was an offense that rendered a quarterback meaningless unless he could down-block a linebacker.

> *"My two-year football career at New Trier was something less than stellar. In fact, I had colleges sending me letters asking me not to apply for admission."*
>
> —Coppock

However, let the record show that somewhere, deep in dust, in some score-book, my name is listed under "points scored." I ended my gridiron tour at N.T. with a grand total of one point. I kicked an extra point against some school during my sophomore year.

Anyway, the Indians and Evanston have been slugging it out it for bragging rights since 1913. In fall of 2009, they were booked to meet for the 100th time.

Think about that, a 100th meeting and a book by me all in the same year. If that doesn't keep you spellbound, I don't know what will.

If you're keeping a running count, Evanston leads the all-time series 53 up, 41 down with five ties. However, the Indians own postseason bragging rights. They've burned the Wildkits three out of three in the state playoffs.

> *"I don't have to create a rivalry. I've inherited a rivalry."*
>
> —Matt Irvin

Okay, let's clear something up. I don't go for all this politically correct nonsense. I was proud to be a New Trier Indian. I still regret the school's decision to go along with the program and change its nickname to "Trevians."

What the hell is a Trevian? If you have any idea, please contact me through my website or my psychiatrist.

Call it dumb luck, but I honest-to-gosh believe I was in the house for the two most unique games in the history of the series. No, I didn't cover the 1913 game. I was assigned to cover the University of Chicago vs. Philadelphia Dental.

In 1962, New Trier opened its year with a crushing loss to Hinsdale Central. The N.T. student body wasn't expecting much from our gridiron entry. Most New Trier kids don't expect much besides a trip to the Bahamas, full use of a country club membership with private golf lessons, and a Mercedes Benz convertible two years before they reach their 20th birthday.

Anyway, the Indians caught fire and set up a season-ending windup with Evanston for the old Suburban League title. If I'd priced that game, I would have made E.T.H.S. a 12-point road favorite with the over/under at 36. Those are logical numbers that would have produced maximum two-way action.

Evanston had won the previous seven meetings in the series by a combined score of 163 to 35. Upset time: New Trier, led by John Smart and John Roche, knocked out Evanston 20–7.

Eleven years later, the Wildkits got jobbed big time at New Trier. The record book shows the Indians won 3–0…but dig a little deeper. The game featured the worst officiating call I have ever seen in any sport. Late in the game, the 'Kits kicked a field goal that would've tied the game at 3. But contemplate this: An official waived off the successfully kicked 3-pointer because an Evanston player—I think it was the kicker—wasn't wearing his mouth guard.

What the bleep?

This is a rivalry game. This is New Trier–Evanston and some wacko in zebra stripes waives off the kick over a mouth guard? I don't care if the call was by "the letter of the law." The decision was criminally insane.

Evanston left the field in Winnetka 3–0 losers.

So here we go, fast and loose. The rivalry's defining figures:

COACHES

Murney Lazier, Evanston. Career record: 125–17–4. He just owned New Trier.

Eugene "Chick" Cichowski, New Trier. One tough son of a gun. Chick swung the rivalry in New Trier's favor during the '70s and '80s. A glare from Cichowski was worse than taking a fat girl to the prom.

PLAYERS DIVISION—THE CRÈME DE LA CRÈME:

Clay Matthews, linebacker, New Trier. Went on to USC before playing 19 years in the NFL. First-round pick by Cleveland in the 1978 draft. Clay played in four Pro Bowls.

Howard Jones, running back, Evanston. Athletic beyond words. Howard won the Illinois state 100- and 220-yard dash titles three consecutive years. Lazier called him the greatest player he ever coached. Sadly, according to prep godfather and former *Sun-Times* heavyweight Taylor Bell, Jones "listened to the wrong people" and went to the wrong school. Lazier had lined him up to attend a junior college that likely would have fed him to Colorado. Howard did play briefly in the Canadian League.

PLAYERS—SECOND TIER

Mike Pyle, center, New Trier. All-State football player, wrestler, and track-and-field man. Captained an unbeaten Yale team in 1960. Mike later co-captained the 1963 world champion Bears. Pyle and I hosted Mike Ditka's radio show back in the early 1980s. In fact, we were in his suite doing his program the night before Mike and the Bears won Super Bowl XX.

Mike Kenn, lineman, Evanston. First-round pick by Atlanta in 1978. Played wire to wire—17 years—with the Falcons. Just imagine what the hell his pension must look like.

Emery Morehead, Evanston, end. Tight end on the '85 world champion Bears.

Chuck Mercein, running back, Evanston. Chuck was an NFL journeyman but, son of a gun, did he have his moment of glory. Go back to the "Ice Bowl," December 31, 1967. Green Bay knocked off the Dallas Cowboys 17–16 in frozen Lambeau Field. On Green Bay's fourth-quarter game-winning drive, Charles racked up the bulk of the rushing and receiving yards. Mercein swears that in the huddle before the game's climactic play, Bart Starr called his number to run the ball behind Jerry Kramer. Bart, however, elected to keep the ball himself and scored on a quarterback sneak. You can't blame Chuck for figuring that if he scored that TD he would have spent the rest of his life on scholarship. As it is, Mercein became an ultra-successful New York businessman.

I've given you the salad, now go enjoy the steak. Check out New Trier–Evanston. It's tough, it's rugged, it drips with tradition. The memories just don't take a walk. They're just too special.

20 *The* GREATEST CARDINAL *of all time*

He was Jimmy Stewart, Alexander Godunov, and Bob Dylan in shoulder pads. He was Pacino, Secretariat, and Ty Cobb in thigh pads. He just never had any kind of supporting cast.

> *"Until the arrival of Jimmy Brown, Ollie Matson was far and away the greatest running back in the NFL."*
>
> —Jeff Davis, football historian

Super Bowl 43 has come and gone. Screw the Roman numerals. That gimmick got sleepy just about the time Joe Namath and the Jets met the Baltimore Colts in "Main Event III" back on January 12, 1969.

Frankly, I'm happy that the Pittsburgh Steelers came up with the win over Arizona. Let's face it. Rooting for Bill Bidwill, the Cardinals' hapless and hopeless owner, is like cheering for Karl Rove or the "bonus babies" at AIG.

We're talking nothing but headaches if Arizona had knocked off Mike Tomlin. Bidwill has no experience winning. He's a poor little rich boy and arguably the worst owner in sports this side of Donald Sterling, the overmatched "basketball man" who's been running the Los Angeles Clippers into the ground since 1981; that's the same year Rick Springfield left this country somnambulant with his recording of *Jessie's Girl.*

I can just see this opera unfolding. Arizona wins the Super. Bidwill receives the Lombardi Trophy and tells guest presenter Joe Namath, "Gee, this is swell. I've been looking for a candelabra for my piano." Or, "Gosh, are the Rooneys going to be hurt by this?"

I was bugged by the Super Bowl buildup. I saw enough Kurt Warner features to last three lifetimes. I got sick of hearing about the genius of Pittsburgh's septuagenarian D-coordinator Dick Lebeau.

I love the 1947 World Champion Chicago Cardinals. Who doesn't? I loved the fact that the "dream backfield" got big play for the first time in 61 years. But by vignette No. 72 on the topic, I had overdosed.

(Name dropping time: Two of the "Dreamers," Elmer Angsman and Marshall Goldberg—both gentlemen's gentlemen—had lockers next to mine at the East Bank Club.)

But here's what really frosted me: I never saw or heard a word about Ollie Matson, the ultimate Chicago, St. Louis, or Arizona Cardinal. Chicago has had three elite, upper-crust running backs during the 20th century: Gale Sayers, Walter Payton, and Ollie Matson.

Please don't throw furniture or burn my membership to the human race. And note I said running backs.

Sayers is number one. Gale was the greatest open-field runner the game has ever produced. But here's the fastball: Ollie Matson was a better runner than Walter Payton.

I said runner—not football player. Sweetness was the most complete player I've ever seen.

Matson was a physical masterpiece. The books list him at 6'2", 220 pounds. Don't buy it. That's crazy. Matson was built like Lawrence Taylor. His shoulders and chest were huge. His waist was probably about 33 inches. His thighs were hunks of sirloin and he bounced off "race horse" ankles. He had to weigh at least 235 pounds.

Ollie joined the old Chicago Cardinals in 1952, but only after he took time to win bronze in the 400 meters and silver in the 4 x 400 relay at the 1952 Olympic Games in Helsinki.

Matson ran like a panther in heat. If he caught you with a knee at full speed, your head was a lock to feel like cream of mushroom soup. Ollie was the league's first back who truly combined size, power, and speed. You need to see tape on this guy. Christ, he was a gazelle.

Ollie played 14 years in the NFL. His talent merited at least a couple of championship rings. No such luck. Ollie played on 12 losing clubs in 14 years—clubs that combined to go 58–117–5. Matson had to figure it was an odd year if his head coach didn't get fired.

Ollie was Rookie of the Year in his first season with the Cardinals. He went to the Pro Bowl and was chosen All-Pro during five of his first six years with "The Big Red"...despite the fact that the Cardinals were punching bags during the "Matson Era." Their idea of a great finish was 5–7. Ollie wasn't "Payton blessed" to run behind Jim Covert, Tom Thayer, Jay Hilgenberg, Mark Bortz, and Keith Van Horne.

Following the '58 season, for reasons that baffle me, the Cards traded Matson to the Los Angeles Rams. Not for a linebacker and two draft picks. Rams GM Pete Rozelle gave up nine players—10 of whom couldn't play...or so it seemed.

Matson came out of the University of San Francisco. Ollie led the nation in 1951 in rushing and touchdowns. He played on the historic Dons club that played nine games and won nine games by an average margin of 25 points.

However, Frisco didn't play a bowl game that season. Segregation was still raging from coast to coast and promoters either didn't want Matson or his African-American teammate Burl Toler...or would accept the Dons if Ollie and Toler stayed home.

Ollie had to know the fix was in. Somehow he finished only ninth in Heisman Trophy balloting. Yes, he was hurt playing on the West Coast and the lack of press that followed. But I really have to struggle to convince myself that 1951 Heisman Winner Dick Kazmaier, outta Princeton, put together a better body of work than Matson.

Hey, this was 1951. This was before *Brown v. Board of Education.* This was years before America was listening to Dr. Martin Luther King. A black man was not going to win the New York Downtown Athletic Club's precious little trophy.

The USF players did the right thing—no Matson, no Toler, no game.

If you truly know the gridiron, you know that Burl later became the NFL's first black official—and a damn good one.

I have to get this in the mix. The young P.R. man at San Francisco was a chain-smoking visionary named Pete Rozelle.

Ollie Matson was a first-ballot Hall of Famer, a running back damn near without peer. He totaled more than 12,000 combined yards playing 12- and 14-game schedules.

Mr. Matson, forget about the media flock that never gave you the time of day in advance of the 43rd Main Event. You were a story any football fan would have loved to hear about. Too damn many people dropped the ball—big time.

21 *He earned his spot with the NFL* OFFICIATING *studs—the Pro Football Hall of Fame should have a bust of* JERRY MARKBREIT

Go back to Super Bowl XLIII. Think about the big play, the difference maker. Ben Roethlisberger, down the stretch, throws on a line in the end zone to Santonio Holmes. Holmes extends. He makes the catch. Did he have both feet in bounds? Did he establish possession?

You know what I loved? Greg Gautreaux, the field judge, was all over the play. He didn't hesitate to make the call. His arms thrust upward. He signaled touchdown with so much damn energy, so much zeal, that he told fans at Raymond James and TV viewers around the world, "There is no way in hell I blew this call."

It was great work on the most enormous one-day athletic stage in the world. And Gautreaux gave football fans what they want: Authority.

> *"The public has no clue just how hard an official works. I used to run four miles a day to stay in shape. I could hardy walk after games, I was so tired. It would take me three days to recover."*
> —Jerry Markbreit

Jerry is now the youngest 74-year-old guy in the valley. He doesn't look a day over 50. You wonder how frequently he yearns for one last shot with the whistle and the yellow flag.

I think the world of Jerry. He's a pal, a teacher, and, at times, a guide dog who feeds me biscuits of football knowledge.

Remember that "tuck rule" controversy in New England back in 2002 during that AFC Championship Game between the Pats and the Oakland Raiders? The referee was Walt Coleman. We'll skip the details since this isn't *War and Peace*. I'm not even sure if it's *Jim Thome's Base-Running Tips*.

I recall this vividly. I called Jerry about ten minutes after the game to get his "read" on the call. Before I could ask a question, Jerry told me, "Don't ask. Walt got the call right." Jerry then covered the details full and complete.

Who's going to doubt Jerry Markbreit? Damn, this guy worked more sandlot games than any human being could possibly remember. He wanted to referee as much as Barack wanted Pennsylvania Avenue.

Jerry became an elite Big 10 referee. He went jaw to jaw with Bo Schembechler, Alex Agase, Duffy Daugherty, Ara Parseghian, and Woody Hayes. In 1971, during an Ohio State–Michigan game, Wayne Woodrow went "Charlie Bauman" on Jerry. Pissed about what he thought was a blown call, Hayes stormed the field, screaming his head off at Jerry. If Buckeyes assistants hadn't stepped in, it had to be even money that Woody was going to try and bust up Jerry's front teeth. Eventually, Woody threw sideline markers on the field. Hayes was what he was. Nobody ever suggested he was a Trappist Monk.

Charlie Bauman? He's the linebacker Woody slugged during Ohio State's Gator Bowl loss to Clemson back in 1978. It was the game that slammed shut the door on Woody's coaching career.

Markbreit will tell you that the NFL's next great official is likely going to be Terry McCauley. Terry was the lead official in the 43rd windup in Tampa. His performance drew mixed reviews. People who know the game understand he was terrific. The guys who bet the under complained about too much yellow.

An NFL game is three hours of drama, movement, and tension. It would leave a marathon runner exhausted. Jerry told me years ago that frequently on Sunday nights, upon arrival back at O'Hare, he would have to stop and just sit down as he walked through the terminal to the parking lot.

Obviously, it was the only TV timeout Jerry was allowed after the games. His body would need three days after a ballgame to feel normal again. Are you expected to feel like a million bucks 20 minutes after you've worked an overtime game in the Meadowlands in 18-degree weather?

The Markbreit scorecard is overwhelming. Our guy was postseason eligible during 21 of the seasons he worked the big league. The results? He worked 24 postseason games. That includes a record four Super Bowls and eight conference title games. You need more action? Jerry was an alternate referee at three other Super Bowls.

Not half bad. And consider this: When Jerry hooked up with the league in '76 as a back judge, he made $325 a game. He was fortunate to land on referee Tommy Bell's crew. Bell was a man's man, a tough hunk of leather with a big-time heart. His motivational speeches were so strong, so husky and passionate, that you half expected guys to run out of the room screaming, "Beat Wisconsin!"

The Markbreit museum piece? Go back to November 23, 1986, at Soldier Field, Green Bay versus the Bears. Jim McMahon was body-slammed on the ballpark carpet by Charles Martin, a guy who fashioned himself as a badass. In fact, he was *j.a.g.* material—just another guy.

You talk about ugly. The play was violent. Martin should have been booked for assault. Honest to gosh, I expected about 60 football players to start throwing punches. I was dead certain that fans were going to charge the field.

Jerry conducted his own rapid-fire U.N. meeting. He preserved sanity. He got Martin off the field. He cooled off a raging Mike Ditka. Somehow, he got Forrest Gregg, the Packers head coach, to shut up.

The situation was handled without flaw.

Now, shift to Park Avenue and NFL headquarters. Art McNally, the league's supervisor of officials, looked at the Markbreit-McMahon-Martin sequence until his eyes crossed. At the time, the league used a grading system.

One to six was the ticket. One was Circuit City—an official had blown a play sky high. Six meant an official had done his job with complete excellence. Sometimes, and this happened about as often as a Chicago politician is found "not guilty," a guy would draw a seven.

Enter Commissioner Pete Rozelle. Pete asked McNally how he scored the sequence. McNally told Pete he gave Jerry a seven. Rozelle looked at McNally and said, "Is that all you gave him?"

Jerry remains part of the action with the NFL—you can't expect this bundle of energy to sit home and flip between Fox and CBS. I always look forward to seeing Markbreit with his notepad in the Soldier Field pressbox in his new role as an "associate supervisor." Jerry now works directly with—he mentors—NFL referees.

Earlier, we mentioned the Pro Football Hall of Fame. The Hall and the NFL should be ashamed. The two parties act like officials don't exist.

It's murder in the first. Jerry Markbreit, Cal Lepore, Jim Tunney, Tommy Bell, Red Cashion, Mike Carey, and Johnny Grier, plus pioneers Ron Gibbs and Bill Downes…they all deserve VIP treatment in Canton, Ohio. Will they ever get the time of day?

This is the NFL. Don't hold your breath. The league is more concerned about players having their jerseys tucked in properly. The league worries more about hustling its association with the United Way than it does about ex-players who made owners wealthy but are busted physically, financially, and emotionally.

Sad, but true to the bone.

22 *Tell Roger Goodell to give* CHICAGO *a* SECOND NFL FRANCHISE

This is a golden opportunity. If Chicago had a second NFL ballclub, it would give the hacks at the Park District 10 more dates to turn out a playing surface that leads the league in divots.

Forget about Los Angeles. The hipsters in Malibu and Hollywood are so consumed by Pete Carroll, Botox, and keeping track of Meryl Streep's cosmetic surgeries that they haven't got time to bother with the "Los Angeles Wranglers" or the "Los Angeles Crimson Tide."

Anyway, this episode is really geared to the 18-to-34 crowd, the disaffected, disenfranchised folks who are sick and tired of hearing about Bronko Nagurski, George McAfee, and—quite frankly—Butkus, Sayers, and Payton. Did I mention Cedric Benson?

Nobody but nobody convinces me that young Chicagoans don't look at the Bears and see their grandfathers' team. These kids—the average 25-year-old in today's landscape is still living at home, so we can use the term kid—has grown bone weary listening to their elders debate the relative merits of Abe Gibron and Neill Armstrong.

Baffled already? Abe and Neill are both former Bears head coaches. Abe's stomach was just slightly rounder than Buckingham Fountain. Neill's wit and wisdom was so dry he makes Lovie Smith sound like Chris Rock.

> *Dear fan of our new team: This is going to be great. You'll no longer feel a sense of abandonment because you just don't know that the immortal Ken Grandberry led the Bears in rushing in 1974 with a whopping 475 yards.*

While we dream, we have to deal in reality. Go back a few years. The last lease the Bears signed with the Park District wasn't just good, it was fantastic. The deal left roughly 29 other NFL clubs screaming bloody murder.

Check out ESPN legal expert Lester Munson:

"At the time of the 2003 Soldier Field renovation, the Bears had the best lease agreement in the entire National Football League. That might not be the case now, but the team still has an incredibly one-sided document."

The package, no surprise, also gives the Bears exclusive use of the lakefront ballpark. No runs, no hits, no second tenant.

Don't be delusional. This wasn't the "genius" of the McCaskeys at work. This was team president Ted Phillips carrying the ball after Michael McCaskey had pissed off Mayor Daley to the point that Daley wanted to drop kick Yalie-Mike off the Sears Tower.

Daley is the lever in this "arrangement." What the mayor wants, the mayor generally gets. His batting average makes Ty Cobb's lifetime B.A. seem about as relevant as Mötley Crüe.

The mayor would have to play some kind of hardball to get the McCaskeys to give up exclusivity. No problem, the mayor was born to play hardball.

One suggestion: The new tenants pay the Halas heirs $125 million for the right to use their playpen. I know that sounds heavy. But I hear that's what the Pritzker family spends annually for upkeep on their downtown residences.

Second suggestion: Play the embarrassment game. The mayor can grab a mic and start screaming to local taxpayers that most of the McCaskeys—roughly 84 percent—have never worked an honest day in their lives. Or he could bark that any team dumb enough to draft Stan Thomas in the first round of the 1990 draft owes the public the chance to expand its football menu.

> *"I love the Bears. I still have 20 season tickets. But I'll volunteer to do public address for the new club. I did P.A. for the Bears from 1974–80. My starting salary was 35 bucks a game. My wage my final year was something like 36 bucks a game. But, hey, I had a swell parking spot."*
>
> —Coppock

Is our new team going to draw? Will it have people standing in line just dying to put down cash for PSLs and season tickets? No brainer. Our new club would sell 55,000 season tickets within a month of arrival. And that figure may be low.

> *Dear 22-year-old: This team will be your team. You can tell your old man you don't care that Red Grange was All-NFL in 1931. Or that Brad Muster, good old "Softy Brad," led the Bears in receptions in 1990 with 47 catches. Uh, out of those 47 grabs, Brad never did find the end zone.*

Merchandise? Glad you asked. It will just burn the radar screen. I can see 15-year-olds from Waukegan to Gary, from the Hancock Building to DeKalb, wearing new jerseys that swear allegiance to the "Chicago Thunders." Okay, smart guy, you got a better name?

Finally, the new club shall be required to sign a "give back" agreement. The first phase of the document will mandate that said football team agrees to use the vertical passing game at least three times a quarter and respect wide receivers at all times.

23 *The current Bears need* ED O'BRADOVICH

I'm going to be as gentle and as proper as I can be. Ed O'Bradovich, the ex-Bears defensive end, was about as subtle as Hurricane Katrina.

I would have killed to see him play for the 2008 Bears. Believe me, if you think you were ticked at Bob Babich, the Bears' D-coordinator, Eddie O' would have been busting Lovie's little Bobby roughly 25 hours a day. He'd have given the sorry cast at Halas Hall a personality. It would have been tremendous theatre in a season of boredom, a season in which Devin Hester decided that return men shouldn't run north-south, they should run east-west—or backwards.

> *"In my rookie year with the Bears, we were playing Green Bay and Joe Fortunato, the guy in front of me, went down with an injury. Halas told me to get in the ball game. When we huddled up, O'B looked at me and said, 'Do you have any idea what the fuck you're doing?'"*
>
> —Doug Buffone, former Bears linebacker

You've heard of "Manny being Manny." That was O'B being O'B.

Ed had one problem. He arrived about 40 years too soon. If he played today, guys like Terry Bradshaw and Brian Baldinger would stand in line to lionize this incredibly colorful badass who was an All-State running back at Proviso East.

Ed was ferocious, angry, hostile, and top-heavy with killer instinct. He also had a world-class smile that made him a 260-pound chunk of charisma. In other words, he was slightly more fan appealing than Adewale Ogunleye or Patrick Mannelly.

O'B would look at Staley and figure any mascot that pathetic should know the feeling of a strong overhand right.

> *"Never go to bed a loser."*
>
> —Papa Bear George Halas

O'B had a slightly different set of words to live by. Ed's body language and his endless string of slugfests with rival players screamed, "Never end a game without doing your best to leave Fran Tarkenton or Johnny Unitas in a body cast."

O'B's pass rush just never stopped. Really. It wasn't all that strange to see him nail a quarterback a second, maybe two seconds, from time to time three seconds after the pitcher involved had released the ball.

Penalties were rarely called. O'B's 1960s NFL was a league that didn't know anything about turf and figured any running back who was no more than three yards out of bounds was just begging to chew grass.

"Ed was kind of aggressive...if you know what I mean."
—Doug Buffone

O'B played long before the NFL recognized the marketability and the cash to be made by making "sacks" an official stat. Don't be naïve. You can't possibly think the league decided to give stats the time of day just to make Deacon Jones happy. So there are no "official" numbers on how many quarterbacks Edward plastered.

But the 1971 Bears press guide, which is as tiny as a Boy Scout handbook, credits O'B with either direct hits or assists on 71 QB traps from 1967 through 1970.

The crowds at Wrigley Field loved O'Bradovich to death. They knew Ed was an outlaw. They knew he loved to go to war with Halas over contract money. They knew his credit was good all over Rush Street.

I can't confirm this item. Nobody's talking. But for years I've heard that O'B and Mike Ditka, ticked off over a car blocking their auto on North State Street, did what any logical, clear-thinking guys would do. They just went ahead and turned some poor sucker's car over on its hood.

Keep this in mind: O'Bradovich could play. Go back to December 29, 1963, Bears vs. the Giants, NFL title on the line. O'B's fourth-quarter pick on a toss by Y.A. Tittle set up a quarterback sneak by Bill Wade that lifted the Bears to a 14–10 victory.

This was tradition. Halas never shook hands after a ballgame. He figured why pay homage to a Vince Lombardi after he'd just knocked his fedora off. The old man was in the locker room about 35 seconds after the game ended.

O'B stood at midfield and threw his helmet in the stands.

No, I have no idea if Halas took 50 bucks out of Ed's pocket to cover the "lost equipment." But I wouldn't be surprised if he did. It was just O'B being O'B. The guy was an original, he was nails-tough, and he dared to have a personality.

Amazingly, some 40 years after O'B made his helmet toss, the Good Samaritan who caught the headgear returned it to O'B. Why? He was obviously a decent fella who recognized that the statute of limitations freed him from any counter claims by the loafers at Halas Hall.

Take this to the bank. Dick Butkus will tell you that O'B's ability to contain and beat double teams gave "Crunch" a world of opportunities to drill Lions, Vikings, and Packers ball carriers.

A modern-day O'B would turn Halas Hall into a fun house instead of a library. Guess that tells us the obvious. Eddie would never be Jerry Angelo's kind of player.

24 MOUNT CARMEL: *The best* HIGH SCHOOL *football team in* ILLINOIS *—north of East St. Louis*

"Yes, I'm old fashioned and I won't change. I know my way works. I tell other people, 'I'm not sure your way does.'"
—Frank Lenti, head football coach at Mount Carmel H.S.

Frank and the Caravan dared to lose 10 ballgames during the 2003 and 2004 seasons. The experience must have been at least mildly disconcerting. Actually, the two-year window was probably overwhelming. Since the "off-years," Mount Carmel has won 47 games while losing just seven times.

Keep this in mind. Lenti and Mount Carmel really don't have a classic rivalry game for one no-brainer of a reason. They're the X, the check mark, on everybody's schedule. That's what happens when your program wins nine titles and plays in the Illinois state championship game thirteen times under one coach's direction.

Think about that, just contemplate the numbers. Lenti has run the show at 64th and Dante for 25 seasons, and his teams have played the main event 13 times. I wonder if the Cincinnati Bengals can relate to those type of numbers. Jeez, could Bobby Bowden or Mack Brown relate to a scorecard that gaudy?

So what makes Lenti tick? You visit with Frank and he's as comfortable as a La-Z-Boy. He seems more like a retired insurance salesman than a football coach. Listen a little closer and you realize you're talking with a pugnacious bulldog, a guy with an edge who says he can accept a loss but beats himself up

Frank Lenti, legendary coach at Mount Carmel High School.

if he sees a kid, after four years under his guidance, leaving the school saying, "Woulda, coulda, shoulda."

> *"Frank loves the kids, and they love him. But he puts the fear of God into them."*
> —Sue Doheny, Frank's administrative
> assistant and troubleshooter

Frank's office is a football overdose, but it's not The Frank Lenti Hall of Fame and Museum. There are a handful of photos and plaques that put a big-time spin on a truly unique football career, but the take-home point is Frank's display of reverence for the coaching fraternity.

The walls are lined with photos and posters of Bo Schembechler, Lou Holtz, "Bear" Bryant, Woody Hayes, Vince Lombardi, Bill Walsh, and—need I mention—Knute Rockne. There's also a mini-statue of Joe Paterno.

> *"In my wildest dreams, I can't imagine Frank saying 'Rex is our quarterback.' Too vague. Too dull. Too listless."*
> —Coppock

Lenti gets excited when he recalls a private meeting he had with Schembechler that turned into a once-in-a-lifetime coaching seminar in Ann Arbor shortly after he accepted the Carmel job. This was back in 1984. Frank was 32 years young, he had a tough act to follow in Bill Barz, and he wanted to tap into Bo's cranium.

"I had some kids going to Schembechler's camp," Frank recalls, "and I asked Bo if he could find time to spend a few minutes with me to offer me some advice."

Schembechler—in that gruff voice that made him sound like he'd just downed a gallon of sawdust—told Frank, "Grab a box lunch and follow me, kid." Bo took Frank to the press level at Michigan Stadium, where they convened with a third party, ex-Notre Dame Coach Ara Parseghian.

Last time I checked, Bo and Ara knew slightly more about football than the average John Madden video game. After a fresh round of introductions, Bo told Lenti, "All right kid, ask questions." Hey, that was Bo.

Think about this—the big stage! The State playoffs! Frank Lenti's teams have gone 88–15 over the years in postseason competition.

You are so right. It is imperative that we schedule Frank for a meeting in October with Lou Piniella. Crane Kenny can join the fray to explain just why he has the nerve to tell people he's "a baseball man." Better yet, Kenny can just pick up Lenti and drive him home. Otherwise, "Crane Baseball" will just get in the way.

Figure this one out—Lenti never played high school football during his prep days at Mount Carmel. In fact, after grammar school, the only time Frank wore shoulder pads was when he played two years of club football at Loyola back in the day. History tells me that's not the traditional way a coach creates a path that produces a career record of 284 wins and just 47 losses.

Maybe Frank learned the game in a roundabout way. While prepping at Mt. Carmel, he spent numerous afternoons helping to coach a grammar-school team south of the Carmel campus. Were lessons learned? No question about it.

Frank admits he's had about a dozen offers to leave Mount Carmel to coach at other high schools and he was flattered when Holtz talked out loud about adding him to the staff at Notre Dame back in the late 1980s. Other colleges have whispered in his ear over the years.

Is Lenti a candidate for a U-Haul and a new gig? Does he have the eyes on becoming defensive coordinator at Alabama or running some high-school club in a football-rich Florida county? No dice. Frank couldn't be more content. As much as he loves the job, the job loves him back.

You know what I'm really curious about? I wonder just how hard Frank and his staff have to recruit. (Yes, the Catholic League still recruits.) My guess is very little. Look at the Caravan's body of work. If you're a kid and you've got the goods, why wouldn't you want to play for Mount Carmel?

Put it in these terms: St. Patrick and De La Salle *play* football. Lenti and the Caravan *are* football.

Frankly, this baffled me. When Frank and I met in the winter of 2009, he told me he still had not heard from Rich Rodriguez, the Lloyd Carr replacement at Michigan. If I'm Rodriguez, I would be working overtime to establish a relationship with a coach who's turned out—good morning—25 All-State players.

Mention retirement, and Lenti plays a mean game of dodgeball. In other words, if Frank walked away from the kids and the clipboard, he'd be out of his mind in roughly 36 hours.

Lenti doesn't win with frills. Forget about "five-wide" or the "Hawkeye." He still runs his traditional three receiver sets with offensive lines that are generally tough enough to chew, rather than pound, tackling dummies.

I wonder what the heck Lombardi would think of this: During one run, Frank's teams won 24 consecutive playoff games. Is that a bigger play than having teams that posted double-digit win totals for 17 consecutive seasons?

Lenti's Caravan still play their home games at good old Gately Stadium at 103rd and Cottage Grove. If you attend a game, you have at least one guarantee—Frank's ballclub will never get knocked off because they're unprepared.

25 BEARS FANS, *the statute of limitations has run out—cut* WANNY *some slack*

"I remember the Monday after we lost my first game as head coach to the Giants. I pulled up for 6 AM Mass at St Mary's in Lake Forest and just began to throw up. There I was, by the side of my car just throwing up. I was just so mad, so sick that we'd lost that ballgame."

—Dave Wannstedt,
former Bears head coach

Wanny can still see Phil Simms connecting on the on a 38-yard strike to Mike Sherrard, deep in the fourth quarter. That play catapulted the Giants to a 26–20 victory. He questions himself 16 years after the fact. Did Dave beat himself by rushing three instead of four down linemen? He'll be questioning himself 10 years from now about the same sequence.

Dave suffers from the "coaching syndrome." All the front men have the same internal demons. The wins? They're a brief sigh of relief. Nothing more.

Defeats never seem to find a finish line.

I may as well spell this out right off the top: I'm a big Dave Wannstedt guy. We met, no kidding, the instant he got off an aircraft from Dallas at O'Hare the day before he was formally introduced as Mike Ditka's successor as front man for the Bears. Do I need to feed the meter? That was back on January 19, 1993.

Dave didn't just stroll down the terminal. He set a world record for the 50-yard dash en route to the baggage carousel. He looked like a guy who'd just heard that a slot machine was coughing out jackpots every 15 seconds.

Keep in mind, back in '93, Wannstedt wasn't just hot; he was Knute Rockne meets Vince Lombardi meets Chuck Noll. Dave had just won a second Super Bowl with his buddy and mentor Jimmy Johnson and the Dallas Cowboys. He was—don't even debate this—the hottest NFL defensive coordinator since Buddy Ryan had departed the Bears for Philly back in '86. Wannstedt had a signed contract from the New York Giants resting on his nightstand back in Dallas. A bundle of clubs were interested.

> *"The Giants were offering me $425,000 a year to take their job. Mike McCaskey asked me 'What do we need to do to get this done?' I said the Giants are offering 425. Mike said, 'We'll match it,' and I took it because I really wanted Chicago."*
> —Dave Wannstedt, on his tough Scott Boras–style bargaining stance with the Bears

That kind of negotiating isn't taught in grammar school, let alone the Harvard Business School. No doubt, Dave left 50-large in McCaskey money "on the field." But it was big-time scratch, "fantasyland money," for a kid whose dad and granddad both worked the J & L steel mill in Pittsburgh. And it was a far cry from the 12,500 bucks Wanny made coaching tight ends at Pitt back in 1978. Keep in mind, Dave thought he won the lottery when pal Jimmy brought him to Oklahoma State to coach the Cowboys' defensive line at 21 grand a year.

Confession time. Nod your head if you're one of the many fans who booed Dave Wannstedt during his tour with the Bears. You had a right to scream bloody murder in '97 and '98 when Dave walked off 4–12, 4–12. Dave, himself, knew his window of opportunity had come and gone.

I just want to know this. Did you ever really give him a chance? Was there a part of you that actually wanted the guy to fail because he made one mistake at birth—he wasn't Mike Ditka's twin brother?

Give it up, admit it, you little old personal seat license holders.

Go back to '94, Wanny's second year. Do you remember Dave and the Bears winning the old NFC Central and just knocking the living crap out of Denny Green and the Vikings at the Humphrey Dome in the NFC Playoffs? Do you recall the following year when Dave went 9–7? Wanny held up his end of the bargain. He won nine and he should have been looking at another playoff ticket.

But the 49ers swallowed their tongues in Atlanta. San Fran kissed off a game it had signed, sealed, and delivered. That left 'Frisco in the gutter and sent the Falcons to the dance over the Bears.

Go back to opening night 1996, the world champion Dallas Cowboys on the lakefront. Christ, the buildup was huge. Scalpers paid off mortgages. The game could have drawn 110,000 people. Were you telling Wanny to fuck off when the Bears licked Deion Sanders and the Cowboys 22–6? No, you were cheering like hell. Did your wife look at Dave and see 225 pounds of charisma? You know she did.

Here's what burns me up. There is still this common thread in Chicago that says Wanny's a second-rate coach. I say to those people: You're out of your minds.

Dave's 2008 Pitt Panthers won nine games. The season was a continuation of the club's '07 season-ending knockout punch when Wanny—a 28-point dog on the road—beat West Virginia in the steel mill heavyweight championship.

Dave is a winner, a winner who all too often has been underappreciated. After Chicago, Dave followed Jimmy down to South Florida, first as D-coordinator, then as the head honcho. Miami never caught on to Wanny. Dave won 44 games his first four years on the job and, somehow, picked up a rap as an "underachiever."

Wait. The guy won 44 fights in four years. If that isn't Michigan Avenue shopping, what is Michigan Avenue?

His fifth year was an abortion. Ricky Williams, 60 percent of his offense, traded shoulders pads for ganja. Injuries decimated the club and team owner Wayne Huizenga had a lot of things on his mind, but Dave's back wasn't one of them.

Wanny stepped aside before the year was half over.

> *"I'm not doing this for money. When I leave the game, when I retire, I don't really want to go to Europe or go on a cruise. I like simple things."*
>
> —Dave Wannstedt

Wannstedt can't say it, but this is legit. In his role as the front man at Pitt, he's the highest-paid coach in the Big East. He's under contract through 2012. Besides his Pittsburgh-area residence, he maintains a getaway pad in the western Pennsylvania mountains and has another home in Florida.

You're right; throw in a San Diego beachfront condo and Wanny becomes MTV-VH1 material.

Conversations with Dave are a "rush…a no-charge pep talk." He's an explosion of energy. Wanny jumps from his 2008 win over Notre Dame in South Bend to the fish sandwiches and beer he shared with buddies Friday night at a Pittsburgh shot-and-beer joint.

The buzz moves to the new offensive coordinator he just hired. No, nobody ever taught him more about football than Jimmy Johnson. His wife, Jan, wishes he'd just drop the whole shebang so they could move to Florida and commute to Chicago every two weeks to see their grandkids.

Chicago, I just wanted to let you now that Dave is thriving. The kid who was told a thousand times, "You can't work in the mills, you can't be like your old man," is at peace with himself. Of course, peace to Wanny means 14-hour days in an office that actually sits on the site of the steel mill where his family members toiled for all too many years.

> *"The Bears, the fans, and the media were more than patient with me."*
>
> —Dave Wannstedt, March 1, 2009

You still got an ax to grind with this guy? Drop it. He's a class act, always has been, always will be.

26 *The educated guide to* SOLDIER FIELD TAILGATING

I just can't stand this. Why is there a certain portion of our local populous that figures a day of tailgating at a Bears game isn't full and complete unless they vomit on your North Face parka?

That's bothered me since Jim Dooley was coaching the Bears, which should give you a pretty good idea of how little I've had on mind, other than teasers, over/unders, and who's going to quarterback Notre Dame.

Actually, N.D. fans can be worse than Bears fans. The fact is, the only thing more insufferable than an Irish fan when the football team loses is that fan when the team doesn't cover. Touchdown Jesus will confirm that one.

You know I'm always looking for ways to improve the "fan experience." With that in mind, I've come up with a list of "can do's" and "can't do's" that are henceforth and forever shall be Bears tailgating rules to live by.

Number 1: Any and all fans, regardless of age, are forbidden to play the song "Crazy Train." Let's go a step further—anybody who has "Crazy Train" on iTunes is a certified nut case, which means they are qualified to work for the Bears as an assistant special teams coach.

All fans entering the tailgating area also agree to never play "Copacabana," the remarkably touching song by Barry Manilow, the patron saint of lousy hairpieces.

However, fans may sing the following lyrics to the tune of "Copacabana": "His name is Harris/He plays at half speed….Once he got his bread/He just played like he was dead…"

Number 2: This goes back to our original point. If you're going to be completely slopped up by 9:30, just stay home in your garage, turn on the engine, and—please—lower the door.

Number 3: Allow yourself 10 good minutes to discuss just who is the funniest McCaskey sibling. Is it Patrick, who sings off key ever year at the Piccolo Award presentation, or is it Michael?

Think "Urlacher, Urlacher fills gaps and makes tackles…orange and blue…cover two…we hope he plays forever." That's Patrick.

Mike, of course, was handed the ballclub after Papa Bear Halas died for any number of reasons: business acumen, vision, a keen ability to evaluate football talent, and the instincts of a young Pete Rozelle. I should probably mention that his mother Virginia figured he was the only logical choice. Believe me, despite 11 kids, her options were terribly limited.

Damn, do you realize it's been almost a full decade since Mommy Virginia told Michael to get lost after he screwed up the hiring of Dave McGinnis?

Number 4: It is no longer fashionable to wear a Curtis Enis jersey. Frankly, honoring Curtis is like celebrating the invention of the thumbtack.

Number 5: The cooking of salmon or other fish dishes is strictly off limits. I suggest you try the Susanne "End Zone" Wood gastronomic treat. Got the apron on? Get five bags of homemade baked beans. Now throw in 24 large strips of bacon. Mix slowly for 11 minutes. Now add chunks of beef and 3.5 shots of Tequila. Mix for another 11 minutes. Calories: 750 per tablespoon. Recommended daily allowance: one four-ounce cup.

Number 6: Quit spewing the "F" word all over the fuckin' parking lot. It's not your neighbor's fault that you lost your house on Colorado State, plus-13, versus Oklahoma State in Stillwater or that you went "all-in" on the Naval Academy minus-3 at Louisiana Tech.

Number 7. All Catholics shall forever sing "Bear Down Chicago Bears" in Latin. I'm a converted Protestant, so I can get away with that one.

Number 8. If a keen, penetrating interviewer like WBBM's Vince Gerasole sticks a microphone in your face and says, "Who's gonna win?" Give him this sane, logical, and thoughtful reply, "The team that scores the most points, you illogical, witless testament to misery." You may then call security.

Number 9: Expand your Bears horizons. Each week, study the team's press guide to memorize historic Bears playoff moments since 1986. Trust me, this won't cut into your drinking time.

Number 10: Do not play bocce. Throw a football. Bocce is reserved for ladies—five-tattoo minimum—who tailgate at the Cell.

We appreciate your cooperation. Now, take the Bears and the over.

DIAMONDS
in the ROUGH

27 If we can forgive Nixon, we can FORGIVE BARTMAN

In the grand scheme of life, what was dumber—Steve Bartman reaching for a foul ball during Game 6 of the 2003 NLCS or Cubs' "Baseball Man" Crane Kenny calling in a Greek priest before the 2008 National League play-offs to rid his "little chokers" of evil spirits?

If you answered "Bartman," you're dealing with arrested development. If you answered "Crane the Baseball Man," you qualify to win an 8 x 10 auto-graphed photo of Sammy Sosa's busted boom box. But if you did swing and miss, don't feel bad. We'll send you a copy of Felix Pie's sensational bestseller, *Secrets to Hitting Adjustments in Late Game Situations*. Foreword by Corey Patterson.

> *Section 4, Row 8, Seat 113 at Cubs Park—the Bartman seat. It amazes me how many people/tourists/psychos with nothing better to do will take photos of the chair. What are these people doing, waiting for Bartman to turn up at a nickel-and-dime card show to autograph photos of a night that turned his life into a living hell?*

Apparently, Bartman isn't keen on a "score." He turned down 25 grand a few years ago to do a photo signing at the National Sports Collectors Convention. There isn't a doubt in my mind that if Bartman had gone all-in, his appearance would have dialed in about 60 grand in revenue.

I was at the "Bartman" game as a fan back on October 14, 2003. My son, Tyler, and I had been provided with great seats in the front row of the left-field bleachers by then-Cubs Marketing VP John McDonough. I love the bleachers.

As the game moved to the top of the 8th, the situation was "absolutely" blow-proof. Mark Prior—you may have heard of him; he earned $10.35 mil-lion with the Cubs from '04 through '06 while posting 18 wins and one complete game—was working on a three-hitter. The Cubs were six outs away from their first World Series since...oh God, give us a break...1908.

You people south of 90 know that was the same year as a significant occur-rence in the UK: Folkestone, England, hosted the first recorded beauty contest.

I remember saying to Tyler, "Do you realize I'm going to see these guys go to a World Series for the first time in my lifetime?"

Cubs fans, it's time to focus on happy memories like this one and forgive poor Steve Bartman. Photo by John Nunu Zomot

Tyler's response spoke for the entire Cub nation—whether they knew it or not. "Dad, do you know what club you're talking about? These are the Cubs."

We won't waste time with the Bartman details. I'll just tell you my clairvoyance reached a new high the moment Bartman and Moises Alou made the mildest of mild contact and Alou began to do the "cha cha" over the dropped ball. I told Tyler, "Watch closely, that kid with the Walkman is the new Bill Buckner."

Umpire Mike Everitt made the correct call. The ball was in foul territory. No fan interference.

You know what I've always dreamed about? Listen closely...I wish a member of the media had been in the Bartman seat.

You see, the press is conditioned not to react. Nobody cheers. We don't react to home runs or double steals. The press has much simpler concerns. We don't want extra innings, rain delays, overtimes, or NFL replay reviews that last more than 78 seconds. Our motto is, "Get the damn game over."

In other words, we loathe anything that might hold up quality drinking time.

I guarantee you one of two things would have happened if a "reporter" had been sitting in the Bartman seat. Either the guy would have put up his hands to cover his face—that's the traditional press reaction—or, a more likely scenario, a guy with a note pad or a microphone would have stood up, leaned back, and extended his arm to give Alou all the room he needed.

I know that sounds like Candy Land, but it is on the square.

Listen, if a guy fouls off a pitch and it somehow lands in the press box, you can be assured the following will happen: whoever picks up the ball will throw it back in the stands, hopefully to a five-year-old boy. You don't want a 56-year-old man to catch the souvenir. There's no poetry in that kind of move. You want a kid to have his day in the sun. That's Hollywood. That's *Bozo's Circus* and the Grand Prize Game.

Why doesn't anybody ever mention this little item? The Cubs still had a Game 7 and they led 5–3 before going "classic Cubbie" and losing 9–6.

So many people chewed up Bartman. Just creamed the poor guy. You know who you are.

Let it go. The Cubs choked, just as they gagged beyond words in 2008 versus the Dodgers. Yet Bartman remains the ultimate villain.

Five years too late, Alou finally admitted, "I wouldn't have caught the ball anyway." That's great, Moises. Now go do what you like to do before you swing the bat—piss on your hands.

Better yet, let Bartman piss on your hands.

28 It's MORE FUN than watching infield practice—check out the WHITE SOX Championship Moments MONUMENT

You may have noticed this already. It's going to be a few years before the Mensa Society comes banging at my door asking me to speak at their next convention. Frankly, my IQ is much closer to 0-for-5 than it is to a buck-60.

That being said, I just don't understand this whole monument concept. Why can't the names be more basic?

That leads us to 35th Street and the "Champions Plaza" featuring the "Championship Moments Monument" at U.S. Cellular Field. If I ran the show and I commissioned this gorgeous slab of brick and granite, I would have given it a much simpler name.

The natural?

If you're Jerry "I really should be smiling more often" Reinsdorf, go with "Screw the Cubs…Look What We Did." Or, if you want something a little more elaborate, how about this European approach: "This fucker will knock your socks off but please don't gawk for more than three minutes because it means traffic is down at the Minnie Minoso hot dog stand."

Get the message?

Now, let's get down to business. The Sox "Moments" monument is 25 tons of tremendous imagination. A.J. Pierzynski, Juan Uribe, Orlando Hernandez, Joe Crede, and Geoff Blum—remember his 14th inning Game 3 homer?— come leaping off the multidimensional sculpture. Other images ingrained on the face of the monument, which is roughly two-thirds cookie cutter and one-third planet Earth, make this sucker a must-see.

Cookie cutter…planet Earth…just keep in mind what I said about the showoffs at Mensa. Did you know ex-heavyweight fighter Bobby Czyz is a member of Mensa? That's living proof that good genes can overcome the inability to deal with a left hook.

You can almost see Uribe's ninth-inning highlight reel plays that locked down the '05 World Series win over Phil Garner and the 'Stros. Crede and Paulie are in full "swing." Hernandez—"El Duque"—is pointing his finger toward the ticket windows.

You tell me that isn't a subtle message.

The monument's unveiling was truly a spirited event. Then-governor Rod Blagojevich, who actually sleeps in Glenn Beckert pajamas while cuddling a Crane Kenny-Greek Priest Teddy Bear, was booed like crazy. Crane was dying to be there but he had an unavoidable conflict. He was speaking to a gathering of Greek priests in Athens, Ohio. But look on the bright side—Mike Madigan didn't attend the unveiling.

We should also mention that Rod showed up for the event in his finest pair of spandex jogging pants. Only kidding. Actually, he sported a game-worn Matt Sinatro sport coat with a tie personally signed by Mike Quade.

If you're headed to the Cell, take time to yank out the portable phone and get a photo of your kiddies with the Sox Championship Moments Monument. It's the most gorgeous sports monument in Chicago this side of the George Halas statue at Soldier Field (which is hidden—literally—underneath the stands on the west side of the lakefront ball park).

Give the Champs Monument a solid A-.

29 Play tourist. Get a photo taken with the CUBS PARK MARQUEE in the background

I'm running a risk with this one. I'm going to let you know about a major itch I have to scratch ever year.

Let me lay it out for you. This is complex. Just a few days after the stores begin howling about "pre-Christmas...blowout...no-interest for 24 months...sales," most people are worried about the essence of the yuletide spirit. I mean the true meaning of Christmas.

If you have family, you know what I'm talking about. Your Santa-spirit generally breaks down to deciding where you are going to sit your dysfunctional second cousin at the family dinner. I'm talking about the one who figures "tis the season to be jolly" means if he hasn't downed a pint of "Old Grandad" by 10:30 AM on Xmas Eve, he just isn't ready to sing "The First Noel," let alone any song by the Kinks.

I do something different. I have no choice.

I quit drinking 25 years ago. Damned if there hasn't been a day that I haven't missed sitting in some juke joint slapping quarters, later dollars, into the old Wurtlitzer. If it ain't a Wurlitzer, baby, it ain't a jukebox.

No, I wasn't a falling-down drunk. Hardly. I just figured with my first child due, it might be nice to spend more time with her than with Red Label.

Here's how I get my Christmas fix. (And mind you I didn't begin this routine two years ago. My "addiction" began when I was about 19...or roughly three hours after Grant and Lee stopped glaring at each other at Appomattox.) Around nightfall, I hop in my car and wheel over to 1060 N. Addison Street. Now here's where we really get deep. Here's where the shrinks will start suggesting in barely audible whispers, "He probably was never breast-fed."

(I don't know. My memory only goes back to about 2006.)

I just park my car and spend about 10 good minutes staring at the Cubs Park marquee.

I yearn for the days when the old red sign at the oldest ballpark in the National League didn't have neon. The past few years, I've had stomach cramps thinking about the eventuality of a "redesigned" board. You know, a marquee that says "Circuit City Stadium at Wrigley Field." Well, maybe not "Circuit City," but you get the point, right?

One of Coppock's favorite views in the world, the Wrigley Field marquee at the corner of Clark and Addison. Photo by John Nunu Zomot

Maybe there's that that sentimental part of me that just internally screams, "Is that you out there, Moe Thacker? Dick Bertell? Karl 'Tuffy' Rhodes?"

I know I think about the early '60s, when the Cubs were run by the legendary "College of Coaches"—a move so positive, so ingenious that it left players confused and the upper deck closed due to lack of ticket-buyers about 68 games a year.

The only positive I can offer up on that P.K. Wrigley experiment was that nobody died. In hindsight, P.K.—the absentee owner and chewing gum heir—did his best to hand Chicago's baseball fan base over the White Sox.

P.K. didn't worry about who was going to play right field or his lousy farm system. However, he would break out in hives if he saw a dead leaf in the left-field ivy.

You know the tired NFL phrase, "On any given Sunday"? During the "college days," the Cubs came up with a new battle cry. Whether it was Elvin Tappe, Vedie Himsl, or Harry Craft—or one of the other fumblers in blue pinstripes running the show—Cubs players generally screamed from their bellies up, "On any given *Tuesday*, your guess is as good as ours, as to just who the hell might fill out our lineup card."

I always think about 1981…not for baseball reasons. The Cubs sucked. It was the year Jack Brickhouse, my hero of heroes, departed the WGN broadcast booth. It was beyond the end of an era. I like to remember the huge number of fans chanting "Jack-Jack" in tribute to the "Brick" as he left the ballpark after his final "official" home telecast.

Frankly, I cried more than Jack did…and Jack was sobbing.

I think about a really special moment in '62. The Cubs hosted the All-Star Game. Don't ask me about the final score. Ask me about how spellbound I was listening to Casey Stengel spin yarns just to me at Clark and Waveland about the "Babe" (yes, they played together), Mickey, Billy Martin, and his horrible New York Mets while he waited for a cab.

A cab? Casey Stengel? Shameful. I'm still amazed he gave me the time of day.

Here's the pitch. I know it sounds corny. I know Brangelina would cringe in horror. I know George Clooney would ask, "Can I get laid?"

Go to Cubs Park. Get your photo taken with the Cubs Park marquee in the background. Do it for one reason: It's the most adorable marquee in sports. Nothing else compares. No contest. But ask yourself, "Is that you out there, Jerome Walton? Antonio Alfonseca?"

Those guys just scream "O Little Town of Bethlehem."

30 Cubs fans, get used to it— the CELL is the BETTER ballpark

Let's face it, your average Cubs fan is very fragile. I know—by age four I had accepted the fact that my life would include lousy SATs and Cubs teams out of the race by Mother's Day. So Cubbie Nation, we'd best have a heart-to-heart discussion before this goes to the jury. I don't expect an acquittal.

The question: What's not to like about that diamond gem at the corner of Clark and Addison?

The answer: Plenty.

Let's get down to the basics. Remove the historic marquee, the historic ivy, and the historic manual scoreboard and what have you got? Probably the single most uncomfortable ballpark in the bigs.

Cubs fans, be honest. What's worse—waiting for this club to win a World Series or waiting to get into a Wrigley Field restroom, especially after the fifth inning?

Don't get me started on the main concourse. It's so cramped, so congested it reminds me of the old Union Stockyards. The area has to break at least 12 sections of the city's fire code. Walking down the left field line always gives me one feeling: This should be a haven for pick pockets. For the time being, we'll forget about the grandstand posts on both levels, along with overpriced bleacher tickets.

Meanwhile, on the south side, U.S. Cellular Field has one claim to fame: It housed the 2005 World Champion White Sox. Other than that, the place really isn't running real high on the tradition meter. Nobody screams, "Where is our new Mike Caruso?"

So why do I prefer the Cell to beautiful Wrigley Field?

Let me count the ways. The White Sox have 8,000 parking spaces available. The Cubs have a bunch of shysters and hustlers who just can't wait to gouge you 35 bucks to have your car get battered in their lot while the Cubbies tee it up with the Washington Nationals.

Here's all you need to know about the beauty of parking at the Friendly Confines. A few years back, *Sun-Times* columnist Carol Slezak, a Wrigleyville resident, wrote a scathing piece about parking conditions around Cubs Park. Carol's beef? Some idiot, without Slezak's permission, had parked his car in Carol's garage before a game while she was out running errands.

You're right. You try a stunt like that in Winnetka or Wilmette and you probably get 30 days to life.

The concourse level at Sox Park—it's always going to be Sox Park to me—offers something truly unique: a chance to breathe. I love Chico Carrasquel's dog and polish stand. How can you not get misty-eyed stopping at Tony La Russa's pizza stand?

So what about the ambience around the ballpark? Okay, Cubs fans, you're on the board. Wrigleyville isn't Bourbon Street—it's more fun than Bourbon Street. And it doesn't just offer up booze and boy/girl attraction during the summer months. It's a year-round place to hang out and hustle. You tell me Bernie's doesn't just scream, "Your place or mine?" Or, if you're over 46, "Do you wanna check out my stereo system?"

This knocked my size 13s off: On New Year's Day 2009, after what seemed like three years of buildup, the Blackhawks and Detroit finally went head-to-head in the Winter Classic at Wrigley. There were 40,000 fans in the ballpark and, so help me Alex Zhamnoff, another 8,000 to 10,000 people were within three blocks of the park.

Now, the take-home point: You're paying to watch a ballgame. The sight lines at the Cell, especially on the lower level, knock the Cubs out of the park. If you have tickets in the first 10 rows at Wrigley Field, you know what a test it is to follow the ball. The Cell, with its modest lower-level elevation, offers a far more dynamic perspective of game action.

Don't start screaming about the upper deck. The first 15 to 18 rows up-top at the Cell are just fine. Plus, it's been years since anybody raved to me about the upper deck grandstands on the north side.

Let's talk about box office. I've always maintained that the White Sox would draw Cubs numbers—3,000,000 plus—if they had the benefit of an area dotted by gin mills.

Why not? Cubs fans like seven-and-seven. Sox fans are crazy about Jack straight up.

"I'd love to have the places Wrigleyville has," Sox marketing chief Brooks Boyer told me about the north-side barroom atmosphere. "But I wouldn't give up the parking spaces we offer our fans to get it."

So what about the precious bleachers? A Cubs Park bleacher ticket is sexy. It's bragging rights and one hell of a place to watch a game.

Call it a draw. Again, I enjoy the expanded concourse the Cell offers its outfield patrons. I love to check out the statues that embrace Nellie, Louie, Minnie, Billy, the Old Roman, "Pudge," and Harold. Plus, the easy access to concessions and restrooms is so far superior to Cubs Park, it's really no contest.

Let's wrap it up. If all you want is ivy and hot babes in halter tops, then Wrigley Field is your place. If you want a ballpark that says "We care about your comfort" with hot babes in halter tops—with occasional Bill Melton tatoos—then give the nod to the Cell.

I forgot to throw in this helpful tip. I take care of my consumers. When driving south to 35th Street in heavy traffic, always exit around Jackson Boulevard and take Canal Street. You'll be amazed at how much time you chop from your drive.

A late entry: I also love the pregame video on the Sox Jumbotron. I can clearly see why the Cubs would kill to have one.

Cubs fans, discover 35th Street. Ozzie's waiting.

31 See the single-family mobile home of your dreams: Check out the VISITORS' LOCKER ROOM at CUBS PARK

"The fuckin' place was so antique, I expected Babe Ruth to come walking out of the shower."
—Paul Hornung, talking about Wrigley Field's
Turkish prison...aka the visitors' locker room.

Just how cramped is the visitors' dressing room at Cubs Park? Let's put this in elite, show-biz terms. If Britney Spears walked into the place, she'd be so frightened she'd call her agent, tour manager, makeup artist, personal fitness trainer, and shrink—before her anxiety attack. My gosh, if Cher walked in, there wouldn't be enough room for her outfit changes. If this was Cook County Jail, legal eagles would be lined up begging inmates to sue, charging human-rights violations.

Visitors' locker rooms aren't supposed to be Four Seasons hotels. But if you put a sign on the dump that sits above the Stadium Club on the south side of Wrigley Field that said, "25 bucks for three hours—pillow and sheets extra" it would seem, you know, reasonable.

Think of all the magnificent hunks of talent over the years that have sweat through their shirts standing inside this war zone. And I'm not talking about ballplayers, I'm talking about the press.

"It's so Spartan. It's like trying to live in a shoe box. When you wait to get in, you wonder if you might wind up like those people who attended the Who concert in Cincinnati back in '79."
—Mark Gonzales, veteran *Chicago Tribune* baseball writer

This really isn't funny. If there was ever a flash fire in the visitors' quarters, God only knows what the level of misery might be. I guarantee you, this series of cubicles violates at least 25 paragraphs of the city fire code. But, hey, who's going to screw with the Cubs?

And keep in mind this place was renovated before the Cubs hosted the 1990 All-Star Game. As best as I can tell, the renovation consisted of sweeping the floor, adding two more ashtrays, and leaving half-price coupons for drinks at the Westin Hotel.

"The place is the black hole of Calcutta."
—George Castle, author and Cubs beat writer
for the *Northwest Indiana Times*

Castle, who began covering the Cubs near the close of the Dave Kingman era, says there's actually a positive to the mosh pit atmosphere. "It's a reporter's dream," Castle says. "There's no place for the players to hide."

You have to see the place during a cross-town classic ballgame between the Cubs and Sox. When Ozzie Guillen holds court in the manager's office, it's a miracle that someone doesn't get decked by a camera or wind up with a busted arm trying to position a mic for one of the "Oz" man's messages. Wrigley Field, in general, brings out the best of "Ozzie being Ozzie." Any chance he gets to bum rap the place, he'll do it. The Cubs, being the Cubs, of course, just have no idea how to react.

Quick. Timeout! This is a test. What's the most screwed-up aspect of the "Wrigley Field experience?"

A. The visitors' dressing room
B. The home dressing room
C. The god-awful price people have to pay to sandwich their cars into some guy's backyard

The correct answer: none of the above.

The height of Cubs contempt is down the street at 3717 N. Clark. That's where the Tribune Company and the ballclub gave us "Wrigley Field Premium Tickets." Stop by, get screwed, pay scalper's prices through the ballclub. Don't deal with poor slobs on the streets: Stop by "Premium" and get clobbered by the corporate giant.

Bruce Levine has become a Chicago baseball legend covering the Cubs and Sox for ESPN-1000. He says the visitor's dressing room isn't the issue. "The home dressing room is a disaster," Levine will tell you, adding that the quarters don't exactly boost player morale. "When the Cubs go to Miller Park, they dress in a state-of-the-art facility that's just palatial. The place even has a separate dining room."

Actually, the Miller visitors' locker room has enough TVs to qualify as a sports bar.

The football issue: I attended more than my share of Bears games at

Wrigley Field before the club zipped over to Soldier Field in 1971. You talk about a dive. Soldier Field in '71 was one of those rare athletic venues where it actually rained indoors. At the time, it needed three major upgrades to qualify as a housing project.

Anyway, I'll go to my grave wondering how Gino Marchetti, Johnny Unitas, and the Baltimore Colts or my guy Deacon Jones and the Rams' old "Fearsome Foursome" didn't give in to claustrophobia before games in the old Cubs Park visitors' locker room. I'm guessing they had to adjust their shoulder pads with pliers. A misplaced hip pad had to be lost—maybe for good—in a sea of hair and calf muscles.

So much for Cubdom.

Fifteen minutes have passed. Isn't it time for the ballclub to raise ticket prices?

32   *Learn the gospel, the funk, according to* THE "HAWK"

> *"I love to piss off Cubs fans. I want them to know I have one thing in my mind when we play them. I want to kick their ass."*
>
> —Hawk Harrelson

Wow, can't you just feel the love oozing from every pore? Hey, this is the "Hawk." This is Kenny Harrelson. What would you expect him to say? "When we meet the Cubs, I always look forward to truly competitive ballgames between two evenly matched teams"?

Here's a tip: If you see Kenny Harrelson at a golf course and he says, "How about you and I playing a one hundred dollar Nassau?" run for your life. And if Hawk wants to play a few hands of gin, just hand him your wallet. I guarantee you it's a cheaper way out.

> *"I'll play anybody a hundred dollar Nassau, but I'd sure as hell rather play for a lot more money than that."*
>
> —Hawk Harrelson

I hear complaints about Kenny all the time. He's too big a homer. His stories on Dick Williams, "Catfish" Hunter, Rico Petrocelli, and "Yaz" have grown stale. I don't buy it. I only have one complaint abut the Hawk. If the Sox are down 11–3 in the 6th inning, he won't quit on a broadcast, but he will get brutally quiet. And, if you're scoring at home, when the Sox really take the pipe, Hawk will "close" the 'cast in record time. You get a feeling he just can't wait to wash his hands and head to the next joint.

> *"Listen, I could have made a heck of a lot more money doing network baseball—and I've had the chance. But I don't want that. You can't say, 'Put it on the board…YYYEEEESSS' for both ball clubs."*
>
> —Hawk Harrelson

You think Hawk didn't have big-time supporters? Howard Cosell was among the network studs who told Kenny to drop hometown baseball and concentrate on developing his network niche. The Hawk and Howard? Tell me that wouldn't have been appointment TV.

The Hawk has changed over the years. When he arrived in Chicago back in 1982, he was a sidekick to frontman Don Drysdale. The chemistry between the two was fine, but you knew something was missing. The broadcasts were just too methodical.

You can blame that on Drysdale's insistence that the game be called "straight up-down the middle." Don just never got giddy about Ron Kittle. In turn, "Double D's" approach did nothing to bring out the down-home personality of Harrelson.

Go back to 1984. Hawk was doing a ballgame one day wearing a "Zorro hat" with a jet-black shirt and slacks. Really. Don was wearing his customary brown polyester slacks with a lifeless golf shirt. It always made me wonder, *How can these guys be such great drinking buddies?*

Is it really possible that the Hawk's second tour with the White Sox is now almost 20 years old? Yes, he's been the Sox front man since 1990. He thrives on the past, but will tell you, "I enjoy the game more now than I ever have. When the old-timers call me up and ask how can I compare the current ballplayers to the old days, I tell them because I've been around baseball for the past 50 years."

Hawk ain't lying. He begins to reel off his all-time All-Star team. Eddie Murray, Robbie Alomar, Alex Rodriguez, Ivan Rodriguez, Barry Bonds, and Ken Griffey, Jr. all come rolling off his southern-fried tongue.

"I don't like Barry Bonds. I have no interest in meeting him. But, screw steroids. He may be the greatest baseball player of all time."

—Hawk Harrelson

Yes, this is a man who craves the spotlight. You want Hawk's worst nightmare? He finds out tomorrow he's done calling Major League Baseball. No batting practice, no airplanes, no clubhouse chitchat to cover. No chance to visit with longtime friends in New York or Anaheim. You know what happens. Hawk goes nuts in about two days. Or, the real killer—he loses his ability to hit the wedge from 130 yards out.

The Hawk reminds you, "Think about this. In 2011, I will have been around this game for parts of seven decades."

Christ, did Hawk play with "Shoeless Joe" Jackson?

No, but this is on the square. Go back to 1968, a year after he arrived in Boston. He drove in 109 runs for the Bo's during the pitcher's era. He thrived on game situations. Inch for inch, pound for pound, he was the most complete offensive player in the American League.

Hawk is far and away the most dynamic baseball announcer in Chicago. It's really no contest. And I say that with all due respect to Len Kasper, who's improved ever year since he arrived at Cubs Park back in 2005. Pat Hughes, the Cubs' sterling silver radio voice, is also tremendous.

If you don't dig the Hawk, you don't dig rock 'n' roll. And Hawk is a hell of a lot closer to 70 than he is to 60. Kenny is still talking away as we move from baseball to golf and what a 3-iron can do to clobber your nervous system.

"Pressure is the greatest performance killer…you know Jack [Nicklaus] was longer off the tee than Tiger…lots of guys can shoot 65 on Thursdays but on Sundays their assholes are wound so tight…."

Hawk, you're what every broadcaster wants to be. A full-blown original. YYYYYEEEEESSSS.

33 *Get with the program—check out the* JOLIET JACKHAMMERS

This is "Las Vegas comes to Joliet." This is what I figure a guy like Mark Cuban would do if he had a ballclub playing out of a flashy, new-age, bells-and-whistles ballpark. Take a tip from the fat kid: Get 20, maybe 25, of your closest friends and pay the tab for a one-night stand to watch Joliet Jackhammers base-ball from the legendary DesRochers Spa & Party patio area at Silver Cross Field.

You get patio furniture along with party lights and optional catering. Plus, here's the crème de la crème—the patio also includes a hot tub. If that isn't the national pastime, I don't know what is. Think about it, you and your babe and a bunch of pals lounging with a beer in the hot tub during a pitching change.

Only in America.

Okay, let's get down to the basics. I love Silver Cross Field for a bundle of reasons. First off, the press box sight line seems to hang right over home plate. It's a vivid reminder of just how cool the view from press level at old Tiger Stadium used to be. I only saw the White Sox play about a dozen games at Tiger Stadium, but each time I did, I always had one particular feeling. I could almost reach out and grab Lou Whittaker, Kirk Gibson, or Cecil Fielder.

It's a far cry from the media section at U.S. Cellular Field. The press box at the Cell is so far down the right field line, you feel like you're closer to Bronzeville than you are to the home plate umpire.

Before you walk up to the ticket window, you're already ahead of the game. Why? Because parking is free. In other words, there isn't that miserable feeling of being gouged before you've actually dipped into your wallet just to buy tickets.

Tickets are beyond affordable. Let me put it in very simple terms. According to my math, a family of five can get in to the "Cross" for a little less than it costs to park in the downtown Chicago lot at the corner of Clark and Lake. And, to be frank, I don't want to clobber the guys who run the Clark and Lake lot—but it's been years since they had a bat-day promotion.

Promotions are a way of life with the Jacks. "There's something different every night," according to longtime Joliet play-by-play man Bryan Dolgin. "It's impossible to walk out of the ballpark without some kind of prize."

Dolgin is a keeper. Eventually, he'll get the call from some big-league team to be their "voice."

Back to my beloved hot tub. Did I mention that if you sign on for a night, you and your guests will also receive complimentary towels with the official team logo?

By now, I'll take a wild guess that some of you are asking this question: Just who are the Joliet Jackhammers? Let me cover the tabs. The Jacks are an inde-pendent ballclub playing out of the Northern League. Their rivalry with the Fargo-Moorehead RedHawks is just an inch below Alabama vs. Auburn or Texas vs. Oklahoma.

"Independent" means the Jacks have no affiliation with any major league team. Does that mean the product is a waste of time? Forget about it. What it means is that you have pitchers who throw 91 instead of 95 or guys with bat speed that's good but just not good enough to threaten the legacy of Andre Dawson. The line between the bigs and minor league is paper thin. Northern League players just happen to be on the wrong side of the paper.

A lot of the Jacks are just baseball lifers. They love the game. They play hard and, while many won't admit it, they just never give up the dream that one day a scout from the Atlanta Braves is going to go back to headquarters and tell the front office, "We can't live without this kid from Joliet."

I don't like the term "fan-friendly." It's as overused as the question, "Who is quarterbacking the Bears next week?" Just say this: The atmosphere, especially in the grassy areas down the left and right field lines, is just tremendous. The place is just cozy, relaxing.

I know it's not the big leagues, but so what?

This is an inexpensive opportunity in a rotten economic environment that allows the old man to take his wife and little guy to the ballpark and not have stomach pains afterwards wondering how he's going to pay the ComEd bill.

I have to get this point on the table: Silver Cross also has something Wrigley Field hasn't seen in years—a nice wide concourse that allows you to walk without the feeling that you're a blocking back for Matt Forte. The concourse at Cubs Park is a lunchroom prison riot at the U.S. Pen in downstate Marion.

Hey, the Jacks are fun. Players sign autographs. The product is very good. Book a date to see the Jacks play the Gary SouthShore RailCats. And, if you want Las Vegas Boulevard, hop in the hot tub.

34 Hey CUBBIES, build two commemorative STATUES for SAMMY SOSA

Mr. Coppock appreciates your kind and rapt attention. We will now open the platform to questions from the audience.

Q. Does Sammy Sosa belong in Baseball's Hall of Fame?

A. You have to be kidding. Billy Pierce, Bert Blyleven, and Tommy John don't have plaques in Cooperstown and you want to toss the bouquet to "Sammy Cut Off Man?" No dice. Did we mention that legendary Cubs manager Whitey Lockman has also never received the call?

Q. Before Sosa played for the Cubs he was a member of the White Sox. What's your most vivid memory of Sammy on the south side?

A. Two things. One, he didn't control the clubhouse boom box. Two, Jay Mariotti was still five or six years away from becoming Sam's full-time P.R. man. Mike Kiley, a Mariotti sidekick from the *Sun-Times*, was Sammy's associate P.R. man. More on that later, maybe.

Q. Why was Mariotti so hot for Sosa? Why did he treat Sam like "the second coming"?

A. Easy. Adam Katz, Sammy's agent, fed Mariotti stories on Sosa in the same adorable way that young children feed dog biscuits to collies.

Q. Just how much has Sosa impacted baseball since he last played for the Rangers in 2007?

A. Think Arkansas Governor Mike Huckabee or former New York Mayor Rudy Giuliani in the 2008 Republican presidential primaries. Does that cover it?

Q. What was Sam's impact on the box office at Wrigley Field?

A. Overwhelming, over the top. Even bigger than "Floppy Hat Day." It pains me to say this, but Sosa had far greater impact on Cubs Park attendance than Ernie Banks or Ron Santo. Sosa was DiCaprio in *Titanic*, Da Vinci and the Sistine Chapel, or the old Faces Disco on Rush Street—strictly one of a kind, pal.

Q. Why was Sammy so intriguing to the fans in right field?

A. Those fans knew—I mean they just *knew*—that every 12 to 15 games, Sosa would hit the cut-off man. Sosa's throwing arm wasn't exactly a Winchester rifle. It was more like a sprint car going end over end on an Alabama dirt track. Not that I want to be negative.

Q. What should the Cubs do to honor the legacy of Sammy?

A. For openers, they should immediately retire his number. And while they're at it, how about some jersey love for Damon Berryhill? The Cubs don't have nearly enough uniforms in mothballs. When George Halas was alive, the Bears used to retire numbers every 20 minutes. I mean, don't you get warm and fuzzy thinking about famed offensive guard Danny Fortman?

Q. Is that all you do for a guy who hit 551 home runs for the lovable chokers/losers/heartbreakers/dream-weavers (and other assorted adjectives that were all the rage back in the '70s)?

A. Of course not. I want two statues built for Sammy. Here's my dual concept. Statue "A" features a robust Sammy, in granite of course, bat on ball in what is obviously a home-run clout. Round two, since we want a full-figured/featured Sam, we steer a different course. This would show Sosa doing what he did so frequently and it will test the sculptors' ingenuity. Just how do you build a statue that illustrates Sammy—in a 9th inning game situation—swinging and missing at a slider, low and away and nine inches off the plate?

Q. Will there ever be another Sammy?

A. C'mon, was there ever another Michael Dukakis? Sam the Sham and the Pharaohs? Was there ever another Starsky and Hutch? Will there ever be another Antonio Alfonseca, or for good measure, Michael McCaskey?

Q. Sammy's numbers compare favorably to Reggie, the Mick, and Willie Stargell...does that mean anything?

A. Let's get back to the cut-off man. Just curious...how many World Series at-bats did Sammy rack up?

Q. Anybody get damaged when Sosa signed that four-year, $72 million deal with the Cubs?

A. Mike Kiley, Sosa's pillow and blanket, had to be kept from sharp objects for a month. *Tribune* scribe Teddy Greenstein was working the Cubs beat at the time. T.G. will tell you, "That Kiley was devastated." (You have to remember at 3:35 every day Mike and Sammy would have their little whispering session.) "Kiley couldn't believe what happened."

Q. Does that mean Kiley got scooped?

A. No, knucklehead. He got burned. Greenstein, by the way, had the story full and complete about two days before Kiley reached the recovery room.

Q. Does Crane Kenny have any more idiotic plans to trot out a Greek priest to purify the Cubs dugout...you know, like he did in that '08 playoff series when our north side heroes were gonna pound the living hell out of Joe Torre and the Bums?

A. Stick around. Good things come to those who wait.

35 Cover the CHICAGO BASEBALL scene for one week with ESPN 1000's BRUCE LEVINE

"My goal early on was to have someone pay me to go to a ballgame."

—Bruce Levine

You talk about bland. Gene Michael's managerial career with the Cubs was so indifferent, so uneventful, it eventually made Jim Riggleman's dugout tour on the north side look like the second coming of Earl Weaver. Frankly, I only have one memory of Gene in Cub double knits. He got tossed out of the first game he managed for the ballclub. He also replaced Jim Frey during the summer of '86 when Cubs boss Dallas Green decided that "Frey just didn't want to manage."

However, Michael's exit from the Confines was above and beyond storybook. By September 1987 "Stick" knew his days in the Cubs' dugout were on the "death watch." The only real question was the obvious. Would G.M. Dallas Green drop-kick Michael on Monday or Tuesday after another 162-game Cubs ticket to oblivion?

Enter Bruce Levine, who is now, and has been for years, the best and most complete Chicago baseball reporter since the great days of Hall of Famer Jerome Holtzman. Bruce had forged a strong friendship with Michael. Levine had Gene's ear—big time. What Bruce didn't realize was that he also had an impact on Michael's thought process.

A month earlier, "Stick" had told Levine over dinner he knew he was on the "hit list." Levine told Gene, "You know it doesn't have to go down this way. You could resign and go out on your own terms."

End of conversation.

But on Labor Day 1987, Michael invited Levine to his office in the dressing room at Cubs Park following a ballgame. "Do you remember that conversation we had about me resigning?" Michael asked Bruce. "Turn on your tape recorder." Michael then threw the 98 mph fastball. He told Levine, "This is it. I will not come back next year to manage the Cubs."

You get the picture. Michael quit. There was just one minor issue: He'd quit through one reporter. He'd never alerted, you know, his employers.

Michael, in a gesture that said "get lost," didn't bother to call Green...and Dallas was about to hit the roof in anger.

Levine immediately called in to my radio show *Coppock on Sports* on old WMAQ Radio. We broke the story sky high and truly cemented a friendship we've both enjoyed for years.

Green, of course, was livid. Dallas tore into Levine. He nailed him for not telling him about "Stick" deciding to walk before he dished the story out to the press. Green knew better. Dallas understood the media game. If he'd been in Levine's shoes, he would have done exactly the same thing.

Bruce made both downtown papers look foolish and he left Green with just one play. Dallas, gushing venom from all pores, fired Michael the following day.

Bruce Levine is full-blown original. I will always owe a debt of gratitude to Cheryl Rae-Stout and Jerry Kuc, a pair of "MAQ" colleagues for hipping me to Bruce. Kuc, by the way, should have been a star in this town. His work ethic was boundless.

Go back 23 years, to 1986. Tony La Russa was on death row at Comiskey Park. G.M. "Hawk" Harrelson, in his one-and-out year running the club, just didn't want Tony calling the shots. The friction between the two went beyond the boiling point—two days into spring training.

While Tony suffered, I got tipped by Levine that Billy Martin was in town to meet with Harrelson. I made a request to Kuc that should have earned me a royal "fuck you" in return.

We had called hotels up and down Michigan Avenue looking for Billy, with no luck. Not registered. So, Mike Wallace here asked Jerry to go back to all the joints we'd called to see if he could actually find Martin. I also told Jerry, "Just go to the bar. He won't be anywhere else."

About three hours and nine gin mills later, Jerry had his man—on tape. Ironically, the Yankees were also in town, which just infuriated the New York writers. Damn right, that makes you feel good.

Hawk and Martin never did punch out a deal. But, jeez, we had a great story.

BRUCE LEVINE'S WORLD is one of 12-hour days, a massive contact file that never stops growing, and Bud Selig's home phone number.

Just kidding—to a point. Bruce created a new era.

For years, a baseball story wasn't legit in Chicago unless it appeared first in a local newspaper. That was gospel. Levine killed off that ridiculous concept by establishing records for breaking stories that will probably never be touched.

If the White Sox have a 7:11 tee-off, Levine figures to be on 35th Street by around 2:30. When he first began working the Cubs some 25 years ago, it wasn't unusual for Levine to be at Wrigley Field by 8:30. Levine has to see both managers to feel complete. He has players to visit on both sides. Rumors to be checked. Whispers to pack away for future use.

Bruce is a stud reporter. So today's concept of "gang-bang interviews" with players and managers drives him nuts. He wants what I want, what guys like WGN's Rich King want: A world where you still live and die on your own questions.

These days, press guys protect each other. There really is no competition within the electronic media. Tape at 10. We all feature the same "Ozzie Guillen" sound bite or Jim Thome saying, "This shows we can come from behind." Solid reporters are frustrated. Lightweight reporters aren't exposed and ballclubs live happily ever after. Sports teams live for the "controlled" sound bite.

You think our guy doesn't cover all bets? Levine will check in with various nondescript ballpark employees just to pick their brains. In 1987, a Wrigley Field handyman told him that a company was coming in following a game to do a sight survey for the installation of night lights.

Bang. Levine broke the story that the Cubs would debut night lights in 1988.

The job is taxing. Who likes rain delays? Or day-night doubleheaders? Who wants to cover the Cubs in September in 47-degree weather? Especially if the Cubbies are running 13 laps behind the Pittsburgh Pirates—and the Bears own the front page?

The answer: Levine.

Bruce actually gets his best "stuff" from scouts—guys who hold radar guns, baseball lifers who try to determine if Felix Pie will ever develop "patience" in the batter's box. Levine credits legends like Hughie Alexander, a brilliant talent evaluator, the Babe Ruth of scouting, for taking him under his wing and providing him with unconditional friendship and direction.

You talk about a rock-solid list of contacts. I've done three-hour radio editions of *Talking Baseball* with Bruce on WMVP, where he's talked with at least four guests on-air while connecting with seven different baseball people on his cell during commercial breaks. Freakin' commercial breaks.

You don't walk in and order the respect Bruce has picked up over the years. You earn it. You report honestly. If you piss off Lou Piniella, you sit down and hash things out. You guard your credibility.

You learn to live with a lack of sleep. You never turn your cell phone off.

Full-time baseball reporting is brutal. Guys never really have days off. They live in fear of bring licked by the competition on a "major story." Exhaustion is a frequent companion. It's a far cry from Halas Hall. The Bears orchestrate the news. Lovie performs on cue. If you want five minutes with Jerry Angelo, you better damn well not press Angelo on his failures to draft the "right" offensive players.

So where does Levine see himself in five years, 10 years? Bruce is playing with a full deck. He knows he won't be working the beat when he's 82. But I can see him doing his baseball number when he's 75. That gives him 15 more good years to pick the brains of an endless flock of baseball contacts.

Not bad. Think about it, this guy used to manage restaurants during his college days at Southern Illinois in Carbondale. His dream is fulfilled and ongoing. He gets paid to go to ballgames.

36 Dear Baseball Writers of America... Wake up and vote ANDRE DAWSON into the HALL OF FAME (among other things)

Don't turn that dial—later on during our show, Coppock explains why he thinks the BBWA is a complete waste of time!

Grab the soap box, hand me the microphone. I'm mad as hell, and this won't change a damn thing, but it might help me ingest my dinner in a more comfortable manner. Andre Dawson was a remarkably gifted player. I could spend the next 15 minutes running you through his numbers, but let's move in a different direction.

I saw my first Major League Baseball game sometime during the glory days of Dwight Eisenhower. And let me clear up one point, those days weren't nearly as halcyon as the "historians" would have you believe—unless you got jazzed watching *Circus Boy* or *The Steve Allen Show* on a 12-inch black-and-white television with a fuzzy picture that required the man of the house to perform juggling acts with a "rabbit ears" antenna.

Anyway, there are three prolific National League throwing arms I've seen over a 50-year window. Three guys who were just in a class by themselves. Willie Mays, Roberto Clemente, and Andre Dawson. And for the hell of it, let's throw in Dave Parker.

Dawson's arm was a rifle. I recall a game at Cubs Park when he recorded two outfield assists at home plate in one inning. Andre was also a consummate "clubhouse" guy. Guys like Greg Maddox and Ryne Sandberg rave about what a terrific fellow the "Hawk" was to have at the Confines.

Now, this is what I really dig about Dawson. He played through pain that the average person just cannot contemplate. His knees were bone on bone. His cartilage began to crumble while he was playing high school football in Miami. Dawson's pregame routine just to get physically warmed up to play was grueling. Following ballgames, "Hawk" would need to cool down in the trainer's room to deal with knees that burned.

Fred Mitchell, the veteran *Tribune* writer, was on the Cubs beat when Dawson was with the Cubs. "He'd keep us waiting an hour after games," Fred recalled. "But we didn't complain. We knew he was suffering."

Dawson was a superb offensive and defensive player. He was a solid gold teammate and he did what most guys don't do any more—he played when he felt like absolute hell. He suffered, but he played. Andre Dawson's career screams "Hall of Fame" and he may well get the call in 2010.

What I want to know is just how 31 percent of the BBWA's voting members didn't deem Andre HOF-ready in 2008? They have to be drinking cheap scotch.

Dawson, 1987 National League MVP. Two runner-up MVP finishes. 8 Gold Gloves. 1977 Rookie of the Year. 4 Silver Sluggers. 2,627 hits. 438 Home Runs. 314 stolen bases.

Let's examine the Baseball Writers of America, this august body that determines who gets a plaque in Cooperstown, New York. My issues with the BBWA run deep. Why shouldn't MLB's longtime broadcasters, guys like Vin Scully, Marty Brennaman, or, here in Chicago, Pat Hughes, have the right to a Hall of Fame vote?

Won't happen. The BBWA thinks baseball announcers are overpaid shills who could never deliver a fair and honest ballot because of their "affiliations."

Oh, please. Furman Bischer, who began covering sports in Atlanta when Jack Dempsey was a teenager, once told me he voted for Dale Murphy every year because he was "our guy."

Look at the voters. The *Tribune*'s Phil Hersh is a truly gifted writer. But why does he have a vote? Phil's basically been covering Olympic sports for roughly a generation. In other words, he can give you a full rundown on press boxes in Lillehammer, Norway, or Beijing, China, but I doubt he's ever seen the batting cage at Minute Maid Park. He was off baseball during the entire steroid era.

This guy has a vote? That's the Theatre of the Absurd. What does he really know about Reed Johnson or Brian Anderson? Nothing personal. I like Phil. In fact, when it comes to conversation, I find writers to be 10 times more engaging than broadcasters.

Okay. I feel better. BBWA, give Andre his HOF ticket sometime before I arrive at that last great 9–4–2 double play in the sky and give announcers the time of day.

Is that asking too much?

37 Join the Beer Town pilgrimage— attend a CUBS-BREWERS game at MILLER PARK

Give me a show of hands. How many of you baseball diehards recall that the White Sox, starved at the Comiskey Park box office, actually played nine home games at good old Milwaukee County Stadium back in 1968?

Let's try again. How many of you attended the Bears' historic 2–0 preseason victory over the Green Bay Packers in the "Midwest Shrine Game" at County Stadium in August 1971?

I was in the house. In fact, I worked that game for Brent Musburger and WBBM-TV as Brent's spotter. By the third quarter, both Musburger and I were taking intravenous fluids.

But here's my own County Stadium "Rolex Presidential." In 1957, I saw my first World Series game—Casey Stengel and the Yankees versus Hank Aaron and the Braves—at "The County."

What a remarkable year, 1957. The Soviet Union scared us half to death by launching Sputnik. Sex Pistols guitarist Sid Vicious was born along with professional wrestler Brett "Hit Man" Hart and singer Donny Osmond.

Tell me, who doesn't break down and sob when they hear a young Donny, still years from puberty, belt out "Puppy Love"? Donnie, at 11, was Wilson Pickett, Sam and Dave, and a busted tuning fork.

This is just amazing. The '57 Braves, World Series Champeens, drew 2,215,404 fans. What about the Cubs? They hosted several youth groups from Carbondale and every Friday was Ladies Day. Total house count: 670,629.

Did I mention I also saw the Rolling Stones at County Stadium?

Now that we've won lifetime membership in The Greater Milwaukee Chamber of Commerce, let's dig in to the real purpose of today's lecture. Treat yourself to a Cubs-Brewers game at Miller Park. A life without the 6th inning Klement's Sausage Race is a life that's, quite frankly, incomplete.

Are you as amazed as I am at how many Cubs fans turn up at "The Miller," a gorgeous facility, whenever the Cubbies are up north? There are several obvious reasons. If you live north of Deerfield, maybe even Wilmette, the drive to Miller Park is simple, relaxing, and devoid of red lights. It can actually be much easier than trying to fight the traffic war to get to "Crane Kenny" Stadium.

I didn't dream this up 20 minutes ago. If you're parked within a block of Wrigley Field and you wait a half an hour after the game to get back to your car and you live in Glencoe, you're looking at a miserable two-hour drive back home. It could be upped to three hours if there's road construction or a guy with an overheated engine blocking two lanes.

Side note: Cubs fans, you all need a wake-up call. How many of you suckers have been getting off at Irving park Road or Addison Street for years to make your way to Wrigley Field? It's crazy. It's like spending a year learning German so you can travel to Norway. Drive down to Diversey Avenue or even farther south to Fullerton and double back on Southport or Racine.

I know this message will fall on deaf ears. Cubs fans are nothing if not creatures of habit. One hundred years, Chip Caray, and the Bartman Ball will do that to a person.

Honest to gosh, I think Cubs fans have been brainwashed to believe that being stuck in bumper-to-bumper pavement "hell" is a traditional part of the "Fan Experience."

> "[Cubs fans] enjoy watching their team at Miller Park because it isn't a dump like Wrigley Field."
>
> —Bob Wolfley, columnist, *Milwaukee Journal*

Guess what? Miller Park doesn't gouge you to park. General weekend parking is just 10 bucks. You want to upgrade? The "Preferred" tab is 18 dollars.

This is just too obvious. You want another reason Cubs fans put on their Ryne Sandberg jerseys and Geovany Soto T-shirts to make the trip to Milwaukee?

Tickets in the upper deck grandstands at Cubs Park have become damn near as tough as tickets between the 30s for a Bears-Packers game.

You know the Cubs Park drill. If you haven't got tickets, here are your options. Deal with a broker—that's legal scalping. A street scalper, that's illegal scalping but also an American way of life. Or you can walk to Wrigley Premium Tickets.

"Premium" is generally referred to by the clergy as "These jerks haven't won a damn thing for a century and now they have the stones to gouge us with corporate scalping?"

Miller Park has great sight lines, a retractable roof, tremendous restaurants, and the fans sing "The Beer Barrel Polka" during the 7th inning stretch.

Cubs Park features ivy, a manual scoreboard, usherettes who were flappers during the Al Capone era, and the tranquilizing aroma of a men's room that offers a swell chance some drunk will piss on your leg.

Here's the main event, my last reason to sport your Cubbie colors at Miller Park.

How often does a Cubs fan feel like he's "The Man?" It happens at Miller Park. The Cubbie Nation overloads the place to such an extent that it makes the ballpark feel like Wrigley Field North. You half expect Bud Selig to come by and sing "Take Me Out to the Ballgame."

Miller Park is a winner—big time. You won't feel like you're getting knifed by the hostile parking lot operators at The Confines when you park your vehicle at Miller. You can hear Cubs fans cheer louder for Mike Fontenot than Brewers fans cheer for Prince Fielder. And the bonus—if the game gets dull, stop by the Potawatomi Casino. It's right next door.

How do I say this? Potawatomi isn't quite the Bellagio in Vegas. However, the joint does have reasonably loose slot machines. Plus, Potawatomi leads the nation in second-hand smoke and cheesy ads that feature a guy in a tux trying to look like a member of the Rat Pack telling you that this casino is almost as much fun as bratwurst.

End of issue. I'm headed to Millerville.

38 *Let your* IMAGINATION *work overtime...the* CUBS *have actually just* WON *the* WORLD SERIES

Cubs win, Cubs win, Cubs win…

My God, can you imagine how ticked off, pissed, and otherwise disgusted Kenny Williams is right now with the guys 71 blocks north? Kenny has a football mentality. He was on the gridiron during the classic Stanford-Cal "lateral" game back in 1982. It didn't help that the Golden Bears won 25–20. If you see Kenny banging his shoulder against the Harold Baines statue inside the Cell, don't let it bother you. Kenny just figures it's cheaper than buying a tackling dummy.

Stranger things have happened. In 1943, naval engineer Richard James invented the Slinky. Ford was dumb enough to mortgage half the company to try and force feed the Edsel down the American public's throats in the late 1950s.

Let's not overlook Alcibiades, the famed Athenian statesman who is generally credited with leading the charge toward the invention of the hammock. Alcibiades, born in 450 BC, later went on to sing backup for Hootie and the Blowfish. But of course you know that.

So now that the Cubs have won a World Series, I have a full list of items that need to be done, taken care of, or otherwise handled by you—the Cubs fan, a fan who all too frequently has had to endure Josh Mora's post-game interviews.

One, Gail Fisher from Comcast will show her appreciation by giving Lou Piniella a table dance.

Lousy idea. Let's have Lou Piniella give Gail Fisher a table dance.

You will forgive Al Pacino and Robert De Niro for their work in the impossibly dull flick *Righteous Kill*.

This is a must. All TV stations, most notably Channel 2, will be barred from doing man-on-the-street interviews. In particular, Vince Gerasole will be handcuffed the moment the Cubbies record the 27th and final fourth-win out.

Did you see Gerasole interviewing folks at the Barack Obama election celebration in Grant Park? His questions were so piercing, so penetrating I thought he was talking to nine-year-olds at a Hannah Montana concert.

Man-on-the-street interviews insult the human race. Do you really need some drunken broad yelling, "We're the greatest" while her dead-drunk boyfriend strains to look at the nearby monitors to make sure he gets face time to wave to his homies?

This is a collective effort. Remember that Sunday in Auburn Hills back in '91 when the Bulls closed out the Pistons 4-zip in the NBA's Eastern Conference Finals? We'll join hands to forgive Isiah Thomas and Bill Laimbeer for walking off the court like gutless cowards with time left on the clock rather than offering handshakes to M.J. and friends.

I have to dig deep on this one. We will forgive—but for 12 hours only—all the downtown restaurants that rip off their customers by charging 11, maybe 12 bucks for valet parking.

We will do the right thing. We will forgive ex-Bull Eddie Robinson for stealing money during his tenure with the club.

And you thought I forgot the NBC Network. We'll forgive the suits in Peacockville for failing to hire Jennifer Aniston when she applied for a spot on the *SNL* cast back in her early 20s.

Speaking of NBC, I will forgive the brass at Channel 5 for firing me back in 1983. I'll even forgive Paul Beavers, the listlessly clumsy news director, for leading the charge to fry me—when my wife was six months pregnant.

This is pressing the issue. We will forgive Ben Affleck and Jennifer Lopez for their work in *Jersey Girl.*

I will forgive the Blackhawks for firing P.A. announcer-without-peer Harvey Wittenberg to give the job to Gene Honda. That was like ditching Bruce Springsteen to hire the house band at a joint on Lincoln Avenue.

We will gently remind Ronnie Woo-Woo that he's already driven about 1,328,000 people nuts with "Cubs-woo…Sosa-woo" and ask him to apply duct tape to his dentures the moment the celebrating kicks into second gear.

Sammy? We will tell him we love him despite the fact that he set world records for striking out on breaking balls low and away.

We will forgive ex-Blackhawk Alex Zhamnov for being "Cold Woos on Ice."

I will personally forgive all the "oldies" stations that refuse to stop playing "Born to be Wild."

All booze joints in Wrigleyville will be urged to have 10-cent beer night for a period of six months.

The Steve Wilkos show will be banned due to lack of something unique—quality.

Here's where I really get tender. I'll forgive the late Stanley Kubrick for producing/directing and fumbling a piece of cinematic junk called *Eyes Wide Shut.* The film's only positive was Nicole Kidman's ass.

Go ahead and try on your Cubs Championship T-shirt—and don't worry. When you wake up tomorrow, you'll remember it was all just a dream.

39 Meet Bob ROSENBERG, the Chicago White Sox OFFICIAL "home field" SCORER

"Official scorers, like journalists, have to be professional and ethical. It signals a loss of credibility when you're wearing attire that represents one of the teams involved…especially the home team."

—Mark Gonzales, White Sox beat writer, the *Chicago Tribune*

I can't stop laughing. Gonzo wasn't delivering a new section of the Gettysburg Address. Mark was suggesting that it might be a little more appropriate if Bob Rosenberg were to ditch his supply of White Sox sweatshirts.

Rosey is fascinating and quirky all at once. He's also in love with the White Sox. I swear he must have a Bill Melton teddy bear on his nightstand. I wouldn't keel over if somebody told me that he uses dish soap shaped like "Bull" Luzinski.

It's also not unusual to see Bob on the job, scoring a ballgame at the Cell, wearing a shirt or a jacket that qualifies as official White Sox apparel. The garb has a knack of telling you that, by golly, Bob will do whatever he can to give Jim Thome a base hit when E-6 seems to be the only logical call. Actually, Bob doesn't need to sport his White Sox colors. If you follow him over seven or eight home games, you'll see the trend emerge. Rosey is actually the Sox' 10th man.

Years ago, Bob and I were casual friends. I recall taking him to old Comiskey Park as my guest to see a Roller Derby game back in 1972 that—you can look it up—drew 52,000 fans. The two teams involved were the legendary Midwest Pioneers and the equally historic Los Angeles Thunderbirds. I get tearful thinking of both clubs. Rosey cheered so hard for the Pioneers, I swear he thought the game was on the square.

Side note: This tells you anybody can earn a buck in this industry. For a couple of years, back in the early '70s, I was the national TV voice of the Roller

Derby. Don't laugh. We were carried in over 200 markets. I once got fan mail from Guam.

In the ratings game, which is all that matters on the TV scorecard, we made it a locked-in regular occurrence to beat the living hell out of the NHL whenever our "routine" went head to head with hockey's "game."

NBC's Peter Puck never did find a way to beat Roller Derby villainess Anne Calvello. By the way, there was this night Annie and I got loaded at the Barclay Hotel in Philadelphia and it was around 2 AM....well, let's respect the deceased. God, for a 43-year-old babe, Anne Theresa Calvello had a great ass.

ROSEY AND I have even worked together. I was the public address announcer and he was part of the stat team for the long-gone WHA Chicago Cougars.

Since I'm doing Rosey's life history, I may as well throw in this item. He's been the Bulls' official scorer since day one. Contemplate this…at last count, he'd scored more than 1,650 games. Reportedly, he has missed just two nights of action.

That gave Bob a ringside seat to see the tandem genius of Jordan/Pippen. It also put him in the front row to hand out assists to enough stiffs over the years to fill the Ressurection Cemetery. Think Tate Armstrong or Cliff Pondexter. Or new age superstars like Trenton Hasell and Marcus Fizer. Wasn't Marcus going to be Tim Floyd's ticket to the Basketball Hall of Fame? I do believe that for at least a few years, Marcus led the NBA in tattoos on his calf muscles—quite an achievement.

Mr. Rosenberg has to be ready for a 100,000-mile maintenance check. Keep this in mind. Bob was also the official scorer for the old NBA Chicago Packers when the team began play in 1961 at the International Amphitheatre. In '62, after a lousy year at the box office, the club changed its name to "Zephyrs" and moved to the Chicago Coliseum.

Side note: Bet anybody five bucks they can't tell you where the Chicago Coliseum was. It's my lock of the year.

After another lousy year at the ticket window, the club moved to Baltimore. Honest to gosh, absolutely nobody noticed or cared. Think of it in these terms. What would have happened back in 1861 if the Robert E. Lee and the South had fired on Fort Sumter and missed? Get where I'm going?

Back to baseball.

It's become a running press box joke over the years. Rosey, almost nightly, will make a scorer's call that leaves the media club groaning over its hometown feel. One of his close friends told me, "He can't help himself, he just gets a little more carried away every year."

This will happen someday before I die. Rosey, in his crackling, busted falsetto, will tell the guys on deadline, "Attention Press. Change the walk to Paul Konerko in the fourth inning to a double."

Trust me, I'm not ticked off at Robert. I think he's one of the better acts in town. With proper training, he could elevate his game to the Crane Kenny level.

The *Tribune's* Teddy Greenstein sees a fellow who's big on attention. "Bob loves the camera more than Paris Hilton," Teddy joked. "I'm convinced he likes to make at least one change a game so that he'll either get face time or his name mentioned."

If you're scoring at home, Rosey makes $135 a game—the going MLB rate—as the official scorer. I don't know if the clubhouse guys give him complimentary bats or chewing tobacco. But I wouldn't bet against it.

However, I do know this. Ozzie Guillen, after a 2006 White Sox 9–0 loss to Seattle, turned his wrath toward Rosey. Guillen, mad about everything, called out our hero for one of his scoring decisions. "That should be an error, not a base hit," Guillen said in regards to a defensive lapse by Paul Konerko. "I don't know if [Rosenberg] is getting old…I don't know what he's doing."

Ozzie, take a deep breath. You, of all people, should know that Rosey dreams of the day that he becomes your bench coach.

Hey, Bob, do your thing. It's harmless. But please, no White Sox ponchos.

40 *Dig* RON SANTO, *the* BROADCASTER —when he goes, we'll never see another guy like him

If you think baseball announcers should be required to pay homage to "The King's English" or have the New York Philharmonic eloquence of Vin Scully, just move on to the next chapter. You're in the wrong ballpark.

Four, maybe five years ago on WGN, Santo was reading a fax from a fan asking if a team had ever worn "fooskeea" uniforms. He went back and forth with the word for about three minutes. Finally, Pat Hughes, his broadcast tag-team partner, said, "Ron, I believe the word the gentleman is referring to is fuchsia…the color pink." Santo's response? "Never heard of it."

Ron Santo. So many good vibes…good memories.

There was that lazy Saturday when former Governor Jim Edgar wandered into the Cubs booth to hype some Illinois state program in need of a pop. Edgar, by the way, is a very rare bird. He's an ex-gov who doesn't leap out of his chair when he hears the words "minimum security."

Pizza Ron, obviously reading off prepared copy, made about three or four tries to get the question out. Frankly, Santo never quite got past first base. By the time Edgar got to his spiel, he could be forgiven if he thought he was on hand to talk about a garage sale in Danville.

I love Ron Santo. So he clobbers three-syllable words, who cares?

WGN and the Cubs are paying him to sell tickets and create love for a franchise that hasn't won a damn thing since former President Washington picked up his first pair of wooden false teeth.

By the way, George and I were both born on April 30. I don't know about Washington but, for the fat kid, I wear 48XXL sport coats, XXL sweaters, and 46 long slacks. Please enclose receipts with all gifts. I can be very moody.

In 2008, I was brunching at U.S. Cellular Field before a Sox-Cubs tee-off with Santo and ESPN Radio's Bruce Levine. Just three guys talking baseball and having a great time doing it.

It got me to thinking. I saw Ron play ball for the Cubs during his rookie season back in 1960, the same year Don Cardwell, in his first start with the Cubbies, threw a no-hitter versus the Cardinals. You talk about delirium. Cardwell was so overwhelmed by his brilliance that he closed the rest of his Cubs career 29–44.

I remember Santo's electric pose on a 1969 cover of *Sports Illustrated* that carried the headline "Chicago's Raucous Cubs."

I can talk about honors galore. But why bother? We clearly know them better than baseball's idiotic Veteran's Committee.

God, do I recall Ronald Edward Santo's last hurrah. After 14 years with the Cubs, Santo closed his career in a one-year straitjacket with the White Sox. I wish you could have seen Ron on Opening Day. He looked like Santino Corleone in Bonasera's Mortuary in *The Godfather*. Ron looked about as blown apart as Jane Byrne looked after she got bumped out of the mayor's chair by Harold Washington.

Baseball can play mind games on guys. Some ballplayers wake up in late April and realize they'd rather face a firing squad than play one more day with the club that employs them.

Nobody can convince me that Santo didn't begin to hate life with the White Sox about 20 minutes before he got to the Sox' old spring training site in Sarasota. The Sox-Santo marriage had a shorter shelf life than Dennis Rodman and Carmen Electra. It was over and out in less than seven minutes.

Maybe that's why Ron made such a clean break from the diamond.

After Ron retired, he spent the bulk of his time hitting 265-yard drives at the very fashionable North Shore Country Club in Glenview. It was a rare occurrence when he turned up at Wrigley Field.

Anyway, let's get down to business. Santo frequently joined me on TV and radio shows during the '80s. That came to an abrupt close in 1990 with one phone call. We'll touch on that later.

It's really a great story. It's about vision and thinking 15 miles out of the box. In other words, elements that are on the canvas—with the count at 9—in today's world of talkers and talking heads.

WGN sent Bob Brenly, a guy with no Cubs ties, and Ron down to Florida for a unique "audition" in 1990. Essentially, it was a head-to-head winner-take-all competition between Ron and Bob to see who would team with young Thom Brennaman.

Brenly didn't just win. He knocked Santo out of the park. Bob was smooth and free flowing. Ron was Ron. He figured after day one of the tryout, he was in a losing clubhouse.

But Santo had an angel, Jack Rosenberg, the longtime sports editor at WGN. Rosey is a living, breathing saint. The title "sports editor" doesn't begin to define the scope, the energy, or the passion he brought to his job. Rosey had conducted the Brenley-Santo audition. He could see a ray of sunshine where 99 percent of the people in this racket would have seen less than nothing.

Jack went back to WGN and delivered his own pitch to the station's front office. Tradition says that broadcast executives are conditioned to say no. Rosey outlined a game plan that was simplistic but stellar.

"Brenly has the job for sure, right off the bat," Rosenberg told the station brass. "Santo will take time, but when Ron walks in to meet an advertiser, that guy's going to buy because he's Ron Santo. Put them both together. Go with a three-man booth."

WGN, with no small degree of hesitation, bought the Rosenberg concept.

Remember that phone call I talked about? Santo called me just minutes after he got the job to tell me he couldn't appear on my radio shows anymore due to his WGN deal. I wasn't mad; I was thrilled for the guy. He was a hero to me in 1960, and he's a hero to me 49 years later.

Here's the deal—appreciate Ron Santo.

Dig the gags about his hairpieces and his groans when Alfonso Soriano waves at a slider that's not only off the plate, but south of the first base dugout.

Sadly, Ron Santo and old-school broadcasters like Dizzy Dean are as out of date as Latin. New-age TV and radio execs would never put their wrists on the table to hire a guy like Santo, regardless of his playing credentials and fan appeal.

Take a chance in today's "game" on Ron Santo?

He's not conventional. He'd drive the Medill School of Journalism nuts. He's funny. Listen to his pre-game interviews. Every boss he's ever spoken with…Baylor…Dusty…Lou…they're always "the fine" manager of the Chicago Cubs. Broadcast executives want a guy who knows the full and complete history of the balk rule and does flawless reads on Windex commercials.

All Ron does is dare people to have a little fun. Maybe forget their overdue rent for a little while.

Ron, give us 10 more good years. Jack Rosenberg: I still owe you that lunch at Jack's on Touhy Avenue.

I asked a Cub executive a few years ago if Santo really knew all the players on other National League clubs. How about this for a retort? "Other teams? I'm not sure he knows all the players on our team."

IT DOESN'T MAKE a damn bit of difference. Somewhere inside that Santo cranium there is a button that reads "entertainment." Ron is a trip to the fun house. He's too smart not to know he's hysterical.

You want conventional baseball? Put yourself to sleep with Kenny Albert. If you want to giggle along with the greatest homer in Cubs history—jeez, that even includes my beloved Jack Brickhouse—then wait for Ron's next malaprop.

Ron Santo—is he eligible for some broadcaster's Hall of Fame? If so, tell that hall we want No. 10 inducted by acclamation.

41 Guess what, gang? STEROIDS will always be part of MAJOR LEAGUE BASEBALL'S subculture

Hand me the bullhorn. I want to scream this until my sternum breaks. I got this feeling after the Alex Rodriguez made-for-TV steroid apology in February 2009. Some people thought the "confession" somehow brought "closure" to the horrific era of baseball and juice.

The press conference was so laughable I kept on waiting for Martin Scorsese to scream, "Clear the set. It's a wrap. We'll try again tomorrow…Get Affleck in here to fill Brian Cashman's chair."

Folks, get with the program. There will always be a certain number of ballplayers who will go beyond the limits in the never-ending quest to gain "an edge." It will never reach the enormous volume we saw earlier in the decade, but it will always hang around in one form or another. Come to think of it, just how big was that so-called "volume"? The A-Rod "leak" contained a list of 104 names that tested positive. Based on 25-man rosters, that doesn't qualify as a drop in the bucket. Do the math—that's about 14 percent using illegal enhancers.

Look at the city council. I'd be thrilled if our very august aldermanic branch of government only had 14 percent of its members wind up in the joint.

Of course—here's where I kill my own argument—another 34 percent of ballplayers using high-end stuff probably skated through the testing without detection.

Please try and be realistic. As you read today's sermon, don't think for a minute that there aren't steroid "designers" all over the globe creating new performance-enhancing products that, at least for now, cannot be picked up during random testing.

Check out the rival sides. In a battle between chemists who are spending 18 hours a day in the lab versus MLB's testing procedure, would you bet your kid's allowance on the testers?

If so, please contact Vince McMahon and tell him you just can't wait for the XFL to reopen.

Speaking of the McMahon one-year fumble, don't you feel a sense of grief when you remember the checkered career of Rod Smart, aka "He Hate Me"?

While we're at it, the Bears should liven up the Halas Hall picnic by calling Tommy Harris, "I got mine—why play."

I mean, has your equilibrium been jolted by an overpaid third baseman using juice? Be honest, you're more worried about the White Sox having a good fourth starter or the Cubs winning their season series versus the Pittsburgh Pirates.

I gave up on this steroid routine long ago, long before the feds botched their case against Barry Bonds. Let's just say that since 2005, I've just said I like baseball—unconditionally. I accept that there are cheaters, but I still want to see Ozzie being Ozzie or Manny being Manny or watch Jim Thome gallop from home to first in 13 seconds.

Could that be any simpler?

Here's part of the reason why steroids don't really have a profound affect on me—because any seven-year-old Cub Scout with a Wolf badge can tell you the owners really don't care either.

MLB club owners are just like players. They're really glorified mercenaries.

Can you look in the nearest vanity mirror and actually convince yourself that a club owner is losing sleep over one of his players he thinks, or has been told outright, is on the "stuff"? Is there an owner in a cold sweat wringing his hands if he gets the low-down that a power-hitting right fielder on a rival club is using the androgen metabolism of rhesus monkeys to somehow get a better rip at a 96 mph fastball? C'mon.

> *"Don Fehr [MLB Players Association union chief] is a brilliant lawyer. He hasn't caught on to the steroid problem. He just doesn't get it. He thinks it's treated in rehab. No, Don, it is cheating."*
> —Lester Munson, ESPN legal expert

The steroid "concern" doesn't play. Let's go back a year or two. Bruce Levine, ESPN Radio's baseball heavyweight, tossed me a quote from a prominent general manager. You tell me this baby doesn't giftwrap the package.

"I don't know what my guy was on," the G.M. said, "but whatever it was, I wish to hell he'd get back on it, because right now he's killing us."

The last time I checked, fans at Clark and Addison are more concerned about how Lou Piniella plans to platoon at second base than they are about steroids. You want to debate? I didn't think so.

I admire Bud Selig and the effort he's put forth to crush the 'roids epidemic. I also don't think Bud's overpaid a nickel when you realize that baseball had reported revenues of $6.7 billion in 2008. Selig and MLB are winning—

big—while Chrysler's losing streak has begun to threaten the misery on Sirius XM Radio. Or visa versa.

Bud knows the score; he knows there will always be cheats. It's the great American way…death, taxes, Roger Clemens, and Sammy Sosa's interpreter.

I just love how things work on Capitol Hill. Politicians, sniffing votes, love to jump MLB. Has Congress ever given you the impression that it's a little edgy about the fact that the average NFL offensive lineman will weigh roughly 380 pounds by 2013?

42 BASEBALL'S *next "great" trend…* *the* FIVE-INNING *quality start*

It's not often I offer up this kind of expertise at no charge. I have a tip for the Cubs and the White Sox for a truly unique joint marketing plan. This will create turnstile frenzy at whatever ballparks the two clubs are playing in, roughly four decades from now.

In 2008, our two local baseball entries combined to produce a whopping six complete games. Naturally, this left ownership on both sides of town scared to death that their pitchers were being "overworked." Sam Zell was said to be apoplectic.

By the way, the payroll-rich New York Yankees, a team that keeps the Florida Marlins in business through "revenue sharing," had a grand total of one complete nine-inning effort, so help me Whitey Ford.

Whitey, the gifted lefty, somehow—and this had to scare the hell out of Casey Stengel—completed 167 games during his Hall of Fame career.

> *Did Bernie Madoff, the Ponzi scheme heavyweight champ,*
> *ever get his gloves on anybody connected with the Bombers?*
> *Any educated 13-year-old knows the Yankees bat boys make*
> *more than the average utility player for the Minnesota Twins.*
> *Here's hoping Bernie has found new life as a prison "bitch."*

Back to business. Sox, Cubs, look down the road. This has five times more pop than the DOA Sox marketing scheme titled "The Kids Can Play." Of course, your average Irish wake has more sparkle than "The Kids Can Play."

Get ready to erect the billboards that proclaim, "Bert, We're Running You Down. You Just Can't Stop Us."

When does the Hall of Fame deal in reality and finally give Bert Blyleven an invitation to its cozy little club in Cooperstown?

The line on Rik Aalbert Blyleven: 287 career wins, 4,970 innings. But here's the meal ticket: Bert also finished his career with 242 complete games.

Where are we going? If the present trend continues—I just love going all CNN—if the White Sox and Cubs continue to average a combined six complete games a year, by 2049 Team Hendry and Team Williams will be within striking distance of Blyleven's complete game total. In 2050, we pour the Dom Perignon. The two clubs ask for a Michigan Avenue parade as they eclipse the "Dutchman's" complete game mark.

Trust me, it won't happen. I have seen the future and I see the obvious: It's only a matter of time before baseball determines that three runs over five innings is a "quality start."

You're kidding yourself if you think it's not going to happen.

Just who the hell invented the quality start? Who determined that starting pitchers should go six, followed by two "bridge" men and a closer? Whoever the schmuck was, he created a sport where pitchers aren't guided by determination and grit; these clowns are guided by fear of overuse.

Ferguson Arthur Jenkins: 267 complete games, 4500 innings pitched. In 1971, Fergie, the greatest Canadian athlete this side of "Rocket" Richard, went 24–11 and walked off with the National League Cy Young Award.

Think that's a magic year? Now get ready to have your socks blown into Lake Michigan. Jenkins had 39 starts with *30—30—*complete games.

Gee, I'm amazed his arm didn't fall off. I do know this—Fergie had to be terribly distraught over his excessive mound time. Look it up. In 1972, he only won 20 games with—you talk about a year off—just 23 complete games.

Jenkins finished just third in voting for the Cy. You're right, he still owes the Wrigley family a rebate.

Damn the pitch count. It's turned every big-league manager and pitching coach into nursing home custodians. A special "damn" goes out to the nasty slider, which has done two things: freeze hitters and make Tommy John surgery almost as common as a hamstring pull.

You can almost feel stomachs, in the stands and the owner's box, screaming for Rolaids if the pot-bellied manager and his pitching guru see a starter take the ball into the seventh inning.

I just love this phrase, "Our guy needs to get stretched out." Huh, isn't that why Florida and Arizona have spring training camps?

Twenty-six years ago, October 1983, the Baltimore Orioles beat Britt Burns and the White Sox at old Comiskey Park to capture the ALCS. Tito Landrum delivered the game breaker. His one-out, 11th-inning home run off Burns did the trick. Burns deserved a better fate. The Landrum blast came on his 150th pitch of the ballgame.

I was in Sox manager Tony La Russa's office after the show was over. I don't remember anybody with a microphone or a notepad pressing Tony because he hadn't gone to the bullpen. Why? Burns still appeared sharp. He just made a mistake and hung a breaking ball.

> "I've asked Dusty [Baker] and Lou [Piniella] who started this six-inning crap. Why can't guys go nine? To me, it's an absolute joke. These guys are in better shape than we were. The whole thing is stupid."
> —Militades Sergios "Milt" Pappas

What the heck does Milt know? For heaven's sake, he only won 209 games with a paltry 129 career complete games during his stay in the big leagues. You talk about a different world in 1961. Milt threw just 177 innings for the O's but still had nine complete games.

Here's one big problem. Pitchers want "abs of steel." They're workout freaks. They condition year-round—which is out-and-out idiotic.

Pappas said he always tried to get to camp about five or six pounds over-weight. He knew he had seven weeks to get his weight and his arm sorted out.

I'm just curious, how many pitchers win in July because they bench press on Christmas Eve?

> I'm deeply concerned about the wear and tear on CC Sabathia. He won 17 games in '08 with the Tribe and Milwaukee. CC also delivered 10 complete games. What a show-off. At this rate, Sabathia, with a seven-year $160 million package with the Yankees, won't pitch a lick after he turns 39.

Back to Milt: "Pitchers lift way too much. When was the last time you saw a machine get anybody out?"

Here's the modern baseball culture. Pitchers are brainwashed to be protective, to the point that they figure their arms will blow up if they get carried away during a side session. Agents tell their pitching clients not to overdo it. Family members send out texts reminding little Jimmy not to throw 93 mph all day because he's in a "walk year."

How often do you hear baseball broadcasters get panic-stricken when a guy's count gets to 103? You get the impression that if a guy goes "eight full," he should get a week of rest in Hot Springs, Arkansas.

We don't have pitchers anymore, we have baby kittens.

In 1961, just as he reached his 41st birthday, Milwaukee Braves Hall of Famer Warren Spahn began a typical three-year run in the office. He racked up 62 wins with 65 complete games. Boy, his managers Charlie Dressen and Birdie Tebbetts were truly screwed up. Or maybe, they just said, "Leave this guy alone. He doesn't know we have a bullpen."

I see you coming. The five-inning quality start is darn near in focus.

43 *You might ride an elevator with Carmen Pignatiello*—attend the CUBS CONVENTION

I don't want to play hard ass, but, frankly, the Cubs Convention has been a source of bewilderment to me since the sucker began way back in 1985. I'll show up maybe once every three years for the Friday cocktail hour. I always stroll through the vendor booths looking for any kind of funky memorabilia. Other than that, I'm lost in a sea of Alfonso Soriano batting gloves.

Sometimes I think the convention is a glorified costume ball. Walk through the halls of the Hilton Hotel. Check out that guy with the foam rubber cowboy hat that rises three feet above his head who's also wearing a license plate that says, "Sox Suck."

Uh, he's a downtown attorney.

Lurch your way up to the Grand Ballroom and watch the 70-year-old babe (who still dreams of one good night in a second-rate hotel with Hank Sauer) listening to Jim Hendry preach the North Side gospel. She's wearing "face buttons" that pledge allegiance to Elvin Tappe, Cuno Barregan, Elder White, Turk Wendell, and other clowns who have made a mockery of the national pastime.

The buttons are attached to a Keith Moreland throwback jersey. She's also wearing those oversized Harry Caray sunglasses and a floppy hat—at least 36 years old—autographed by Yosh Kawano, the Cubs' longtime clubhouse man, and Preston Gomez, one of the most forgettable in a long list of completely forgettable Cubs managers.

You get the picture. As much as these fans are overwhelmed by watching Geovany Soto wolf down scrambled eggs, they're actually here on another mission. The convention is Mardi Gras for fans from coast to coast. At least half the house sees the event as Halloween in January. The other half has to be asking this question: *Why did I leave San Diego to hear TV weathermen screaming about wind-chill factor?*

> *"My biggest shock is that no one thought about doing this kind of event before we did."*
>
> —John McDonough, former Cubs executive
> and the originator of what began as
> the "Diehard Cubs Convention"

But John did know almost from the get-go that he was riding a winner. McDonough recalls that during the convention's second year at least seven big-league ball clubs—along with Major League Baseball—sent teams of scouts to Chicago to figure out just what the "lovable losers" were doing with this off-season springboard.

"My idea was to bridge the year," Mac, now president of the Blackhawks, told me while we gabbed with his sidekick, Jay Blunk, in the Hawks' United Center conference room. "I just didn't know why we had to give away the off-season to the Bears, the Bulls, and the Hawks."

By 1989, tickets had reached elevated status. The event was a sellout and scalpers were hustling up and down Michigan Avenue. If you're a promoter and you have scalpers moving your product, consider yourself a winner.

"What this did for us was to get spring training rolling in January," McDonough tells you.

Let me clear up one misconception. The players—past and present—don't make big dough to attend the convention. Blunk told me that over the years the basic tab held steady at 500 bucks, along with a free room and plenty of booze. The old-timers might work "N.C." They're so gratified to be back in the spotlight, to feel the fan energy, that the cash is just an extra set of Jockey briefs in the Christmas stocking.

The immortal Moose Moryn one said, "The first time I was at the convention, I felt like I was one of the Beatles."

Let me see, how would that play? John, Paul, George, Ringo, and Moose. You be the judge.

If you don't know who Moose Moryn is, go to the back of the line. Moose, an average outfielder, made a running dipped-glove catch on a drive by the Cards' Joe Cunningham to preserve Don Cardwell's no-hitter over St. Louis back on May 15, 1960, at the confines.

Damn right I was at that game. My old man always maintained that Moose was so slow that he turned what should have been a routine catch into a highlight with about 15 lifetimes.

You talk about devotion—or insanity. McDonough remembers fans sleeping in the halls on Friday nights to be in line early Saturday to get autographs. These are people who paid good dough for rooms. But let's set our priorities straight. What would you rather do, sleep in a nice, comfortable bed with a mint on the pillow or be among the first 15 people to get a signed photo of Jerry Mumphrey?

Eventually, the Hilton banned the "campers" to avoid a 15-rounder with the fire marshall.

Go back to the early '90s. I recall a crowd in 15-degree weather lined up out the door and onto the street waiting to get autographs from Mark Grace. Jeez, imagine what kind of impact Mark would have had if he had been a long-ball hitter.

You know what really doesn't matter when you talk about the convention? Which players who are going to the main event actually attend. They are all Cubbies, they are subjects of unconditional love, and they were forgiven 35 seconds after the gag and choke versus the Dodgers in October 2008.

That just never really happened.

Someday Sammy Sosa will return and the event will have to be moved to Allstate Arena. Corked bats? Screw it. Let's talk about heart taps and tape measures.

"If the Cubs never played another game," McDonough suggests, "the convention would still sell out."

Who would possibly disagree?

Cubs fans are just so damn sympathetic. If Jerome Walton attends the 30th Anniversary convention in 2009, Cubs fans by acclimation will suggest that he be given the keys to the city and three comp dinners at Manny's Restaurant.

44 A cozy feeling 450 FEET from home plate? Yes! Enjoy a Cubs game at SKYBOX ON SHEFFIELD

Think about that tremendous Miller beer commercial. You know the one where that big old dude, just High Life hysterical, comes strutting into a luxury suite and asks two La Salle Street types what inning it is? Both, of course, have no idea.

You'll find a big chunk of that at the "Sheff." But who the hell really cares? Skybox serves many—in bold type—purposes, and there are plenty of big-screen monitors inside and on the "double-deck" rooftop to keep diehards abreast of just what the Cubbies are doing versus their archrivals, the San Diego Padres.

Dave Abrams, life-long Chicagoan and front man at the Skybox, has created a multi-dimensional facility that offers up, in a very simplistic way, a baseball experience that in a heck of a lot of ways is more fun than actually being in the park. For openers, Abrams promises you'll never sit behind a post.

You want celebrities? Dave's joint has played host to Keanu Reeves, Kathleen Turner, "King" Richard Petty, hoops hero Rick Barry, Billy Williams, and the Jersey Boys. You've got it. The only things missing at "Sheff" are a red carpet, Joan Rivers, and a deal on face lifts.

Do you love a dramatic sunset? Book night game boards for the "Sheff" sometime in July or August. Arrive about 6:30. Follow the path of the sun as it glides behind the roof, winks at you through the gaps behind the grandstands, changes colors from yellow to orange to various shade of blues before finally—gosh I love TV talk—fades to black. Do it after two-three beers and you might hear distant sounds of Jimi Hendrix.

The illumination from the 21-year-old nightlights at Wrigley Field create a visual experience that is just magnificent. I mean, it's not Neil Armstrong on the moon, but it will have you talking overtime at the office water cooler the following day.

I have to warn you about something. If you're the kind of guy who figures a trip to Clark and Addison is a waste of time if you can't see the whites of Lou Piniella's eyes, or if you have to figure you're no worse than 5 to 1 to catch a foul ball, this isn't your place.

Washroom concerns? Glad you asked. A trip to the men's room at Cubs Park is a lengthy reminder of just how nice life is if you avoid residence at a state-run maximum security prison in Texas. Abrams provides clean facilities and should really post a sign that says, "maximum wait time: 45 seconds."

Okay, so much for the warmup. Here's the real charm when you talk about the "Sheff": Chicago isn't Shelbyville, Indiana, or a little hamlet 65 miles west of Iowa City. We're a city of deal makers, power players, crooked politicians, wise guys collecting "street tax," and aldermen on the take. We're also a city where wintertime "dibs" is a way of life. If you don't know what dibs means in Chicago, you must be a lifelong resident of Schaumburg.

Dibs is a an old dining-room chair, a busted baseball bat, or a $20 Sears golf bag, locked in a street-side snowdrift and making a reasonably strong statement of intent: Park here after 5:00 PM and my psychotic brother-in-law will tattoo your head with a bowling ball.

How does this relate to our guys at Skybox on Sheffield? The "Sheff" is first, last, and always about networking. TV salespeople show up in droves, along with Michigan Avenue advertising executives and guys just dying to add one more three-level condo in Lincoln Park to their cache.

Even our town's most notorious three-dollar bill, Jerry "The Crasher" Berliant, shows up from time to time—but only on a one-hour pass. "The Crasher" has this odd habit of driving most people nuts in no more than 24 seconds.

Abrams, the best maitre d' this town has had since Johnny Blandino was running the old Palm restaurant on East Lake Shore Drive back in the day, has an uncanny ability to get the right people together.

I'm just country enough that I loved this. During Game 2 of the Cubs' 2008 October crash and burn versus Joe Torre and the Dodgers, I watched about six innings of the ballgame with members of the Ricketts family. The name ring a bell? You got it. That's the Ricketts family of TD Ameritrade fame who, at the time, were just dying to buy the Cubs from *Tribune* emperor Sam Zell, the king of employee buyouts and would succeed the following summer.

What was up with this powerful family with eyes on a franchise that hasn't won a World Series in a mere 10 decades? No, Team Ricketts wasn't swapping ideas about relocating the press box or adding another layer of luxury boxes down the third base line. They were just munching on the Chicago-style dogs and wondering if Alfonso Soriano might actually come up with a base hit or at least avoid swinging at a breaking ball two feet off home plate.

No, the "Sheff" is not Gibson's restaurant or the mayor's office but I would love to know just how many millions of dollars in deals on the table—

and under the table—have gone down at this place just during pitching changes.

The newcomer's guide to the "Sheff:"

—The beer is always cold.

—The hot dogs are damn near as good as the carrot cake at Gibson's, and the carrot cake at Gibson's is so damn good it should be outlawed.

Abrams—and this had to be a bad day—once tried to bolt the door on Eddie Vedder, the lead singer for Pearl Jam. As Dave told me, "I knew the band; I just didn't know him."

Amen.

45 The new revolution: TALK SHOW BASEBALL

Okay gang, this one is going to require all of us to think "out of the box." (Out of the box? There's a pop culture line that should be placed on injured reserve or, better yet, full-blown retirement.) Think about watching baseball on television and think about how much "action" is truly presented. No, I'm not talking pitch-by-pitch or 6–4–3 double plays. What we're looking at is drama, sequences that ultimately determine just who the devil is going to win this sucker.

Time out: Suppose baseball had never been invented and some guy tried to hustle Madison Avenue and the TV networks on this wonderful game that features far too many guys scratching their crotch and far too little "live drama." Plus, there's no Vanna White and nobody ever gets kicked off an island—they just get sent to Des Moines or Birmingham.

You got it. The guy wouldn't get in the front door. But he would get couch therapy.

Let me go back a few years. ESPN 1000's Bruce Levine, simply the best baseball reporter in Chicago, and yours truly were dining in the Bard's Room at the "Cell." Bruce and I do this about 35 times each summer for two prime-time reasons: One, he's a great storyteller; and two, for eight bucks, you can eat at the Bard's like you're one day way from a six-month tour on Nutri-System.

Levine threw the first pitch: Why not give baseball a talk show format? Essentially, as we began to roll through ideas and concepts, we reached this conclusion: The MTV generation is entering middle age and the younger generation—I hate to be so avuncular about this—leads the nation in one category: channel surfing.

So here's what we suggest.

TALK SHOW BASEBALL!

A talk-show host, an eclectic guy who knows baseball, rock 'n' roll, politics, and pop culture, becomes your front man. He's joined by the traditional sidekick—a career lefty who played for five different big league clubs, including the Kansas City Royals. You get a solid, "challenging" baseball guy—fresh out of the bigs—to work the home and visitors' team dugout.

We immediately mandate that ballclubs allow the reporter interview access at all times during the ballgame. What's the problem? Is Ozzie Guillen's thought process going to be capsized because, for example, broadcaster Mark Grace just asked him why he didn't play the percentages and go lefty-lefty in an eight-inning sequence? The correct answer is, of course not.

But now let's go up top. Show the game on three quarters of the screen. Condensing the graphics won't be any kind of challenge.

Now the big ticket: The "play-by-play man" has to be well-schooled in a world that goes beyond the left-field wall. If Barack Obama and Hillary Clinton are sparring with each other or the Stones just announced another windup tour, make those stories equally, if not more important, than the actual play by play. Take the radio approach. Get a political expert on board. Have Jam Productions boss Arne Granat relive his greatest on-stage memories of Mick and Keith. Tell me this wouldn't be a great chip when it's 98 degrees in August and the Cubs are trailing Atlanta 9–2 in the fourth inning. If the game gets "hot," widen out to full screen and get into a traditional mode. On a normal day, it won't happen more than seven-eight times.

I don't think anybody above the age of nine needs to know that nothing much over the past 118 years has changed when it comes to handling a ground ball to third.

Take phone calls live on the air. Convince club owners, who see their TV product as nothing more than a three-hour advertisement for the great hot dogs the club is peddling, that a guy railing about the Cubs centerfielder of the week with visual reactions from the two guys in the booth will be tremendous.

Where do we start the revolution? Cubs Park. Len Kasper is a fabulous broadcaster. I don't doubt for 10 seconds that he could be a gold cup winner under the Levine-Coppock approach. Trust me, Len knows the Iowa caucus, the 43rd Ward, and just how badly the McCaskeys are fumbling at Halas Hall. Lennie can riff about the Replacements, DM3, the Romantics, and Superdrag. He's a club scene regular at joints like the House of Blues, Double Door, the Metro, and the Vic. He'd flourish in this environment.

Bob Brenly is still a teenager at heart. If Robert is dealing the cards face up, he'll tell you he'd rather jam with Pete Townshend than talk about the history of the double switch or the importance of long relief. That's the kind of guy we're looking for to push our new approach.

This is the revolution. Baseball on TV needs a new feel. It must dare to be different.

46 *Pounce on* HARRY CARAY'S *calamari during a* CUBS-CARDINALS *weekend*

Before we go lunging into today's sermon, I have a couple of items on the "Mayor of Rush Street" agenda I want to put in your lap. First, Harry Caray was what all of us secretly want to be: a person who knows the rules, understands the rules, and figures it's a lousy day in the office if you don't break the rules at least five or six times.

To me, this was the essence of Harry. When I was doing *Coppock on Sports* on WLUP/WMVP in the late '80s and early '90s, Harry was practically a regular contributor. The old guy was very shrewd. He knew that every time he appeared with me, he was violating his broadcast contract with WGN, just busting it sky-high.

So what was WGN going to do—tell Harry to go to his room? Make him do 25 pushups? WGN knew the obvious. Harry was so popular, such a moneymaker, the brass wouldn't dare tell him to live by the terms and arrangements of his deal.

You talk about a knockout. Harry once announced his "retirement" with me on 'MVP...and he did it on the same day the Cubs were running their annual fan convention. Naturally, WGN was out of its collective mind with anger. The local media couldn't wait to get to Harry. When Harry saw the blitz of microphones and notepads, he saw one thing for certain: a win. He'd upstaged the convention while claiming he'd only "suggested" to me that he might leave the booth. That was just Harry being Harry.

Meanwhile, I don't want to sound disrespectful, but Harry's funeral was the greatest roast you could ever hope to attend. I'm telling you, Dean Martin on his best day—surrounded by Frank, Sammy, Don Rickles, and Lucille Ball—never put on a better act. Just two things were missing: booze and ash trays.

The eulogies, led by Pete Vonachen, Harry's long-time drinking buddy and owner of the Peoria Chiefs, were hysterical. You're right. It is an odd feeling to sit in Holy Name Cathedral and laugh your head off over an icon who's just gone to that last great 6-4-3 double play in the sky.

Let's talk about Harry's Kinzie Street restaurant—fabulous steaks, world-class pasta, impeccable service. Let me clear up one misconception: The place doesn't live and die on tourists from the middle of nowhere who can hardly wait to sample the shrimp cocktail. We're talking in some respects about a neighborhood place. The bulk of the crowd, especially at the bar, is made up of regulars. And as anyone who understands the biz knows, in the restaurant game, more often than not, you live and die off the booze, not the desserts.

You want some A-listers who've turned up at Harry's? Alex Rodriguez darn near lives in the place whenever the Yankees come to town. Of course, Joe DiMaggio ate there. So have Ludacris, Crosby, Stills, Nash, and Young, and the Doobie Brothers.

Don't you wish we could turn back the hands on the clock? Wouldn't you love to hear Harry duet with Neil Young on "Cinnamon Girl" or "Ohio"? I'll go you one better: Stan "The Man" Musial turned up in the house one night and played the harmonica while Harry tag-teamed with Tanya Tucker on "Take Me out to the Ballgame." I bet "The Man" just begged Harry to follow up with AC/DC and "Highway to Hell."

That reminds me of a terrific yarn Bruce Levine, the WMVP baseball expert, likes to spin. Bruce remembers a time when ZZ Top, at the height of their popularity, showed up at Cubs Park. Harry, of course, had no idea who they were. When he learned they were ZZ Top, Harry's reaction was, "What religion is that?"

Call me self-serving, but this was cool. When Harry Caray's first opened the doors back in 1987, I was downright thrilled that my photo was on display in the restaurant entrance. You'll be happy to know that the folks at Harry's finally discovered common sense and exiled me to a second-floor banquet room. I think.

We haven't got time for a 20-minute lecture on Harry's ties to the St. Louis Cardinals or how many young broadcasters he influenced. Just keep this in your back pocket—kids, young adults, and 63-year-olds carrying too many credit cards from Missouri and southern Illinois revere the name Harry Caray. So—no surprise—Harry's joint becomes a sea of red whenever the Cardinals are in town for a series with the Cubs.

"Cardinal fans have waited in the bar and the front of the restaurant for up to four hours to get a table," according to Grant DePorter, managing general partner of the Harry Caray restaurant group. DePorter is also a brilliant promoter.

Tony La Russa, Ozzie Smith. If you're a part of the Cardinals family, it's better than even money that you've dined at Harry's.

One more for the road: Back in 1972, I was covering White Sox spring training down in Sarasota with the late Jack Drees, a truly brilliant sportscaster. One night after a long dinner, Jack asked if I wanted to stop off for one last belt. I'm 21. What am I gonna say, no? So Jack finds this little honky-tonk off Highway 41. We walk in and all we can see are these female hard bodies in a circle obviously watching someone dance. I move about 15 feet closer and, you got it, the chicks are digging Harry. These babes in their twenties are just knocked out by Harry doing a little foot-stompin' that was sort of like Fred Astaire meets James Brown meets Paula Abdul. I guess you had to be there.

I know I'll never forget this. While Harry entertained the troops, he yelled to me, "Hey, kid. Hop in, there's plenty for all of us."

47 The natural toss play: BUD SELIG gives the keys to JOHN MCDONOUGH

Give me one good reason why this doesn't make sense.

John McDonough's tenure with the Blackhawks has already earned him "early" retirement. Whatever Rocky Wirtz, son of Papa Billy Wirtz, pays big John, it's the cheapest buy in a city where buys are a way of life. I don't pretend to know what McDonough's salary is, but if it's not well into seven figures—$2 million per year would seem reasonable—then Wirtz should be ashamed of himself.

Side note: Rockwell's smile always reminds me of the old Celozzie-Ettleson "Hard to find—tough to beat" TV commercials…or a guy who just looks too rich, too privileged for his own damn good. Close friends of the Rock tell me he's as business-savvy and as tough as his late father. That's saying a lot. Sam Zell is Sally Field in *The Flying Nun* compared to William W. Wirtz.

Do you want me to document the complete facelift Mac has given the Blackhawks? He's done the impossible. In real-life terms, let's just say he's balanced the federal budget, removed U.S. Troops from Iraq, and bounced all the crooked cops from the Chicago Police Department—and put a hold on their pensions.

That's a pretty mean trick, given the fact that John doesn't have the benefit of "The Matadors." Or "Benny Bull." Or a bunch of nutcases running around the ice with signs saying "Make Noise."

I wonder how often this happens. John drives home from another United Center house of 21,000-plus—you know, against some glamour team like the Nashville Predators, the Atlanta Thrashers, or the Columbus Blue Jackets— and asks himself just where all this is going. And why does the brain-dead league have franchises in Columbus, Nashville, and Atlanta? In other words, John should be asking, "Where do you dance when the music stops?"

Sellouts, check. Blackhawks Convention, check. A deal I would have bet my daughter and my rent money he couldn't get done with WGN-TV, check. Are we going too fast? An Ice Classic at Cubs Park, the return of Pat Foley, merchandise up a bundle.

This should have been given greater consideration. John has done so much for the Blackhawks over such a limited window of time, I think Obama fumbled when he didn't name Mac Secretary of the Interior.

But our boy Mac is no dummy. He can see the big picture. He knows he turned a local graveyard into a "WIRTZ" gold mine. But he also knows ESPN told the NHL to get lost. He knows the league runs the bulk of its national telecasts on Versus, a network so obscure that when I Googled them, all I got was "no results."

The NHL in Chicago is major league. The NHL across the board is a minor league. Its revenues, player identity, and team recognition leave it just a notch above Arena Football and the MSL.

Does Vegas do any action on the NHL? I don't think so either.

I've said this to both John and his sidekick Jay Blunk before. They're throwing one helluva party on the west side. But keep in mind the lessons of George Halas and Pete Rozelle, the remarkable football visionaries. Your league is really only as strong as its lightweight franchises. Quick, name one player on the Calgary Flames. Christ, I'd bet that John doesn't know one player on the Calgary Flames. I'd bet five more yards he can't tell me all the teams in the old Norris Division. Who cares? John sells dreams.

Let's simplify. McDonough took Phyllis Diller and turned her into

Beyonce in about three weeks. As recently as 2004, ESPN declared the Blackhawks the worst franchise in sports. Think about that. The worst.

People who had Hawks season tickets in those days were also seeing Marv Albert's dominatrix.

So here's the play. Bud Selig is on the clock. He's booked to retire in 2012. And don't tell me Bud has to apologize for anything. Save Rozelle, he's the greatest commissioner in sports history. Screw David Stern. He gave the media empty sound bites while Bird, Magic, and Michael took the league out of the gutter. Stern is more overrated than Notre Dame football.

Selig can look at a game that produced nearly seven billion dollars in revenue in 2008, a staggering number. His detractors, and they are a legion, don't look at the big picture with Bud. They don't look at revenue sharing, the wild card, the additional playoff round, legitimate drug testing over the protestations of Don Fehr…all they see is a tie—due to a lack of pitchers (pitchers?!)—in the 2002 All-Star Game.

John McDonough is a natural choice to replace Bud. He has the business background, he's a facilitator, he could deal with the egos of the Steinbrenner kids, Frumpy and Dumpy. This is so natural, so perfect, Bud and John should be talking by phone six days a week about a "smooth transition."

McDonough needs action. Mac's on so many charity boards and "blue ribbon" committees that if he takes time for lunch at Carmichael's on Monroe Street, he has to have 37 voice mails before he cleans off his club sandwich. The Hawks will eventually bore him. How many times can you fill the house and beat the Buffalo Sabres before you say "no mas"? Patrick Sharp and Johnathan Toews seem to be good kids. But they just will never have the fan appeal of Brian Urlacher or Carlos Zambrano. That's just a fact. Hockey players in general—laborious sound clips.

John McDonough, Commissioner of Major League Baseball. Jay Blunk, the trusted right-hand man, becomes President of the Blackhawks. Rocky gets a manicure and counts his money.

The gloves fit—perfectly.

John, for openers, get rid of the DH.

HOOPIN'
It UP

48 *Tell the* NBA *that* FAT GUYS *shouldn't be* DANCIN' *at halftime*

"Do we really need this crap?" —Coppock

Okay, no fat jokes. The fact is, I've been above and beyond my playing weight since Jimmy Carter was tossing us double-digit inflation. But let me suggest this. Should you plan on buying a "Matador" as a Christmas decoration, skip the traditional scotch pines and evergreens. Buy a pair of sequoias and hang the poor blubber gut between the two trees with chain-link fence. That would support your new "Fatador"—maybe. No guarantees.

This verse isn't really about the Matadors, it is about an NBA that's deathly afraid of letting its product stand alone. If there isn't constant music, constant scoreboard activity, or kids running around with signs that read "Make Noise," the league is convinced it might lose it audience to curling or table tennis.

If you can explain the appeal of the Matadors, the Bulls' outrageously stupid dance troupe, please call me immediately—but only if you're in the 312 area code.

Outsiders assume all charges.

Do these massive hunks of apple pie have secret followers they correspond with on the web? Are there babes in cyberspace who just dream of shacking up with a Matador? I don't think so. But I could be wrong.

Hey, Drew Peterson—he leads the nation in missing wives—seemed to find a new chick about every three days.

Ever heard the line, "Nothing makes a girl's heart beat liked a badass?" Maybe it should read, "Nothing makes a girl get hotter in a hurry than a fatass."

Now stop. I don't want to pick on anybody. It's not my nature. The Matadors' choreographer is Cathy Core, a wonderful lady. Cathy and I have been casual friends since the long-gone days when the Bears were trotting out the Honey Bears and Cathy was teaching the young cuties how to be "coquettish."

Trust me, once Virginia McCaskey goes to that last great end zone in the sky, the "Honey Bears" will be back quicker than you can say "Kordell Stewart."

Side note: The Matadors are protected—big time. When I called the Bulls office and told some secretary I wanted to write about the "Big Mats," you would have thought I'd asked for the keys to Air Force One or Vinnie del Negro's playbook. I actually "conversed" with some third-tier employee who wanted to know if I "could write a note to discuss what I wanted to talk about."

Talk about what? How's health for openers? How's about a pathetic sideshow, an act so dismal that anyone who laughs should be shot at sunrise?

And maybe we should mention that these poor guys make a whopping 30 bucks a game? Thirty bucks a game, plus two cheap seats, to show off your belly and man breasts that aren't quite in the same league visually with Carmen Electra.

The ballclub doesn't care if these guys weigh 900 pounds. You want to be a Matador, you sign a waiver that clears the club if you have the misfortune to be at the east-end free-throw line when you have a stroke.

> *Message to all Matadors: Is this your ticket to the executive suite?*
> *Ever wonder about your vital organs? What do you eat for breakfast,*
> *your next-door neighbor's dog?*

Jeez, one night, I'm walking into gate 3½, the press gate at the U.C., and I see some guy with a dyed red punk/Mohawk dragging on a cigarette. My first thought? He must be the road manager for Johnny Rotten and the Sex Pistols. No, he's a "Mat-Man." Or he's a circus fat man. As a last resort, he's Haystacks Calhoun.

The Matadors don't get big ovations when they perform. They don't even get murmurs. They may get a few high-fives in the main concourse or in the runway after they "perform."

So what, lawyers high-five dentists at the United Center.

But that's about the extent of "Matador love."

Bulls, ask yourself, do you need this? Is it generating box office? Are you going to lose three season-ticket holders if you stop endorsing obesity?

You never know. In the NBA world, the game alone isn't enough.

49 Retire the "MOVING VAN'S" number

"I demanded respect. Nobody called me Normie or 'little Norm.'
If they did, I kicked their ass."

—Norm Van Lier

"Norm was a guy who feared no one. He'd fight guys who were
6-foot-10. His only goal in life was to win at all costs."

—Bob Love remembers his teammate, the last angry man

Norm Van Lier wasn't really a basketball player. He was a human floor burn, a guy with elbows that came from blueprints for meat cleavers. He was at his best when he squared off the with the NBA back-line heavyweights of his era, guys like Big "O" Robertson, "Clyde" Frazier, and the quirky but brilliant Earl "The Pearl" Monroe. What about the paint? "The Dutchman" wouldn't hesitate to drive the hoop against the big Ws: Wilt Chamberlain, Wes Unseld, Willis Reed, or Walt Bellamy. Frankly, Norm would take it to the rack if he was staring at Dick Butkus and Dick the Bruiser.

Norm's playing time is long gone. To the end, in the winter of '09, he harbored a tremendous degree of anger over the Bulls ordering him to take painkillers just to stay in uniform before eventually tossing him in the gutter when his tired knees could no longer propel his 170-pound jetstream of body down the floor.

This is a must for all people—and age is no issue.

Get on the phone and dial this number…*today.* 312-455-4000. Demand that Jerry Reinsdorf and his posse over at the west-side Ball-Mall do what should have been done 25 years ago: retire the number "2" worn by the Dutchman. Norm deserved the red carpet, the video tribute, the words of praise from "Chet the Jet" Walker, "Long Tom" Boerwinkle, and Jerry Reinsdorf. That could present a problem. Jerry usually spends most of his nights worrying about Paul Konerko's batting average.

Most of all, put the spotlight on his long-time running mate Jerry Sloan, whose number "4" is already gathering dust in the rafters. Let Jerry hoist Norm's banner together in a display of respect to one of the greatest basketball backcourt tag teams in NBA history.

> *"I had a routine. At 2:00 on game days, I shut down. I didn't answer the phone. I didn't wanna talk to anybody. All I thought about was the game. I didn't have to work up any anger, the anger was already there."*
>
> —N.V.L.

Raw numbers are a waste of time when you talk about Van. Why? Because while Norm earned plenty of accolades, he was ultimately a team man. Every bit as much a team man as Michael Jordan.

You didn't need a calculator to keep track of Norm Van Lier's shots from the floor or free throws made. You needed a calculator to keep track of just how many times Norm busted a passing lane or made the move on a switch to prevent a rival bucket, how frequently he disrupted offensive sets or burned his lungs to get back on "D" to KO a team on the break with "numbers." Uh, can you say "fundamentally brilliant"?

In other words, Norm Van Lier did all those things that average basketball fans only think about when they complain about how ridiculously overpaid today's NBA players just happen to be.

Look at the current Bulls. If Joakim Noah or the immortal Tyrus Thomas had half the passion on game night that Van Lier brought to the table, they'd do something new and unique—justify their paychecks. Ben Gordon? If he had Norm's competitive drive, he'd be surging his way toward Kobe Bryant-type money. (Oh shucks; now he's Joe Dumars' problem.)

"I think I'm as competitive as anybody who ever played this game."
—N.V.L.

And you know what, he might be right. This guy from Midland, Pennsylvania, who was so far under the recruiting radar that he played college ball at St. Francis, wasn't an annoyance. He was a root canal to the guy in the other uniform.

Book it. If Norm Van Lier would've been 6'3" with a frame carrying 218 pounds, he might have been heavyweight champion of the world. Why not? Van was an accelerator of an athlete. Catch him in a restaurant, mention the name Joe Namath, and he'd bend your ear about passing records that belonged to Joe that Van Lier busted during his high-school days in the football cradle known as western Pennsylvania.

Yes, Norm belonged to a different era, a time when a man's handshake was still legit. A time when NBA teams regularly played three games in three nights flying commercial. Per diem money in 1971 was eleven bucks a day. Good God, isn't that what guys pay for Chivas Regal on the rocks at a Peninsula Hotel?

But Norm changed with the times. I take a great deal of pride in this. Back in 1989, I told Van he should try his hand at broadcasting. Watch tapes of Dutch on the air. He was at once folksy, edgy, and entertaining with a big dose of attitude. In other words, Norm, the announcer, was a full-blown showman.

"My biggest problem is I tell the truth...always have. A lot of people just don't want to hear it. A lot of people are afraid of it. But nobody can say I'm not honest."
—N.V.L.

Hey, Bulls, get honest with Van Lier. Retire his number as soon as possible. Yesterday would be just fine.

Postscript: The "Dutchman" is gone. Norm passed away on February 26, 2009. He was just 61. We never did hear about "cause of death."

This is just my opinion: Norm appeared to be sinking into deep throes of depression. This "Pied Piper" of a man just never found a way to unload a significant load of bitterness.

Van went to his grave angry with the Bulls over a number of issues, most notably the fact that the club just never saw the outright logic in retiring his number 2.

Norm had also felt sold out, betrayed when the club didn't invite him to participate in its tribute to a dying Johnny "Red" Kerr. The club said it was an oversight. Norm felt, as did countless people, that it was an inexcusable omission.

Ironically, Red and Norm passed away on the same day.

Several days later, on the spur of the moment, I was called upon to eulogize Van during his funeral service at the Fourth Presbyterian Church on Michigan Avenue. I felt honored. I wanted to cry, but I was too busy thinking about all the laughs we'd shared for nearly 40 years. That's the way it should be.

Norm was a character, a fighter, a guy who defined "guts' and "passion."

You hate to lose those kinds of people.

50 Visit the MICHAEL JORDAN statue

"Jordan was a barracuda. He'd kill you to win a game."
—Chuck Daly, former Detroit Pistons head coach

"I made good dough and got great exposure doing television commercials for Chevy with Mike."
—Chet Coppock, noted hustler

Everybody has some kind of dream. Some guys want to get it on with Cameron Diaz. Some guys want to be A-Rod's gofer. I've got a far more simplistic approach that wouldn't do a damn thing for the national economy but would bulk up my sagging financial picture.

Here's the drill: I'd like to have 10 bucks from every person who's had a picture taken by the Michael Jordan statue who wouldn't spend five dollars to actually attend a Bulls game.

A young MJ was initially distracted by Coppock's classic '80s sweater, but His Airness regained focus to deliver his usual killer interview.

You talk about traffic. Everybody talks about busloads of Asian tourists bringing their cameras to M.J.'s granite spectacle. I'd like to know how many busloads of people from Iowa blow off a trip to Water Tower Place to get their kids photographed by this magnificent "Mikeness."

> *"Yes, I've seen the Jordan statue. I like to believe that it's my hand extending upward trying to stop him"*
> —Craig Ehlo, former Cleveland Cavaliers guard

Ehlo is a class guy. He can laugh about the moment of misery. He can talk in happy terms about getting burned by "the shot" Jordan dropped on the Cavs on May 7, 1989, to lift the Bulls to a first-round playoff series win. The shot gets replayed roughly 300,000 times per week on broadcast and cable television. The audio is classic. Red Kerr, screaming "Bulls win....Bulls win" doesn't sound like a basketball call—it sounds like a guy who just dropped a slot machine on his baby toe.

So it's warm-up time. Here are a few things you should know about the spectacularly detailed hunk of 2,300-pound brilliance on the west end of the United Center. Did you know it honors a guy who was cut not once but twice from his high-school basketball team back in Wilmington, North Carolina? Michael Jordan, cut from a prep basketball team: Jeez, would his coach have looked at Bill Russell and said, "Hey kid take up water polo?"

Remember the happy-go-lucky slogan "I wanna be like Mike"? Here's why none of us will ever be quite like M.J.:

1. No athlete ever looked better wearing an Armani suit. Or, for that matter, overalls.
2. He's made so much darn dough over the years that he could probably pay cash to buy the Columbus Blue Jackets. Hint: That's an NHL hockey team. M.J. + hockey. Tell me that isn't a marriage made in slap-shot heaven.
3. Praise from the Godfather. Before the 1984 NBA draft, Bobby Knight tried to convince the Portland Trailblazers to draft Michael with the second overall pick and play him in the post!
4. I have no doubt that M.J. could play blackjack nonstop for 24 hours…36 hours if he was down at least $500K.
5. Mike should be the guy to light the flame for the 2016 Olympics if the games are conducted in Chicago. What? You want Dusty Baker or Joe Crede? Or ex-Governor Ryan?
6. The phrase "The Jordan Rules" was created by former Detroit Pistons assistant coach Dick Versace. No, the concept was not based on Bill "I am and always have been a spoiled brat" Laimbeer or John Salley busting Mike's jaw. Its technical approach was changing defensive sets depending upon where Jordan was on the dance floor.
7. Ehlo, a frequent Jordan rival, said the nastiest thing Mike ever said to him was simply, "Craig, don't you know you can't guard me?"
8. Forget about Devin Hester trying to haul in passes. M.J. was so quick, so instinctive, that he might have been a poor but not very poor man's edition of Jerry Rice or Art Monk.
9. Michael Jordan was Tiger Woods before Tiger Woods was Tiger Woods.
10. Jordan and golf are locked at the hip. But Mike is no threat to Jack Nicklaus. I've met too many Chicago-area players who've told me he's just a better-than-average weekend player.

I don't think this required a great deal of heavy thought. The inscription on the Jordan statue states very clearly: "The best there ever was. The best there ever will be."

Not bad for a guy who bit .202 back in 1994 playing low-level minor-league baseball with the Birmingham Barons.

My favorite Jordan moment: We have to go back to Ehlo and the old Richfield Coliseum, a building that had roughly as much charm as a landfill. I was in the house working the game for WLUP radio along with Jim Durham and Johnny Kerr when M.J. knocked down the jumper over our poor friend Craig Ehlo to give the Bulls a series win.

You think I don't pick winners? While Mike set up in the paint for his break to the top of the key, I was nudging my way toward Cavs coach Lennie Wilkens. I had no doubt Cleveland was going to win and the first guy I wanted to interview was Lennie. You're right, if I go to Arlington and there's a nine-race card, somehow I'll find a way to lose 10 bets.

Bulls coach Doug Collins was so giddy with joy after the shot that while running—Jimmy Valvano–style—around the court, he nearly took out about six ushers. Doug had to figure he was in line for photo-ops, a press conference, and a brand-new four-year contract. Uh, no. About a month later, Jerry Krause fired Doug because:

A. He couldn't get along with Michael.
B. Doug lost a power struggle with Michael.
C. Collins couldn't coach, which is idiotic.
D. He was having an affair with either a member of the Luvabulls or a wife or girlfriend of one of the team's investors.

Don't tell me you know the answer. This is one of those stories that has so many plots and subplots that it won't be solved before the Apocalypse.

Jordan and the Auto Show—Mike made annual appearances at the show for the Chicago and Northwest Indiana Chevrolet Dealers. M.J.'s deal called big bucks and a couple of Corvettes. I had to work about six years before I finally begged my way into a Blazer. Crowd control eventually burned the date off Mike's calendar. As his star kept growing, the crowds kept building. We darn near had a situation where a mob just dying to get as close to this icon as they could almost turned the makeshift stage into firewood.

Mike and I also did television commercials together for Chevy. Much like Mike Ditka, it was a major upset if M.J. required more than two takes per spot.

The Michael Jordan statue—make it a must.

51 Walk north up Sheffield Avenue... walk left on BELDEN AVENUE... feel the legacy and class of RAY MEYER

"I was just a young basketball coach at Army and I was in Chicago to look at a ballplayer. When the game was over, I asked Coach Ray the quickest way to get to the airport...he said, 'Bob, the quickest way would be for me to drive you.'"

—Bob Knight, talking about the beloved "Baron of Belden" at a
March of Dimes banquet at the Hilton back in 1982

I didn't "carry" that banquet, but I had to cover a bundle of tabs. It was my job to line up a dais and try to squeeze money out of local heavy-hitters. Neither project required heavy lifting because of Ray Meyer.

I love Bobby Knight, but he's a chameleon. In fact, I've seen Bob change his mind three times in the same sentence. I wasn't sure the "General," after a long season, would have any interesting in flying up from I.U. to pay tribute to Coach Ray. Forget it. He gave me an immediate "yes" when I called him in Bloomington. In fact, he seemed flattered.

Bobby loved Ray Meyer...a man who was rediscovered at the age of 65.

Yes, Ray won the NIT—when the NIT, not the NCAA, was "the tournament"—with George Mikan in the hole back in 1945. Yes, he ran an above-board program at tiny Alumni Hall at Belden and Sheffield. From time to time, he had big winners. More often than not, he lacked thoroughbreds. All too often, Ray went to war with Marquette or Notre Dame playing guys off a local street corner.

But before Coach Ray got hot in the late '70s and white-hot in the early '80s, he'd been drifting toward trivia-question status. Chicago has never been a great college roundball city...damn, it was a lousy NBA town before Jordan brought the flight show to the west side. Hell, I can remember hearing whispers in the '60s and '70s about DePaul putting a blade to Ray's throat.

And here's what's unique about the man: He would have accepted the exile. He wouldn't have screamed bloody murder. He wouldn't have gathered up a couple of friendly columnists and given them a free ride. He wouldn't have bum-rapped other coaches who cheated their way to players he wanted. Ray would have packed up and just moved to the next stop. Other than a blind rage when the Demons, led by A.D. Bill Bradshaw, fired his kid Joey in '97, if Ray ever held a grudge that lasted more than 15 seconds, it was the best-kept secret in the world.

It's funny how the course can be altered. During the late '70s, Ray added son Joe and another bright kid, Jim Molinari, to his coaching staff. The recruiting doors swung open with a frenzy: Joe Ponsetto, Dave Corzine, Curtis Watkins, Clyde Bradshaw, Mark Agguire, Skip Dillard, Terry Cummings, and on and on.

Ray became a rock star just about the time he qualified for social security. He became a national hero, everybody's granddad, when the Demons knocked off UCLA in March 1979 to grab a ticket to the Final Four. You just have to see Al McGuire's interview of Ray after the Demons had burned out the clock against the Bruins. Maybe it will turn up on YouTube someday.

McGuire, the ex-Marquette head coach, had found a terrific niche teaming with Dick Enberg and Billy Packer covering college ball on NBC. Al, being Al, was the star while Packer played back-up tuba and Enberg, silky smooth, gave you the score and the scorers.

Al, who never let journalism—and he was right on target!—get in the way of showmanship and just plain fun, ran to Ray and said, "Coach, you're going to the Final Four. How does it feel?" Ray, who probably wanted to know what all the commotion was all about, simply said, "I'm a young man again, a young coach. And these young men have taken me to the Final Four."

God, Ray was cool. Think about this. I get the call from Channel 5-Chicago in January 1981 to replace the departing Greg Gumbel. (I agree with you. I still can't figure out what Channel 5 was thinking. Chet Coppock replaces Greg Gumbel. We're messed up. It's no wonder that our state leads the nation in one category: crooked governors.)

One of Channel 5's P.R. guys called Ray to arrange a photo op with the coach and myself. The guy clearly wanted to warn Chicago and the collar counties that this loudmouth out of Indianapolis—who actually went to New Trier—was coming to Chicago. You deal with most coaches on this kind of issue and you go through seven layers of red tape. But Ray was always the easiest "get" in town. If you didn't speak to him directly, his longtime assistant, Patsy Burns, would tell you that unless the earth stood still or Belden Avenue collapsed, the coach would be available. And he always came with a smile.

Imagine Coach K or Dean Smith or Tom Izzo doing this. To accommodate Channel 5 and Chester Coppock, Ray just skipped out of practice for about 15 minutes while we took photos and did a couple of on-camera promos.

Ray Meyer couldn't say no. When the city fathers needed name value to announce some new youth program, they called Ray Meyer. When a charity needed a payday, it booked Ray Meyer and gave him some kind of "honor," any kind of honor.

Unofficially, Ray was an honorary member of just about every religion in North America.

He wasn't an explosive quote. He wasn't going to give you bulletin-board material. But he was always there, smiling when you knew he was exhausted. Laughing when you knew he'd rather be home watching a rerun of *Dallas*.

That's why I got so sky-high pissed off when Ray's beloved wife Marge passed away in 1986. There were so few writers and broadcasters at Marge's services on the DePaul campus it made me sick—sick with anger. Every media guy in Chicago who'd leaned on Ray to bail out a slow news day, asked him to kill time on campus for three hours, so he could do 90 seconds on the 10:00 news, should have been there. The lack of press attendance remains a disgrace.

I remember chatting with Joel Bierig, a former *Sun-Times* writer, after the service. I told Joel that, in particular, I thought Johnny Morris, the ex-Channel 2 sports anchor, should have been shot for not showing up. Morris had conned and cajoled Ray for years. Naturally, Johnny "I do things for myself and myself only" wasn't in the house.

I'll never forget that sunshiny day in Dayton, Ohio, back in March 1981. Ray and the Demons were 26–1, a strong if not consensus pick to win the national title, but were knocked off in their first-round game by Jim Lynum and St. Joe's, 49–48. The Hawks just outplayed, outschemed, and outdefended the Demons.

This was before coaches' press conferences at the NCAA tourney became so orchestrated they resemble military inductions. The gates were wide open. So I just happened to be the first reporter to get to Ray after the ballgame. The heat in the room was stifling. Ray had just seen his title dream blow up in smoke. I not only interviewed him, I had to ask him to take off the mic he was carrying since we were recording him for "wild sound" for a proposed special. Most coaches would have F-you'd me to death. Ray just smiled, tried to explain a migraine of a loss, and then said, "Oh yeah. You probably do need the microphone back."

That was class, but Ray topped himself in 1982. The Demons, playing scared, lost to Boston College 82–75 in the first round of the dance at Reunion Arena in Dallas. At halftime, you knew the Demons were killing time before the post-game showers.

Now, this is classic. I was on the commercial flight with Ray and his players and about 140 ticked-off DePaul boosters from Love Field back to O'Hare. I knew the flight was going to land about 9:35 Chicago time…and I knew I had a chance to get Ray on live for our 10:00 newscast if everything fell into place.

The plane did touch down on time but—gee, what a shock—the craft sat on the runway for about 10 minutes. Naturally, we hopped off the plane about three miles down at the end of a terminal. Now we're at about 9:55. I asked Ray if he'd mind hurrying up so that we could lead with him at 10 PM.

True story: Ray actually ran past about three gates to join us. He was our lead, loss be damned. Ray knew I wanted him on and it just wasn't his nature to say, "You gotta be nuts." Never was.

I had a similar run with Dave Wannstedt through O'Hare 11 years later. Wanny and I did the 220 through another terminal at O'Hare. It took me years to realize that Dave wasn't running for me. He was just so damn excited about moving in as head coach of the most-storied franchise in the NFL that he couldn't resist jogging to the baggage carousel.

Sadly, Coach Ray eventually fought with DePaul when A.D. Bill Bradshaw fired son Joey as head basketball coach. And Ray—this is just soooo Ray—eventually reconciled with the school.

No sad songs. Ray was just a wonderful man. His level of class was unmatched. And never forget this: he was cool.

52 Is that NEIL FUNK or the unknown soldier?

"Yeah, I remember when Jim Durham left the Bulls back in '91. It was an odd situation. Durham's a stud but his agent, a local babe, told the team she wanted Chick Hearn–type money. Bulls Marketing Chief Steve Schanwald basically told the agent to 'get lost,' and Durham was gone. It was a shame."

—Coppock

Gather up the troops. Let's spend the next two hours talking about our favorite moments of the Neil Funk era in Chicago.

Oh, did I mention to you that the "Funkster" is the "Voice of the Chicago Bulls"? And he didn't arrive via Greyhound bus 20 minutes ago. Neil took over the microphone from Durham after Jim and his front "person" created their own misplaced exit strategy after the Bulls had won their first NBA title back on June 12, 1991.

Durham was not an easy act to follow. I know, I handled pregame, halftime, and postgame shows for the Bulls from the fall of '89 through the first champagne celebration. Durham had sizzle and his broadcasts were top-heavy with steak. Plus, he had a younger Johnny "Red" Kerr, who was establishing global records for screaming every time the Bulls knocked off Detroit. The two of them together were just dynamite.

As 2008 gravitated to 2009, Neil's role was changed. He was moved from radio, where I swear no more than 37 people knew he was on the air, to television.

Funk's tag-team partner is Stacey King. King has network potential. Here's what's funny about Stacey, and I know he's aware of this. He just thrives on bum-rapping players who are soft. Stacey, think about your own NBA career. Did you earn 100 cents on every buck? Your career scoring average, 6.4 points a ballgame, leaves you about No. 3,218 on the NBA's all-time scoring list. You were, in fact, a Jerry Krause first-round bust. You were frequently overweight, never struck anybody as a gazelle on the offensive glass, and were under no circumstances ever a "Go-to Guy." Right? Hell, other than that, you were a cross between Elgin Baylor and Rick Barry.

King just needs to stop taking every bad call against he Bulls so damn personally. It's not like the Bulls have been anything special the past decade and change. Think Bulls—post-Jordan—and what comes to mind? Futility, bad fourth-quarter losses, Tim Floyd, and Vinnie Del Negro. Or, maybe as a last resort, Bill Cartwright's two-hour fling as the club's head coach. The Lakers, the Spurs, LeBron, they get calls. The Bulls have yet to qualify for any special "Zebra treatment."

Anyway, back to the "Funkster." I don't get this. Neil is the Unknown Soldier. He's the WHA. He's the deejay at a teen club in Naperville.

This is no knock on Funk's blow-by-blow ability. He's good, he's functional, he protects the home team's interests. Here's the problem. Neil is what he is: a Philadelphia-style broadcaster who just doesn't create any kind of frenzy. Frenzy? My gosh, how the hell can you go through the Jordan era and all the attached glory and have a profile as low as Mr. Funk?

Neil had M.J., Scottie, Pax, Cartwright, Dennis, and the unforgettable Luc Longley. Any local book would make it 4 to 5 that having an attachment to that cast of characters should guarantee seven features alone in *Chicago Magazine*.

Let's advance the program. Funk has so many championship rings, he should qualify for his own monument in Grant Park. Has any broadcaster, in any sport, ever walked into a sweeter gig? Durham splits. Neil arrives and is ringside for five titles in seven years.

Hardball time. Every time I hear Neil's dulcet tones on Bulls basketball, I find myself asking just what would the Rolling Stones be today if Mick Jagger had become a dentist and Keith Richards had to play off Donny Osmond.

Funk isn't a bad guy. Hell, we hardly know each other.

Neil could learn a lesson from the master. Jack Brickhouse always said, "I like a little gee-whiz in my broadcasts." There are times when Neil strikes me as disinterested, as if he's conveying to me and the house, "Can't we get this damn thing over so I can move a step closer to the off-season and my 3-wood?"

Yes, the Funkster makes me yearn for the glory days of Jim Durham. Jim was hardly a social butterfly—most ex-drinkers are like that—but his ability to seize the moment, raise the level of dynamite, was tremendous. Durham just screamed "Chicago." His play-by-play during that first title run was the seventh game of the World Series. You want Durham's greatest asset? He could keep you locked in when the Bulls were on the short end of a 104–83 ballgame.

What do we see when we see Neil Funk? A guy who used to broadcast for the New Jersey Nets, a nice-enough fellow who probably is so far under the radar he can't get comped at the ESPN Zone.

Funkster, explain this. You've done the Bulls for a generation. Are you absolutely certain Joakim Noah knows who you are?

Okay, let me back off. Maybe I have to give Neil an extended mulligan. Following the "Jordanaires" years, Neil was stuck trying to explain how a club could turn the ball over six times during the pregame layup drill. You try and make Eddy Curry sound like Wilt Chamberlain.

Eddy should be a billboard: "I am all things wrong with the NBA."

Or, "You have every right to punch out your basement ceiling when you look at what kind of dough I've been stealing…The NBA Fantastic."

Maybe this could offer a solution. The Bulls should throw a "Neil Funk Night." Granville Waiters and Wil Perdue can serve as co-emcees.

You know, give Neil an in-house booster shot.

Believe me, it hurts to say this. Neil, forget about "We hardly knew ya." The issue is, "We don't know ya in town."

53 Ditch the Dunkin' Donuts Derby... just PLAY BASKETBALL

Okay, in today's episode I get to perform the role of Grumpy Old Man. Why not? I grew up on Chuck Berry, Vice President Richard Nixon, and Groucho Marx.

Here's the hook. How do you criticize the Bulls for all the bells and whistles and assorted forms of nonsense that are so much a part of their pregame and in-game presentation?

The answer: It's a bitch. This club has played to roughly 98.5 percent capacity *since Michael left town*. In other words, I may dislike their world, but the "family entertainment" gimmicks have to be appealing to guys with big-time disposable cash.

The first Bulls game I attended was back in 1967. Red Kerr was the head coach, the team played at my beloved International Amphitheatre, Jerry Sloan had floor burns, and the Bulls lost to the Boston Celtics with Bill Russell, "Hondo" Havlicek, Don Nelson, and the Jones boys. As best as I recall, the two clubs just played a two-hour ballgame without the world-famous Hinckley Springs grand prix water frolics screaming off the scoreboard.

You talk about good fortune and good timing. From 1988 through 1991, I did the pregame, halftime, and postgame shows for Bulls radio on old WLUP, the forerunner to WMVP. I saw Ehlo's shot, and I generally sat about four feet from either Doug Collins or Phil Jackson. I saw Scottie Pippen redefine the phrase "second banana"—and just to close on the upbeat—the club won its first NBA title the night we did our last broadcast.

Here we go. Keep in mind, life itself should really be tongue-in-cheek. That being said, I just want Bulls and the NBA to give my eardrums and nervous system a break every 30 to 40 seconds.

First off, if I hear Gary Glitter's "Rock and Roll Part 2" one more time, I may deck Vinnie Del Negro. "Glitter" rock was cool during the first Jordan title run back in '91, '92, and '93. Now it's about as dynamic and hip as the *Lawrence Welk Show*. If you don't know Lawrence Welk, you just don't know how wild this country was about polkas and champagne music back in the day.

A typical night at the U.C. really hasn't changed much since the club vacated Chicago Stadium to move next door to a building with all the charm of your local Dominick's. But, by gosh, it is overwhelmed with luxury suites.

About 1:45 into a game, you begin to hear "dot...dot...dot...dot... dot...dot...dot...dot." This doesn't last for 18 seconds; it's still in your brain when you get back to Hinsdale or Lake Forest. It goes on wire to wire. If it isn't the organ punishing your brain, it's the techno pop sound of "Um...um... um...um...." In other words, the Bulls figure anybody who shows up for a ballgame and wants to talk with a seatmate about a post-up or a cross-over must be in from New Zealand.

I love the San Diego/Famous Chicken. Teddy Giannoulis has always been a step ahead of the curve. I just don't dig Bennie the Bull. Watching him try to get a referee involved in one of his stupid timeout gimmicks makes me really believe I was a genius when I said 20 years ago, "The NBA is the one sport that walks a fine line between being an athletic event and being a circus." There must be some kind of house rule at the United Center that says every time Bennie tries to make an official look dumb, the ref has the right to actually call traveling. Kobe, LeBron, and "The Big Ticket" naturally get exemptions. Derrick Rose is on the waiting list.

Explain this: Some clowns wearing McDonald's outfits shoot free T-shirts up in the stands. Those Ts have got to be worth about two bucks each. You know they'll shrink from XXL to medium after one wash. So why are guys sitting in the 100 level, paying around a 150 bucks a ticket, screaming for this stuff like third-world refugees begging for food?

You begin to see the message loud and clear. The Bulls and the NBA have adopted a very simple premise: The game itself just won't sell unless you're blessed with a team that's a lock to win 60. There can be no dead air. No dead time. The fan must be fed nonstop for two-plus hours—give or take a loose ball foul.

Sell till you drop. Trot out the Luvabulls, who are very kinky girls...the kind you don't take to the IHOP. Bring out the Matadors, a collection of overweight guys who remind us that P.T. Barnum actually said, "There's a fat gram born every second."

Once you've been a Matador, what do you do with the rest of your life? Become a trampoline? Or a human two-flat? Hey, I'm overweight, but these guys are cities waiting to sell "naming rights" on their abdomens.

On the night I'm writing this sermon, the world-famous Radio City Rockettes are the halftime entertainment. They exude class, style, and are so 1940s they wouldn't last a week in the Bulls' train-wreck audio corral.

Do I really need the scoreboard demanding that "I make noise" or a bunch of kids blocking sight lines with signs that say "Stand Up and Yell"?

During one timeout, a couple of lucky(?) fans are ushered to half court for a burger-building contest. This rapidly makes me a new fan of Taco Bell. Fans are asked to topple bowling pins. I have no idea why.

The only things worth a darn are the "Bucket Boys" or the Jesse White Tumblers.

The game goes dark. Philly beats the Bulls in OT. And as I drive back to my West Loop condo, I realize something terrible is missing.

You got it. I never heard, "Mony Mony."

Dear Bulls:

Give me basketball, give me a show. Just don't give me a suburban barn-dance with the decibel level of Whitesnake.

Sincerely,

James A. Naismith

54 What—NOTRE DAME plays BASKETBALL?

For openers—and this is big—you don't have to pay to park your car at the Joyce Center.

You want a cheap buy and a chance to see big-time Big East College basketball? Stick around. In about four minutes we'll have you drooling about Notre Dame hoops. But first, let's click on the way-back machine to the most stunning, exhilarating college basketball I've ever seen.

January 19, 1974: Bill Walton, the greatest passing center who ever played the game, and UCLA came strutting into South Bend carrying an 88-game winning streak. *88*—got that?

Side note: You remember 1974? It was the year Terry Jacks recorded "Seasons in the Sun," a song so listless, so sleepy, so outright dull it paved the way for disco. Jacks did more to boost the career of Donna Summer than Donna moaning, "I'd love to love you baby." It was also the year that Dick Nixon was asked to give up his summer home in Washington, D.C. Quick, let's all chant, "I'm not a crook…I'm not a crook."

Back to South Bend. UCLA was invincible. I thought they'd bust Notre Dame by at least 15 points—and, in fact, the Bruins led by 17 in the first half. But with just over three minutes left and the Irish down by 11, Touchdown Jesus waved the magic wand. N.D. ran off the game's final 12 points while Bruins coach Johnny Wooden sat in stunned disbelief. The Gipper—make that Dwight Clay—drained a baseline jumper to give the Irish the lead and the win for good 70–69.

And you thought this stuff only happened when Lou Holtz was still on campus.

Here's the point: Go see a Notre Dame game. The Irish play a Big East schedule, which means you've got plenty of decent, make that tremendous, attractions to choose from. The drive? It's a romp in the park, roughly 102 miles—give or take a left turn—from the corner of State and Madison.

If you tell me you know the following fact, you're conning me. Mike Brey, the N.D. front man, was chosen Big East Coach of the Year twice, in 2007 and 2008. The guy can flat-out coach. Mike only has one real problem. He's allergic to the P.R. machinery. Brey is a stand-up guy who's just content to coach and win. Mike is no threat to Ozzie Guillen if you're looking for an off-the-wall quote.

That's a far cry from my guy Digger Phelps, the long-departed N.D. skip. The Digger specialized in the green carnations, made-to-measure suits, and revving up the crowd. He owned the press. Digger was the Roller Derby with a clipboard. Man, he was colorful.

You talk about a great act. When Phelps coached against Al McGuire, the high priest of Marquette hoops, you were watching two guys who lived to one-up each other. It was Vince McMahon versus Ted Turner. I've always figured Digger thought it was a lousy night if Al did a better job of working the officials than he did. To put it very mildly, neither guy was a shrinking violet.

Now it's conundrum time: Notre Dame does not sell out all its home games. Yet, its student body can be as over-the-top nuts as Dick Vitale's Cameron Crazies.

This is the whole truth and nothing but…March 5, 1977: Bill Cartwright and the 29-0 San Francisco Dons turn up at the Joyce. Tell me this isn't cool. Before the tip, the N.D. faithful began chanting "29 and 1…29 and 1!" The final: Irish 93, Frisco 82. Duck Williams scored 25 to lead N.D. Williams had to be mentally preparing his NBC MVP speech during the final two minutes.

Forget it. The network gave the MVP to the Irish student body.

The student freakin' body.

That happens about as often as I pick up a lunch tab.

Enough said. Treat yourself. Make the drive to South Bend. Check out Notre Dame basketball. If you get antsy during a timeout, stroll over to Charlie Weis' loge box and talk about the Cover 2 defense or ask C-dub when he plans to beat USC.

55 Need a prep ROUNDBALL fix? Attend the PROVISO WEST Holiday Tournament

You have to know a few things right off the top. Jon Scheyer, the kid from Glenbrook North, at last count, holds nine "West Tourney" records. That's on offense. He also holds the record for most overall steals in a single tourney. Those are just a couple of reasons why Duke was begging Scheyer to play ball in Durham. One more item: Jon dropped 52 one night in a "Pro West" game with 21 of those in one quarter. Mike Krzyzewski was in the house to see that performance.

And we thought Joakim Noah was special?

Monsignor Gene Pingatore, the longtime coach at St. Joe's Westchester, has won the event nine times. Trust me—that's as nifty, in its own way, as Chuck Noll winning four Super Bowls with Pittsburgh's Steel Curtain. (Or me breaking 90 on the golf course.)

Different ballpark: WGN sports talker David Kaplan is one my favorite people. We go back about 25 years. I first hooked up with Kap when he was hustling from gym to gym, passing out copies of his publication, *The Windy City Round Ball Review*. He was young, devoted to hoops, and dying to get his "sheet" the time of day from the local press.

David is a full-blown gym rat. He's pulled what I call the "Taylor Bell." He's sat in the 4,000-seat gym at Proviso West and watched not one, not two, but eight high-school games in one tournament day. To put it mildly, both Dave and Taylor, who covered prep sports for the *Sun-Times*, rate high-school basketball just below religion and motherhood on the all-time list. I hope.

You think Taylor doesn't dig prep buckets? If he gets word about an angular kid with Scottie Pippen "hops" 172 miles south of Chicago, T-Bell really can't breathe comfortably until he sees the "gem" in waiting.

Kap and Bell were both regulars on my "COS" radio show during the '80s and '90s. Both, without hesitation, could tell you the name of a junior, backup 2-guard in Decatur who was destined for stardom. They were freakin' encyclopedic. They didn't call college coaches for info…colleges coaches called them.

Side note time: In 1994—good move, great dough, horrible timing—I left Chicago. I dragged my family out to New York, where I worked a TV gig for

Cablevision for about four years. In doing so, I turned down a local offer to work at WGN. Once I'd informed the Tribune Company that I had no interest in their pitch, I tossed out a recommendation: Hire David Kaplan.

My pitch was two-fold. One, I told them at the time that Dave would work cheap. Boy, did that change. Two, I told WGN's Program Director Tisa LaSorte that Dave was a "big-game" player just waiting to blossom. Obviously, time has proved me right.

David, to reciprocate, occasionally allows me to caddy for him.

Why was the New York move a mistake on my part? I gave up a lot of dough in Chicago and great commercial ties with Chevrolet and Coca-Cola. But here's why we call the executioner. When I did return "home," I went to work for James Corno Sr. at the old Fox Sports Net. Corno is without question the most lackluster, boring broadcast executive in global history. He's the kind of guy who raves about a TV test pattern.

The first thing he told me was, "You can't say anything negative about the Sox or Blackhawks. It would hurt my friendships with [Jerry] Reinsdorf and [Billy] Wirtz." In other words, Jim said play "house man" and shut up. It was the worst broadcast experience I've ever endured. All I was missing was a prison uniform and a cellmate.

THE "PROVISO WEST" has always been about star power. In 1977, I attended my first tourney for just one reason. I wanted to see a baby-faced Isiah Thomas. I had heard so much about this wunderkind that I drove up from Indianapolis just to see him play. Trust me, your eight-year-old cousin could tell you "Zeke" was beyond "special."

Think about this: Thomas, Doc Rivers out of Proviso East, and Mark Aguirre, the Westinghouse scoring machine, were the main-eventers on the "Pro West" 1977 All-Tournament team. Doc coached the Boston Celtics to their first NBA title in 22 years in 2008. Aguirre was the first overall pick by Dallas in the 1981 NBA Draft. (That was after he drove Ray Meyer half crazy at DePaul.) Isiah earned Hall of Fame status by bankrupting the old CBA and creating a total Madison Square Garden quagmire as head coach of the New York Knicks.

Okay. I'll bend a little bit. Aguirre took Meyer and the Demons to a Final Four. Thomas led Indiana to a national title in '81 and he was the guy who packed the dagger that led the Detroit Pistons' "Bad Boys" to a pair of NBA titles.

"Aguirre, Rivers, and Thomas were all friends," Bell recalls. "They were such big draws the fire marshall had to come in and close the place down." That's just a modest overstatement.

Perhaps that's been the beauty of Proviso West. It's been a welcome mat that embraces and creates stars. The '60s featured Niles West's Jim Hart. Jim later spent three lifetimes quarterbacking the old St. Louis Football Cardinals. Plus Bob Lackey, "The Black Swan" from Evanston, along with Jim Brewer, a nails-tough kid out of Proviso East.

Take it a step further. The "West" is the Golden Globes of Midwestern holiday basketball. It's darn near a given. If you "play big" at Proviso West in December, you will play deep into March.

Jump to the '80s. Kaplan's all-decade team features Juwaan Howard, Hersey Hawkins, Walter Bond, and Marcus Liberty, all brilliant prep round-ballers. In the '90s, Kap throws out Sherrell Ford, Kevin Garnett, and his Farragut Academy teammate Ronnie Fields. Fields was beyond electric. Bell called him a "rock star." Kaplan says he was "the greatest athlete I've ever seen on the high-school level. He could jump over the moon."

Ronnie's vertical jump was about 44 inches. Sadly, a neck injury, legal woes—and a general lack of direction—has left Fields a minor-league vagabond.

The "West" gym holds about 4,000 fans. But you can bank on this. There have been a bundle of games when at least 4,800 people crammed into the place. Proviso West itself is an easy reach. It's right off the Eisenhower Expressway and tickets are really, in my opinion, too cheap.

Taylor Bell's all-time Proviso West tourney team: Brewer and Aguirre at the corners with, of course, Kevin Garnett, while Thomas, Rivers, Scheyer, and Fields man the back line. Taylor figures that group wouldn't need a true center.

Kap darn near mirrors Bell. His five-man unit features Garnett, Scheyer, Aguirre, Thomas, and Brewer.

Did we mention that Corey Magette, Jeff Hornacek, Randy Brown, and Joe Ponsetto also worked the "Proviso West"?

The event is just a masterpiece. Go out and see eight games in one day. Your life may never be the same. Let's see, eight games times two hot dogs per game, throw in popcorn, pop…oh, just eat and enjoy.

56 DRIBBLE *with the* MASTER: *Get your kid ball-handling tips from ex-Globetrotter* CURLEY "BOO" JOHNSON

"You know what the big problem is with the 'Trotters? Bookies just won't take action on the Washington Generals."

—Coppock

Hum a few bars of "Sweet Georgia Brown." I need a quick lay-up line to get you squared for today's message. But if you only grab one take-home point from our meeting, here's the ticket.

"Boo" Johnson will tell you that in "his prime," he was without peer—he was the greatest dribbler in the world. I don't doubt him for a second.

Now, in the need-to-know category…the Harlem Globetrotters are really a two-man act—the showman and the ball handler. Everybody else is really just along for the ride to fill out the field.

When you have Winslet and Dicaprio or Angelina and Brad, the supporting cast is just politely reminded to stay the hell out of the way. That's the 'Trotter way. Pretty much always has been.

Think about it. Over the years, depending upon your age, after you've seen the 'Trotters, you've raved about Marques Haynes, Reece "Goose" Tatum, "Meadowlark" Lemon, or, maybe, Fred "Curley" Neal.

Or, quite possibly you've been left spellbound by the dribbling brilliance of Curley "Boo" Johnson. Boo played 18 years for the 'Trotters. Call it a tour that screams "all that glitters is not gold." Adulation and a chance to see Melbourne, Australia, or Florence, Italy—and fight it out tooth and nail with an unbearable schedule. Typically, the Globbies play 28 days straight before they get one—count 'em, one—day off.

This is criminal—sometimes the 'Trotters practice on their day off.

"Boo" was blessed by Mother Theresa. He hasn't forgotten dribbling on his knees and back, somewhere in India, on a rubber surface so hot, the flesh on his back darn near became sirloin steak. Hell, he only missed five games in 18 years. Ex-teammates still talk about him playing ballgames with pink eyes so bad, he wasn't sure if he was in Moscow or Dublin.

When "Boo" looks at Barack Obama, he sees the leader of the free world, but that's just part of the action. Curley sees the President as a "nasty defender, who was always hacking me, always in my face." Boo and Barack played pick-up games for years in the fourth-level gym at the East Bank Club. You're right on target. I wonder if Barack would trade Joe Biden for Curley's eye-to-hand coordination.

You think you're a workaholic? Boo averaged 225 games a year during his career with the Globbies. What? That's not enough to fill the calendar? Try this. During his last decade with the 'Trotters, Johnson became the main cog in the team's P.R. machinery. So, besides a playing career that covered 81 foreign countries, Boo figured it was an easy year in the office if he only made about 175 promotional appearances.

Think of it in these terms. Boo might play in Paris on a Friday night before catching a late-night flight to Italy. The following morning, he might do a half-dozen media hits in Rome before playing a doubleheader with game one just a few blocks from Vatican Square and the nightcap in Florence.

You're right on target. If you tried that with NBA players, they'd go on strike immediately. And they'd have the support of the Teamsters and the I.B.E.W complete with picket signs and maybe tire irons.

Boo endured a catastrophic life experience. He was partying with Jayson Williams the night Williams offed his limo driver at Jayson's New Jersey mansion. Curley wasn't three rooms away. He was just a few feet away when Williams pulled the trigger. That's a story, in full, that Boo will unload when he gets around to writing his own book. I will tell you this. The experience was a nightmare. Boo, totally blameless, and a key prosecution witness at the Williams trial, lost 18 pounds he really didn't have to lose within weeks of the incident. His nervous system was shattered.

Here's what I really dig about CBJ. The 'Trotters, of course, have been "playing" the Washington Generals since roughly World War II. The Generals are just kids out of college trying to prolong the dream and maybe see the Pyramids or a hot babe in Lucerne, Switzerland. They don't make any kind of real cash. On and off the floor, they're just bit players in a Globetrotter spectacle. The 'Trotters are the Hyatt Regency. The Generals are the guy "who leaves the light on for you."

Now figure this one out. Curley was the 'Trotters' premiere, prime-time dribbler. He had to put on the show, slide on his knees, dribble on his back in a continuous stream of energy. You have to figure the General who was "defending" Boo was expected to go along with the act. In other words, to use wrestling phraseology, you have to figure the guy "guarding" Boo was expected to "put him over."

No dice. Boo says he always wanted the General "checking him" to play it for real. Why? Because Boo the competitor, Boo the showman, wanted his piece of the pie to be on the square. Plus, he figured it gave the house a better show.

"I remember playing in Madrid one night in a bull ring. The surface was so bad we couldn't dribble. All we could do was pass and dunk. The audience never knew the difference; they thought it was terrific."
—Boo

This shouldn't surprise you. Over the years, a number of NBA players, including Grant Hill, J.R. Ryder, Ben Gordon, and Kendall Gill have worked with Johnson to enhance their ball-handling skills. Johnson's also "schooled" Jon Scheyer, the former Glenbrook North all-everything, who went on to drill jump shots for Duke. "Jon's shooting ability is tremendous. I've tried to help him attack off the dribble, improve his head fakes and jabs," Boo explained.

Have you got a kid who can play or wants to learn the "best of ball handling?" Contact "Boo" by email (curleyboo@aolmail.com) and arrange for him to school your would-be Magic Johnson. Curley is fair and negotiable, but there are no guarantees. Two sessions with "Boo" doesn't mean your kid gets an endorsement deal with Reebok.

Trust me, Boo is a blast—and he's a book of knowledge on where to find great cheeseburgers in the Czech Republic.

57 *To see* JIMMY COLLINS *and the* UIC FLAMES *play a basketball game*

"If a fan comes out to watch my team play, he's going to see an exciting, creative team that isn't looking toward the bench on every possession."
—Jimmy Collins, head basketball coach, UIC

James is darn near as pencil-thin now as he was 38 years ago when he joined Dick Motta and the Chicago Bulls as a No. 1 draft choice out of New Mexico

State. He still has the perpetual smile that makes him seem just about as genuine as a person can possibly be.

We're just rapping, two longtime friends, in his second floor office at the Flames Athletic Complex on Roosevelt Road. Jimmy C. can look out his windows and see three banners that represent trips his clubs have made to the NCAA Tournament and another that serves as a reminder that Jimmy took a team to the NIT.

Jimmy's been coaching the Flames since 1996; he has tenure. Nobody will ever have to run a charity event for the kid from Syracuse, New York.

I see other things. I see a coach who deserves a better break from his administration. Ask yourself this question: What has UIC done over the years to hype Jimmy and the basketball program? Does the school give a damn that its basketball team, lodged in the nation's No. 3 TV market, generally plays to crowds you could fit in a phone booth?

This isn't Collins talking; this is Coppock talking. And I don't want to hear all the lame excuses that UIC is a commuter school.

For chrissakes, Simeon and Westinghouse get more ink than the Flames. DePaul can go 0-for-a-lifetime, draw flies at the Allstate Arena, and still get 10 times better play in the press than Collins. We'll get back to this later.

Okay, I feel better.

Jimmy Collins was a great slice of basketball talent. He was a kid with enormous acceleration who wound up on the cover of *Sports Illustrated* during his senior year under Lou Henson at New Mexico State.

In fact, as Collins and I keep the stories and the jokes running, Jimmy pulls out that *SI* cover from 1971. Seems a fan sent one to him just a week earlier, asking him for his signature.

By NBA standards, Jimmy didn't earn Wilt Chamberlain–type money when he hooked up with the Bulls. But he didn't starve either. Collins' first year with the Bulls included $150,000 in salary along with a signing bonus that upped his number to 185 grand.

He was in awe. Hell, for a buck-eight-five in the early '70s, you could probably have bought the World Hockey Association or maybe two-thirds of *Soul Train*. Jimmy fulfilled a dream.

No, he didn't buy a four-karat diamond bracelet. He paid cash to buy his mom a home and give her a ticket out of the projects back in Syracuse.

Jimmy's problems with the Bulls began roughly 15 minutes after he joined the club. Dick Motta, his new coach, told Jim he "was too fast to run his offense." What?

If you think that sounds nuts, join the club. It makes you wonder why Motta wanted Collins to begin with…or if he wanted him, period. The question still baffles Jimmy.

Thirty-eight years after he hooked up with the NBA, Collins really isn't sure who pulled the trigger on his selection. Was it Pat Williams, the club GM? Was it really Motta? Was it Bob Rosenberg, the "hometown" official scorer?

Anyway, our 170-pound hero moved into Sandburg Village and tried to find his role on a team that was leather tough and veteran mean.

Motta had his agendas. He couldn't fuck with Norm Van Lier or Jerry Sloan because those guys would fuck back; they might haul off and deck him. If you looked at Van the wrong way, he'd break your jaw. Sloan would settle for your cheek bone.

Chet Walker's veteran status earned him a reprieve. Tom Boerwinkle, the high-post pivot, had to be protected. Players had to believe that they could win with "Long Tom." Finally, Bob Love was a fragile guy, struggling with a stuttering problem. Motta had to keep "Butter" content, secure about himself, so he could drop the 15-foot jumpers off the "screens" that were the Holy Grail in Motta's offense.

So Collins became a target of Dick's wrath. Motta could be a bastard. The association lasted two years. Maybe Jimmy was never meant to play big-league hoops.

"I know Motta wanted his style of ball," Jimmy recalls. "And I knew I couldn't walk the ball up against Oscar Robertson, Jerry West, Earl Monroe, or Walt Frazier.

"I often felt Motta targeted me."

Flip the calendar a few years. Jimmy Collins had to face real life. No first-class air fares, no per diem money on the road, and no trainer to hold your hand when you have a blown-out knee.

Real life for Jimmy Collins became a danger zone.

Jim took a job as a felony violation probation officer with the City of Chicago. The gig paid about 30 grand. Life in North Korea might have been more comfortable. And a hell of a lot safer.

Collins served probation violation notices throughout the city. He dealt with a "who's who" of gangs and gang bangers: the Black P Stone Nation, the Latin Kings, the Devil's Disciples. You name the gang, Jimmy knew the front man.

Jeez, Collins got in so heavy he began running an inmate basketball league at Cook County Jail.

Sure, the job was strenuous. Every street corner was an adventure. But Collins says he found the whole experience "adventurous." This wasn't life at Briarwood Country Club or the back nine at Sunset Ridge.

Jimmy packed heat in his cowboy boots. He also carried a piece in his shoulder holster. That was *de rigueur*, just part of the action. What the hell would you do? Carry a slingshot?

Collins is proud that he never had to fire his gun. He was threatened numerous times. Gangs would taunt him like crazy. You never knew who was behind your left shoulder. And what did that guy behind your left shoulder really figure he had to lose?

You get the picture. The job required far more stones than trying to check Pete Maravich coming off a pick. But Jimmy will tell you the lessons he learned taught him a little more about life than you might normally have picked up from stargazing in the old Los Angeles Forum. For example, Collins agreed with me when I suggested that the fine line between a cop and a criminal is basically paper-thin. That's no rap on police officers…it's just a fact.

Eventually, Jimmy gravitated back to Henson. He joined Lou's staff in Champaign at Illinois. It wasn't long before Collins established a huge reputation as a primo recruiter.

Collins doesn't bitch. But he knows he deserved a crack at running the show at Illinois. He also knew the cards weren't falling his way. So the Collins tour moved to Roosevelt Road and UIC.

Jimmy's a realist. He knows that if Tommy Izzo, North Carolina, Jim Calhoun, or UCLA wants a player he wants, he's looking at long odds.

Back to my issues with the UIC "suits."

Collins situation wasn't helped by the school's decision to drop "Prop 48s"—so-called "nonpredictors." That's just stupid.

Let a kid enroll. Hope he can find some kind of academic structure and eventually help you win some ballgames. The last time I checked, UIC was a quality school but no threat to the legacy of Harvard.

Enough preaching. Jimmy Collins turns out exciting ball clubs. They don't burn 30 seconds off the clock looking for the uncontested six-foot baseline jumper. They're active. They won't put you to sleep.

The year 2008–2009 was a tough one in the office for Jimmy. The Flames were blown up by injuries, and he lost his mother early in February. Angry fans aimed invectives at his wife and family during ballgames. But James persevered. He always has.

Go see a UIC ballgame. The team will run and keep you entertained. And maybe the administration will eventually treat the Flames as a major-college entity.

Collins won't disappoint you. The guy defines the word "class."

58 BOYCOTT *the Basketball* HALL OF FAME

What say we just ease our way in to this session of anger mismanagement? Everybody knows the Pro Football Hall of Fame is in Canton, Ohio. Who doesn't know that baseball's shrine is in Cooperstown, New York, a town so quiet the crickets complain about noise?

Now, be honest—do you know where the Basketball Hall of Fame is? Gotcha. Springfield, Massachusetts.

If you're ever in Vermont and get the urge to see a pair of Julius Erving's gym shoes or a uniform worn by the legendary Odie Smith, an unforgettable Cincinnati Royal, just take highway 91 and get off at exit seven. From Maine, take highway 95...

Damn you, Basketball Hall of Fame! Make that damn you to bits. You never did get around to inducting Johnny Kerr into your sacred private club. I know you gave Red a little love down the stretch. You tossed him the John W. Bunn "Lifetime Achievement Award." I checked out old "Bunny" and found out that after he sidekicked with Phog Allen at Kansas, he went on to serve as head coach at Stanford, Springfield College, and Colorado State College.

I gotta tell ya, that just knocks people in Naperville, Romeoville, Libertyville, or any "ville" off their chairs.

Jerry Colangelo made the "Bunn" presentation to Red during his night in February 2009 at the United Center. It was something less than an emotional moment. Colangelo isn't real big on public displays of warmth. I wasn't sure if he was giving Red an award or a summons.

What did you want from Red Kerr that he didn't give you? He played when the NBA was a man's league—not a bunch of 20-year-olds who know more about Kanye West than they do about a screen roll or a fade screen.

Johnny didn't have the luxury of trading elbows with "monsters" like Kendrick Perkins or a feather pillow like Jermaine O'Neal. I'd just kill to see Tim

Duncan—handcheck era—battle on the blocks against Wilt Chamberlain. I'll take a wild guess that Tim might find it slightly more challenging than showing off his drop-step to Marcus Camby. "Dipper Wilt" in a foul mood might have thrown Duncan over the nearest hot dog stand.

Red had to feel the two-fisted hand checks from Chamberlain, William Felton Russell, Nate Thurmond, and Walt Bellamy—all card-carrying Hall of Famers. Johnny grew to accept that his back was naturally meant to be a bright shade of purple.

And he didn't see the tough guys twice a year. Shit, in the old NBA, Kerr might see each of those powerhouses nine times a year. There were too many weeks when he saw Wilt, Russ, Nate, and "Bells" over a five-day window. Think about that. The Dipper, Russ, Nate, and Bellamy, all before the weekend. If Eddy Curry saw that lineup, he'd bolt the NBA to play in Argentina.

A 260-pound human fire hydrant like Wayne Embry, a terrific player, had to feel like a night off for the "Red Head." And "Wayne the Wall" could scare your average third-tier terrorist. A basketball resembled a ping-pong ball in one of Wayne's larger-than-life paws.

Have you forgotten that Johnny played when the NBA thrived on three-games-in-three-nights scheduling? There were no charters. Teams were mandated to take the earliest flights available—when they weren't on a train, for God's sake—to get to the next city on the schedule. Guys like Red had to endure lousy locker rooms, owners operating out of their back pockets, and too darn many 4:00 AM wake-up calls.

You tell Rasheed Wallace he has a 4:00 AM wake up call and he's on the phone with his agent, the Players Association, and the team shrink.

Do I have to remind you that John didn't have the chance to pound lumps on 19-year-old kids out of high school? Think about Eddy Curry, the ex-Bull slouch who entered the NBA about an hour after his Thornwood team lost to universal basketball power Schaumburg in the IHSAA state title game. A 25-year-old John Kerr or Walt Bellamy would have tied Eddy to a chain-link fence. Curry's teammate Tyson Chandler would have required cosmetic surgery after dealing with Kerr's mean streak. Don't ever think Red Kerr was a daffodil. That's nuts. He was an NBA tire iron.

Today's NBA is a perimeter game. Big men seem like an afterthought. Shaq's so far over the hill he may as well be in Sioux Falls. Tyson Chandler, now with Oklahoma City—there's an NBA hotbed—is the creation of New Orleans point guard Chris Paul. Yao Ming wouldn't scare a parking attendant. Yao thinks tennis has too much contact. I'll take Dwight Howard and give you the field.

Shall I mention that Hall of Famer Dolph Shayes will tell you that "Big Red was the greatest high-post center in NBA history?" Dolph's a stand-up guy. He wouldn't say it if he didn't mean it.

Kerr played when the game was about the "Big Man." Our current NBA is all about three-pointers, dribble penetration, and 6'5" two guards. Centers? How many? Where?

Surely you've misplaced the clips that will tell you Red was named NBA Coach of the Year while running the 1967 Chicago Bulls, a freakin' expansion team. Or go back to Syracuse. He played on the World Champion Nats in '54-'55.

Did you ever look at how long Red handled color on Bulls basketball broadcasts? Have you thought about how many people he entertained? Just how much he hustled the product—pre- and post-Jordan. I know…shame on me…I should know that Red was a waste of time because he dared to make people smile.

Red never got carried away with "terminology" or tried to sound like he invented the game. He just gave his heart to the ballclub and, from time to time, screamed off-mic —or on-mic—at Earl Strom, Darrell Garretson, or Mike Mathis.

Think about MJ's shot over Craig Ehlo in that 1989 playoff game at Richfield Coliseum. It's become one of the most electric moments in sports history. "The Shot" has a life all it's own. MJ's move to get the look and his extension over Ehlo was just artistic.

But, you know this—anybody with an IQ over 65 knows this. What made that shot a lifetime highlight was Johnny screaming, "Bulls win…Bulls win!"

Johnny ejaculated in roughly five different languages.

Red wasn't about to go all "Hubie Brown" and tell the house, "See how Jordan worked his way through the painted area…stop the tape…now here is where Larry Nance has to step in…he doesn't…that frees Jordan to concentrate on the in bounds from Brad Sellers."

Get it?

Yes, I'm biased. I spent four years with Red doing pregame, halftime, and post-game shows on Bulls radio broadcasts. But I'm also a realist. And no, I don't know or give a damn what your "voting" procedure is.

I do know this. I will never set foot in your dump until you take care of Johnny "Red" Kerr.

59 Glitter Gulch baby! Watch the NCAA BASKETBALL TOURNAMENT at a LAS VEGAS hotel sports book

I want you to really think about this one. Why would you want to fly to the campus of Bowling Green University to see a sizzling No. 2–No. 15 tourney matchup between Jim Calhoun and Connecticut versus "America's team," Coastal Carolina?

I know you pick up some bragging rights. You can walk in the office and tell your pals—or cellmates—that you scored tickets to "March Madness."

Ask yourself, why did you travel to Clemson, South Carolina, to see that No. 3–No. 14 showdown between Little Ricky Pitino and Louisville versus those Atlantic 10 monsters, the Richmond Spiders?

> *"The sounds that echo from the sports book and the casino during the first two days of the tourney are just contagious."*
> —Chuck Esposito, director of the race and sports book at the Fontainebleau Las Vegas

Chuck is one of the greatest characters and personalities you could ever hope to meet. He was born in Park Ridge, Illinois, but he moved to Vegas with his family when he was just a tot. Esposito's been handicapping for 20-plus years. He left Caesar's Palace, the world's most famous sports book, to break new ground with the stunning Fontainebleau Las Vegas.

A solid handicapper, Esposito's credentials are Princeton material, and he is a living, breathing cash machine for the house.

The 63-story hotel got a bona fide clean-up hitter. Chuck's passion and business savvy are overwhelming. I'm convinced he knew what a teaser was before his mom and dad gave him his first rattle. By the age of six, he wasn't all that tuned in to the alphabet, but he knew the "Vig," the "burn cards," and he had an idea that most Texas fans just don't bet with their heads—it's usually their hearts—when the 'Horns play Oklahoma in the annual battle for Red River bragging rights at the Cotton Bowl.

Chuck's job is simple, but it would play games with anybody's nervous system. He has to look at two ballclubs and establish a "number," a number that will maximize action on both sides. Not just one game, mind you. For openers, there are 256 regular-season NFL games before the playoffs. Don't get me started on the colleges or the NBA.

You think that's Disneyland? Trust me, the burnout rate for handicappers is an annual topic for "The Society of Actuaries."

Let's get moving out to Clark County, Nevada, and the McCarran Airport, arguably the slowest airport in either hemisphere. I don't care if your hunger pangs have your doubled over with agony, don't even think about dining at the "Mac" Airport. Their restaurants would be upgraded if they added a White Castle.

You're going to watch 36 win-or-go-home basketball games over two days. You're going to live in a sports book. Adrenaline will match wits with exhaustion by the time you're done.

You'll notice that you aren't the only person who came up with this novel idea. People will begin arriving at the "book" the day before the action. By 6:00 AM on game day, the joints are generally filled with wall-to-wall flesh.

Sure, it helps if you've got clout. In 2008, my guy Dave Abrams, the Emperor at Skybox on Sheffield, scored four seats, up close and personal, for ESPN 1000 executives at the Mandalay Bay.

Adam Delevitt, an ESPN Radio buddy, has made the "Vegas-Madness" journey too many times to count. He swears he won't do it again. That tells me A.D. is a lock to be in a "book" in 2010. Trust me, this whole process can be addictive.

> *"The Super Bowl is the only event that generates more action than the NCAA Tournament."*
>
> —Chuck Esposito

Vegas, of course, is on Pacific time. So on the "given" Thursday around 9:20 AM, after you've bet, logically, no more than two games to open your day, the tournament begins. The roar, the color, and the wide variety of jerseys will just blow you away. Listen to the babe at the west end of the "book," she's berserk with joy because her alma mater, Loyola Marymount, has leapt to a 4–2 lead on Ohio State.

Here's a tip. There are people, particularly from Los Angeles and Orange counties, who make "Madness" an annual trip or, in some cases, a vacation. Hey, honey, who needs the Bahamas, we're going to bet that sweet 8-9 matchup at the Bellagio or the Luxor.

Beware of the California factor. If UCLA, Stanford, or Cal is really hot, take a long look at the number. West Coast money frequently will drive the number up. If you think, for example (noting that over-thinking in Las Vegas will generally get you clobbered), that the Bruins should be five point faves, but they're suddenly bet up to -7, take a long look.

Chances are that's "public" money as opposed to "wise guy" money that has created an unnatural line. So do you rush to bet against UCLA? No! The handicappers have forgotten more about the "California factor" than you'll ever know.

You really want to unload? Don't forget, during every game, new lines go up at halftime. So if you think Valpo is going to cover the "fresh number" in its 5-12 matchup with Gonzaga, make a move to the window.

The suggested approach? Don't even think about betting 18 games. You may as well hand the book your credit cards and your wristwatch. It's a one-way ticket to oblivion. Look for four, maybe five, games that intrigue you. Don't get carried away by two guys from Raleigh who are telling anybody who'll listen that "this is the best club Duke has sent to the dance since Grant Hill was a Blue Devil."

Be selective. Be reasonable. (You know, sometimes, my level of genius just amazes me.)

Soak up the atmosphere. That's really what this whole trip is all about. I know in March 2010, I'm going to go to the Fontainebleau for the 36-game two-day rush. Of course, the Fontainebleau has 27 restaurants and enough retail outlets to fill Chavez Ravine, so I might not be back in Chicago until April.

I'll do a little hang time with my guy, Chuck, I'll bet some ball games, and I'll probably wander over to the Palms for some late-night slot play. I'm a sucker for the bandits. But over the years, for reasons unknown, I've had some luck at the Palms.

Really, why would I want to go to Bangor, Maine, to watch a 1 versus 16, featuring Pitt and the "automatic" from the Patriot League—if you know a team in the Patriot League, you're leaps and bounds ahead of me.

You love hoops—this is a must. You have to do Las Vegas when the "Madness" begins. It's a rush, it's exhausting, it's unforgettable.

60 Send out the search party— where is LOYOLA BASKETBALL?

Check the numbers. From November 1989 through March 2004, the Loyola Ramblers, under three different coaches, went 156 up and 269 down. That isn't called bad news. That's called box-office poison.

This is really an odd feeling. It's March 2009, and I realize as I walk north on Sheridan Road, I haven't been on the Loyola campus, for any roundball reason, since Yao Ming worked out for NBA general managers on a warm summer day back in 2002.

I remember a few things about the workout: P.J. Carlesimo ran Yao through his series of drills and Bulls G.M. Jerry Krause, with his sidekick B.J Armstrong, glared through the entire 90-minute session.

That wasn't all that strange. By 2002, Krause, in my humble opinion, was so filled with self-contempt running neck-and-neck with anger toward the press, he glared if you dared to offer him two free weeks in a time share in Maui.

We'll get to the guts of today's episode in a minute or two. But first I have to tell you this. I've had a long love affair with Loyola basketball. Part of my passion for all things burgundy and gold has to with a personal weakness: I feel lousy when I don't see other people receive the appreciation they absolutely deserve.

That leads us back to March 23, 1963. George Ireland and the Ramblers, playing just five men, knocked off Ed Jucker and the Cincinnati Bearcats 60–58 in overtime at Freedom Hall (yeah, that Freedom Hall, it has to be older than God) in Louisville to win the NCAA Championship.

So what's the problem? That was high-school time for the chubby kid here. I frequently took the Linden Avenue "El" from Wilmette to Clark and Addison streets to watch a forlorn group of mopes known as the Chicago Cubs...Ernie, Santo, and Billy excluded. Along the way, the train would pass the Loyola campus, where a very small, dismal-looking sign—it had to be about three feet by four feet—acknowledged that Loyola had won the big prize. I just hated that sign. The Ramblers deserved a billboard; they got a Zenith 12-inch TV without rabbit ears.

You think Cincinnati was a collection of water buffaloes? Guess again. The Bearcats were trying for an "early Johnny Wooden." Cincinnati was gunning for its third consecutive national title.

The woebegone sign always looked to me like it should have been pumping Vienna hot dogs or Z Frank Chevrolet.

The 2008–09 Loyola Ramblers averaged 2,200 fans per home game. I'm not sure that pays the cost of opening the concession stands and flipping on the lights. I hope it covers the ushers.

Give me one last stroll down memory lane. You won't believe this—I did color on Loyola basketball for two years beginning back in 1984.

Right place? Right time? Put it on the board!

The '84-'85 Ramblers weren't just good, they were a blockbuster. Forward Alfredrick Hughes led the nation in scoring. Andre Moore was a badass, work-the-glass rebounder on a club that liked to sock people. Ivan Young was a great front-line complement. The Ramblers were on a 19-game winning streak before they finally fell out of the Big Dance against Patrick Ewing and Georgetown in the NCAA round of 16.

Did I mention that I did color while Red Rush did play-by-play? I could do about 24 hours on Red the broadcaster, Red the character, Red the hustler, and Red the card shark. Rush and I rarely talked about the game during TV timeouts. We didn't have time. Red would just give me fresh marching orders to plug Gonnella Bread or some restaurant where he had—no doubt, stone-cold lock—been comped 48 hours earlier.

Did anyone notice that current Ramblers boss Jim Whitesell, a likable guy, won 40 games combined in '06 and '07? I didn't think so. That bothers me.

Why is Loyola such an afterthought? Wait. Let me rephrase. What does Loyola have to do to elevate itself to the level of afterthought? Do you want the tired refrains? Loyola is a commuter school. Loyola doesn't promote itself? I'll buy some of that.

I do know that Ramblers have a right to bitch big-time about the ink it receives in comparison to DePaul. Just what have the Demons done over the past 15 years that I've missed? I do recall Joey Meyer closing his tenure on the Blue Demons bench with a mark of 3–23. Joe always made one mistake as a front man. He took the press seriously. I swear he worried more about hostile columnists than he did about beating Bob Huggins when "Bobby Ducktail" was the head coach at Cincinnati.

There is no battle in the "All-Catholic Media-Coverage Derby." The Demons have crossed the finish line. Loyola hasn't reached the paddock area.

> *Quick—and don't use Google. Name two clubs in the Horizon League other than Butler. Penalize yourself 25 points for not knowing Cleveland State and Wisconsin-Milwaukee. Also, I'll give you a freebie if you didn't know Butler or...this is sad...Loyola.*

I wish I could wave a magic wand. I wish I could produce sellouts at the Joseph Gentile Center, the down-to-earth, no-frills, no-skyboxes, basketball arena on the Loyola campus. Joe, nicknamed "The Baron of Barrington" by yours truly, paid half the freight to build the gym that carries his name.

I'm sorry. I don't have an answer. Just go see a Loyola basketball game. Give Jimmy Whitesell and his kids a break. Parking isn't a giveaway, but it's close. The hot dogs are warm.

Did I mention that Loyola hasn't played a lick of postseason hoops since that 1985 club, which had to endure me as a broadcaster? Maybe I jinxed the suckers.

61 *The* BABES *can shake and bake and take the ball to the rack—check out a* CHICAGO SKY *game*

Let's get this off to a nice fuzzy start. The question: Who is the biggest bitch in the WNBA? The answer: Until further notice, I'm leaning toward William Laimbeer, the beloved former head coach of the Detroit Shock.

I'm just kidding, St. William, but only a little bit. If you're Red Auerbach, I'm the missing member of the Jonas Brothers.

The oath has been administered. I pledge to tell the whole truth and nothing but the truth. I have *never* been a big fan of female hoops. In fact, and this puts us back in the time machine, the first time I ever gave a female roundball player the time of day was back in 1980.

I covered Ann Meyer's "faux tryout" with Bobby Leonard and the Indiana

Pacers. Anne is a marvelous woman and she could play her butt off. Meyers actually looked like a Nebraska cheerleader, all cute and corn-fed. She was the first gal in college history to record a quadruple-double while playing at UCLA. Annie also played on the U.S. team that won gold at the Pan American Games in Montreal back in 1975.

Armintie Price, Candice Dupree, and Sylvia Fowles of the the WNBA Chicago Sky.

Anyway, the Pacers, desperate for cash and increased box office—the club always seemed like it was one bad week away from blowing the payroll—came up with a low-rent gimmick. They signed Ann to a contract reportedly worth about 50-large and brought her in for the "tryout." It was a lousy play from the start.

Ann worked her cute little ass off, but she found it rather difficult to launch a "J" over 6'9" small forwards. Plus, it was clearly obvious that Meyers was fully aware the fix was in on this baby. The project was over and out in about 48 hours. As I recall, Ann earned her paydays the rest of the year while serving a prison sentence: She was forced to do color on Pacers broadcasts with Bob Lamey.

Bob's golden tones always sounded like a guy with a pitchfork tuning up guitars for Mötley Crüe.

> *"Yes, I get in their faces. Yes, I get mad when they play bad basketball. I don't see women basketball players. I just see basketball players."*
>
> —Steve Key, head coach of the Chicago Sky,
> discussing the notion that you just can't
> yell at a female basketball player

Stephen could replace my pal Pat Sajack on *Wheel of Fortune*. His personality is just as warm as a winter blanket, just as appealing as that teacher who looked the other way when you walked in five minutes late from recess.

Key could also serve as a tour guide. Steve never cracked the big show, but after killing time in the CBA for a year, he found his calling and his paydays. He played ball in Europe for a dozen seasons and had a three-year run as head coach of the Dusseldorf Magics.

As a rule, when I make a play on Dusseldorf, I tend to bet them "under," especially on the road.

Now, let's get down to the so-called brass tacks. Key isn't running a sideshow. He doesn't want the Sky playing up-tempo just to please the fans. Give Steve the girls who want to face guard on defense, collect the dimes, and accelerate on the break.

Frankly, that's probably the so-called image problem a lot of us have had over the years with ladies' hoops.

What say we end it now?

I closed shop on "dainty little debs" in cute short pants after I got to know Nancy Lieberman Cline. You think Nancy wasn't a sledgehammer? In her high school and college days, she used to ride the subway from Brooklyn to Harlem to play on the famed red and green court of the Rucker League.

"The Rucker" is bad-to-the-bone, flash-and-dash basketball. NBA studs collide with playground legends. Nancy fought her way through screens set by 240-pound "Threes" and drove the hoop against guys who were more than happy to say hello to her cranium with a loose shoulder She got knocked on her back every week, but she won the most begrudging of basketball elements: respect.

Nancy sidekicked with Meyers on that '75 Pan Am team and later joined Ann on the U.S. Olympic team that won silver at Montreal in '76.

The difference between the two? Meyers might challenege a player to a fight. Lieberman, if she were truly angry, could restart the Vietnam War. If Nancy isn't flattered when someone calls her "one tough broad," she just has to rethink her entire legacy from top to bottom.

Get out to the UIC Pavilion. The Sky play tough, they sweat, and, frankly, they run the screen-roll better than Joakim Noah.

The Sky has a bona fide, in-your-face meal ticket. Sylvia Fowles is a 6'5" streamlined strip of South Florida basketball talent. If you don't know the name, go to the back of the line.

Sylvia, from Miami's mean streets, was a brilliant player at Louisiana State. In the summer of 2008, she led the United States to the gold medal platform at the Beijing Olympics. Key compares her killer instinct and passion for the game to Bill Russell. Jeez, if this chick has half the "hostility" that William Felton Russell brought to the Celtics' old Boston Garden parquet floor, the league should make her play in handcuffs.

"Fowles raises the roof with her windmill dunk. She's got a 34-inch vertical jump."

—Les Grobstein, a Chicago original and voice of the Sky

Les has been a disciple of female buckets for years. Sometimes, the game has left him in cold storage. Remember the old Chicago Hustle? When they finally hit the wall and went belly up in 1981 along with the rest of the old WBL, the club never bothered to mail "the Grobber" the 13-grand he was due for services rendered.

Get the accountant. What's the interest at 6 percent on $13,000 over 28 years?

Here is what the Chicago Sky will do: earn your respect. Steve Key reminds us, "My players have strong basketball IQs. Remember, they all grew up playing against an older brother, the guy next door, or at the local park where they were almost always the only girl."

We'll give "the Grobber" the last turn at the mic. "Real basketball fans will love Jia Perkins. She's just five-foot-eight, but she reminds me of the way Ron Harper used to play defense for Phil Jackson. You know, she was 2007 WNBA Rookie of the Year."

Les, if you're selling, I'm buying.

62 NORTHWESTERN *hoops—welcome to the* "DEAD ZONE"

It has to be 50-to-1 that Northwestern will win an NCAA first-round tournament game in my lifetime. That drops to 35-to-1 if I live to be 96. However, it's a proven fact that Northwestern has played the role of "roadkill" to perfection over the years in the Motor City Classic, the Gator Bowl Classic, the Music City Invitational, and the famed Hoops and Quill Tourney in St. Louis.

This is too funny for words. Whoever wrote this line should be turning out late-night material for Letterman. Page four of the Northwestern basketball press guide states proudly and boldly, "When opponents arrive in Evanston, they know they're in for quite a battle."

Just what battle is that? Northwestern hasn't closed a season with a plus-.500 Big 10 record since 1968. For Pete's sake, that's the same year The Beatles, already bogged down by jealousy and enormous salary-cap issues, released "Lady Madonna."

As I compose this latest epic, the 'Cats are warming up for a home game with Iowa. The tension is about as thick as a White Castle slider. This might be the biggest game N.U. has played since, well, I'm not sure. Wildcats basketball and "big games" don't often turn up in the same county, let along the same hunk of 94-foot plywood.

Pages 84 and 85 of the Duke media guide celebrate the Blue Devils' remarkable record of "National Success." There's no mention of NCAA titles or Finals Fours. Why bother? That's old news. The Blue Devils montage just shows a couple of photos of Mike Krzyesewski with David Letterman, former White House economy crippler George W. Bush, and a slew of Sports Illustrated *covers.*

My gut tells me the only people who've made more appearances on the treasured *S.I.* cover than Duke are Muhammad Ali and Michael Jordan. I might be wrong, but you get the point.

Northwestern knows all about the Final Four. The school hosted the college showcase back in 1956. Bill Russell and the all-powerful San Francisco Dons crossed the finish line with the brass when they beat Iowa 83–71.

Did we mention that the N.U. media guide doesn't have a section on Northwestern postseason basketball? I'm going to take a wild guess that it might be because the 'Cats would just as soon ignore the fact that they've never played in the "Combination Dick Enberg–Billy Packer–Al McGuire–Jim Nantz–Dick Vitale–Clark Kellogg–Month of March–No. 3/No. 14 Showcase."

Uh, not once. Not ever.

Let's talk about Bill Carmody. For those who don't read Missouri Valley box scores seven days a week or worship at the shrine of Jay Bilas, Bill has been the head coach at Northwestern since 2000. William replaced Kevin O'Neill, who closed his final year with a sensational conference record of 0–16.

Here's the quiz—who is better-known in Chicago, Bill Carmody or the maitre d' at Harry Caray's Restaurant? I'll go with the maitre d' and lay the six points.

Are you beginning to get a feel for where this tour is going? Northwestern basketball is the ultimate bastard child, the red-haired stepkid, the all-time basketball afterthought.

Attend an N.U. home game against Indiana, Ohio State, or Wisconsin and half the ballpark will be wearing shades of red and screaming for the rival club. On a bad night, two-thirds of the house will be cheering for the visitors.

Here's the essence of "Purple Round Ball Pride." Otto Graham was an All-American at Northwestern back in 1944. Otto Everett, who could really be a miserable louse, also played for the legendary NBA Rochester Royals.

That's slightly overshadowed by this chunk of gridiron history. Otto wasn't just a good quarterback. The sucker was Johnny Unitas *before* Johnny Unitas. You talk about blast-off numbers. Otto, through his days in the old All-America Football Conference and the NFL, led the Cleveland Browns to 10 divisional titles or World Championships in 10 years. Those are Meryl Streep–type numbers.

No question about it. Jerry Angelo would never have seen Otto as a "fit."

The first 19 pages of the UConn press guide celebrate the Huskies' run of national success. Page 149 of the Northwestern "Book of Anguish" tells the anxious reader that Rich Falk, the pride and joy of Galva, Illinois, is a member of the school's 1,000-point club. Falk later coached the 'Cats for eight completely forgettable years.

This is just cruel irony. In 1983, during the renovation of Welsh Ryan Arena (previously known as McGaw Memorial Hall), Northwestern played their home games at DePaul's old Alumni Hall. (Now, here's where the whole package just goes *Fatal Attraction*.) In '83, led by Jim Stack, Northwestern made its first appearance in the NIT. Guess what? They got knocked off by Ray Meyer and DePaul, 65–63. That goes beyond cruel and unusual punishment.

No NCAAs, but tell the band to play "Happy Days Are Here Again." N.U. returned to the NIT in '99 where they got licked by DePaul. You see a trend.

Northwestern doesn't normally send out "basketball teams." It usually offers its totally indifferent alumni a group of guys working on degrees in business administration who might good enough to land a roster spot with the Washington Generals.

Don't call me a jerk. I'm just a little pissed that my SATs weren't good enough to land me on the Evanston campus. Believe it, my boards were so lousy, the only thing my faculty advisor really suggested was that I see a Marine recruiter.

I've had my share of Northwestern players I've enjoyed. Growing up, I was crazy about Joe Ruklick, Jim Burns, and Jim Pitts. As for players who played after the Korean War or thereabout, I thought Shon Morris and Evan Eschmeyer were terrific. Eschmeyer could have had a solid 10-year NBA career if he hadn't had knees made out of fruit salad.

The following should insult Northwestern. (Then again, over the years Northwestern has proved time and again that it's never quite understood basketball embarrassment. Keep in mind, NU is a *football* school!)

Check out page 20 of the Stanford media guide. It casually mentions that the Cardinal has had seven first-round picks since 2000. No big deal? Just four other schools—Duke, Florida, Kansas, and North Carolina—have turned out seven first-rounders since the dawn of the 21st century.

Northwestern, are you listening? Do you recruit? Do you send your assistant coaches anywhere north of Highland Park or west of Elgin? Do you have a little black book just loaded with preps who were 8th men during their senior years in high school?

Stop the fight. In 1965, Butch van Breda Kolff and Princeton, led by future New York Knick "Dollar Bill" Bradley, won their way to the Final Four. Bradley was named tournament MVP after the Tigers won the consolation third-place game versus Wichita State.

You got it. If other elite schools, turning out future Kenilworth residents, can win big from time to time, why can't the 'Cats do something special?

What is the solution for Northwestern? How does N.U. reach a new level, a new plateau where they do something enormous like post back-to-back 17-win seasons?

I don't believe there is an answer. Because, quite frankly, I don't think N.U.'s affluent alumni or the school's hierarchy give a damn.

It's a shame. N.U. has a gorgeous campus, cozy arena, and kids who, no doubt, care. Northwestern could be a Stanford. It just never has shown the interest. I guess it's content to brag about former student Charlton "Heat Packer" Heston.

By the way, N.U. beat Iowa in that aforementioned ballgame. Hey hey, the 'Cats have now gone to *three* NITs.

Can you spell *dynasty*? Can you spell "who the hell cares?"

ICING
PUCK

63 *Get a picture of yourself or your kids or your girlfriend by the* BLACKHAWKS' "BADGE OF HONOR" *statue*

Here's the drill: Slowly drive down west Madison Street—east to west—and gaze at the Blackhawks "badge." That's round one. Next step, park your car and really get a close-up look at this sculptural masterpiece.

This is not M.J.! Michael's statue on the United Center's west end is a tribute to individual basketball excellence: the slam dunk, midair brilliance, the 39-inch vertical jump. It's a reminder of six championships, the double-nickel game in the Garden. It will return the glow of that playoff game in Salt Lake City when Jordan, battling a miserable strain of the flu or food poisoning, looked ready to collapse but still dropped 38 in a critical Bulls win over Jerry Sloan and the Utah Jazz in Game 5 of the 1997 NBA Finals.

The Blackhawks statue takes a far different approach. There are no blessings bestowed to individual players...no mention of Bobby Hull, Stan "the Man" Mikita, Tony "O," Pierre Pilote, Chris Chelios, or Jeremy Roenick.

This chunk of outdoor mold is about anger, ferocity, rage, morning skates, the hip check, the poke check, the critical third period face-off, and the controlled venom required to play a sport that when it's right—see the Stanley Cup Finals—might just be the best spectator sport in the world, so help me Dick Butkus.

The Blackhawks say this is a tribute to all those players who wore a Blackhawks jersey—I hate the word "sweater"—from the team's inception in 1925 until the statue's dedication in October 2000. That's their angle. Here's my hook. If the face and shoulders just below the Indian-head logo aren't those of a young and toothless Bobby Hull when he still had his own hair, then I want son-of-a-boss Rockwell Wirtz to tell me just who exactly it is.

It's clearly Robert Marvin Hull...however, my "Bobby" figure is wearing an ancient Blackhawks jersey. That got me to wondering the first time I saw the mighty mold if the Hawks and sculpture designer Erik Blome were playing a little mind game on Joe Fan.

Now, be honest. Are you headed toward that coveted A.A.R.P. card? Did you attend Blackhawks games at Chicago Stadium during the '60s gravy-train decade? And the clincher: Did you ever see a Hawks-Montreal game on a Sunday night delayed for an hour because a slow-moving train bringing both clubs back from a game the night before at the Montreal Forum was delayed somewhere near Grand Rapids?

If so, this is your baby. This is a reminder of 70-game schedules that meant Henri Richard and the Habs, Davey Keon and the Maple Leafs, Detroit and Gordie Howe, Andy Bathgate and the Rangers, and "Chief" Bucyk and Boston were booked to play seven regular-season games a year on the west side.

I've said this for years. In the mid-'60s, the toughest ticket in Chicago wasn't the Bears versus Green Bay, or the White Sox and Yankees. It was ANY Blackhawks regular-season game. If you wanted tix for the Hawks and Montreal in March, you had to know a friendly scalper or shove a twenty under the ticket window at the Stadium right before game time and hope for the best.

Are you a hip-hopper or has hip-hop been relegated to the attic? Whatever. When my 24-year-old daughter Lyndsey raves about a sculpture—and she loves the "Badge"—you've pressed the right buttons. While the sculpture doesn't scream "hosanna" for any one Blackhawks player, it does have something I find very cool. The name of every player from the team's debut in '25—that's pre–Stub Hub—through the year 2000 is listed on the statue.

Label this one "just my luck." The first name I noticed on the mold was Fred Stanfield. Why is that unique or special? If you've been around the game a while, you know Stanfield, Phil Esposito, and John "Pie Face" McKenzie were traded to the Boston Bruins for Gilles Marotte, a burned-out defenseman; Pit Martin, a good but hardly world-class center; and waste-of-time goalie Jack Norris back on May 15, 1967.

You talk about a lousy deal. It might be the single worst trade in hockey history.

By comparison, Native Americans got a hell of a deal back in 1626 when they sold a group of Europeans wearing buckskin Manhattan Island for 24 bucks in clothes and buttons—plus the usual "coonskin cap" to be named later.

64 *Ultimate* BLACKHAWKS *anguish:* MAY 18, 1971

"You're pissed off. We gave everything we had and we lost. [Coach] Billy Reay didn't say anything to us after the game…there was nothing he could say."

—Tony Esposito, Blackhawks Hall of Fame goalie

Follow me on a journey to a difficult place. We're talking about a Chicago sports loss that was 10 times more painful than Mike Ditka and the Bears losing to the 49ers and Joe Montana—and kissing off a ticket to the Super Bowl—in the Arctic misery of Soldier Field back in January 1988. This is a tour that took so many people so high they zoomed out of the solar system...before eventually crashing back to Earth. The low still hasn't gone away—never will—for the 257,922 of us who claim, "We were there." And I was.

The spring of 1971 was an interesting window for a young, only slightly overweight Chet Coppock. (How did I get from 214 to 276 in just 37 short years?) I'd wrapped up my one and only year with the Milwaukee Bucks as the club's radio producer. You talk about flying first class. The club went 88–18 through the preseason, the 82-game regular-season card, and the playoffs. And here's the clincher: On April 30, which just happened to be my 23rd birthday, the Bucks closed out the old Baltimore Bullets with Wes Unseld, Gus "Honeycomb" Johnson, Earl "the Pearl" Monroe, and Jack Marin to win the franchise's first and only NBA title.

I packed away so many memories. First, it was a kick to tell guys like Oscar Robertson and a young Lew Alcindor—pre-Kareem Abdul-Jabbar—"Hey, we need you on the air in five minutes." Second, the cheapskates that ran the club never gave me a championship ring. Last, but certainly not least, dealing with Satan had to be four weeks at the Bellaggio compared to enduring the fragile ego of Eddie Doucette, the Bucks' talented but pathologically insecure play-by-play man.

The only positive I can offer up about Eddie is this. He was really born to play Norman Bates in *Psycho*. No, on second thought, he was born to play Norman's mother.

So, I get back to Chicago from Milwaukee just after the Bucks' victory celebration to dig into Blackhawks hockey. The city assumes the product is about to reach the highest of the high notes. The zenith. In other words, take home its first Stanley Cup since 1961.

This just wasn't the same club that in 1968–69 finished dead last in the NHL, right? It was. But in 1971, it was a club with the electric presence of Robert Marvin Hull, "Stash" Mikita, Tony Esposito, "Elbows" Nesterenko, Chico Maki, and a young Keith Magnuson, the red-haired defenseman who retired with 926 losses in 922 career fights. No kidding. I loved Maggie, but he never met a fight he couldn't leave with four face cuts and a chipped molar. You think Maggie didn't love to brawl? He would've gone 15 rounds with Joe Frazier over a lunch check.

Chet was on top of the world celebrating the Bucks' world championship with Oscar Robertson on April 30, 1971. Then he went home to Chicago and the Blackhawks broke his heart.

When the John McDonough–led Blackhawks retired Keith's number "3" in the fall of '08, I expected the number to start screaming, "Not before I get one more chance to smack Jean Beliveau."

I have news for you. As much as I like Patrick Sharp and Jonathan Toews, they just will never see the love that was dished out by Chicago to the '71 Hawks. Won't happen. We're talking one-of-a-kind love affair.

The Hawks were fresh off a scintillating seven-game series win over the New York Rangers in the NHL semi wind-up. That wasn't hockey for fun and "merit badges." It was a seven-game body cast that had to set records for internal and external bleeding. Brent Musburger, then a Chicagoan, told me at the time it was—and I believe him to this day—the greatest hockey series ever played. The triumph over the Rangers advanced the Hawks to the main event—seven games, winner take all, the Stanley Cup final—versus Montreal.

Now, stop the music. From here on out, repeat after me: These things only happen in Chicago.

The Blackhawks jumped out of the gate versus the Habs, winning the first two games of the series. But all the Hawks had really done was hold serve. Montreal won Games 3 and 4 in the legendary Forum to square the series. The two clubs would split Games 5 and 6.

> *"I had nightmares thinking about that seventh game because the Hawks really should have won Game 6 at Montreal."*
>
> —Harvey Wittenberg

Harvey Wittenberg, the former Blackhawks P.A. announcer, was ageless, timeless, tremendous. The best in the business. (Have I gotten the point across?) Harvey, with his distinct nasal tones, worked the house mic for the Hawks for 41 years. Why he was replaced in favor of Gene Honda—a listless billboard for vanilla ice cream—just baffles me.

Harvey was the Blackhawks. Honda should be spinning "Twist 'n Shout" and "The Macarena" at bowling banquets.

> *"We should have won it. It was just heartbreaking. If Bobby doesn't hit the crossbar, we lead 3-nothing and it's over."*
>
> —Tony Esposito

One night. One game. May 18, 1971, in Chicago was hot and cloudless with piercing sunshine. I wasn't expecting the city to come completely unglued if the Blackhawks grabbed the cup. But I fully expected that around 10:00 that night Rush Street would be wall-to-wall flesh and the city would be somewhere between jubilant and hysterical.

I didn't have a seat for the game. I was lucky, very lucky, to score a couple of standing-room tickets that put me below the old hockey press box on the west side of the Stadium.

The heat in the old joint was oppressive. Chicago Stadium had "character," but it didn't have air-conditioning. Throw in body heat from usual "announced" throng of 16,666 sardines—uh, fans. (I'm guessing 22,000 people had to be in the place.) It felt like an August afternoon at Cubs Park after a thick morning shower. You could feel your slacks melting. Your shoes were perspiring.

The ice was better suited for double runners. It was sluggish, sloppy. Players on both sides were trying to accelerate while running the Boston Marathon in combat boots.

By the end of the first period, a thick cloud of smoke hung just above the ice. That was unusual. By Stadium standards, generally it took a full two periods for a thick cloud of smoke to hang just above the ice.

The Hawks jumped out to a 2-nothing lead in front of a crowd that was already whipped into a frenzy an hour before the opening face-off. But somewhere along the way, the scriptwriters went on strike. They put brass knuckles on the doorknobs. They bent the keys. They smacked the Indian-head logo.

Bobby hit the crossbar. Maki and Cliff Korrol had a two-man break on Montreal goalie and series MVP Ken Dryden and they missed the freakin' net. Jaques Lemaire beat Tony "O" with a shot from just inside the red line that Tony just "lost" in the mist, haze, and fog that was rising from the ice due to the god-awful heat. Henri Richard, "Rocket" Richard's baby brother, made Nesterenko and Maggie pay for critical mistakes in the third period.

Yeah, this is Chicago. Henri had been benched during a significant portion of the series because of an ongoing feud with Montreal Coach Allister Wences MacNeil. The same Al MacNeil who was a defenseman/policeman for the Hawks a few years earlier. Al was somewhat hard-nosed. He lived to take slap shots off his sternum. He didn't kick dogs. He kicked human beings. He booed *Ozzie and Harriet.*

Close the curtain. The Blackhawks, dripping sweat, lost the 60-minute steambath. Game, set, and match: Montreal won 3–2. Traditional series-ending hockey-line handshakes between rival clubs are a wonderful thing to watch. But for the Blackhawks, it had to be root canal surgery with a side dish of third-degree burns.

I've never seen a crowd at any sports event so overcome with grief. Not just sadness. Grief—descending in a wave that had to be endured. To describe it any further just heightens the suffering. As they say in the trade, "You had to be there." No, you didn't. Who likes a three-hour Japanese-language film with Swedish subtitles? Or a call from your bookie about that play you made two weeks ago?

I know poor Keith Magnuson went to his grave with that game still anvil-heavy on his shoulders. Christ, it was miserable.

"I didn't say a word after the game. I didn't have to. I just drove home."

—Tony Esposito

65 PAT FOLEY *vs.* LLOYD PETTIT: *The winner is...*

"The game of hockey was invented for Lloyd Pettit."
—Jack Rosenberg, longtime WGN-TV sports editor
and bona fide broadcast historian

Rosey, as always, said in nine words what I couldn't say in two weeks.

This chapter is going to be slightly colored for one particular reason: Pat Foley and I don't like each other. We never have, and I assume we never will.

I agreed with the late Billy Wirtz when he told me shortly after he'd bounced Pat from the Blackhawks broadcast booth in 2006 that, "Foley never really sold any tickets for us."

Wirtz also complained that Foley was unwilling to get out in the community and hustle the club. I'll give Foley a pass on that one. During the last eight or nine years of his Hawks tenure, Pat—in tandem with Don King, Bill Veeck, Vince McMahon, P.T. Barnum, or the girls from the Admiral offering 65 percent discounts—couldn't sell tickets to a product that was just slightly below roadkill.

But I do think Billy was on the square about Foley's "commitment" to help beef up the club's image.

Anyway, that's not the issue. We're talking about two broadcast talents: Pat Foley and Lloyd Pettit.

There is no doubt that Pat has talent. He may well wind up with a plaque in the Hockey Hall of Fame in Toronto. If so, I have no plans to attend. But let the record show, he is not in the same league with Lloyd Pettit.

Lloyd was a tall, dynamic man with the kind of Hollywood-type smile that made old babes think "young Marlon Brando" while making young chicks think "gracefully aging Robert Redford." In other words, Lloyd, physically and vocally, packed about 225 pounds of charisma. Gibson's wouldn't give him a table—they'd give him the dining room and half the bar.

"There is no doubt he could have been an actor...a leading man," Jack Rosenberg told me with without hesitation.

Behind the mic, Pettit owned the game. His golden-voiced baritone, his uniquely polished timbre, his ability to seize on the rhythm of the sport was beyond majestic.

Trust me, if you were a kid growing up in the '60s or a 72-year-old retiree, you could be forgiven if you believed that Lloyd Pettit invented the game. Three guys made hockey connect in Chicago during my growing-up years: Bobby Hull, Stan Mikita, and Lloyd Pettit. And Pettit was just as valuable as Robert Marvin and "Stosh."

Lloyd created, nurtured, and enhanced hockey love affairs for those baby boomers who began to return to the west side in 2007. His trademark expression, "A Shot and a Goal," is a rare slice of phraseology that has been part of Blackhawks hockey for roughly five decades.

Lloyd also knew that part of hockey's charm was the anticipation that at any given moment, the gloves could be dropped and Orland Kurtenbach, the big, bad New York Ranger, could be mixing it up with Hawk "policeman" Reggie Flemming.

At least once a telecast, Lloyd would remind his viewers that, "Our first obligation is to follow the puck." Literal translation? If Glenn Hall was being peppered by the Bruins' John Bucyk and Bobby Orr and 165 feet from the net a fight broke out, Lloyd would begin describing the brawl—nothing else mattered.

I can still hear Lloyd howling, "Now Bobby Hull wants a piece of Bryan Watson and here comes Kenny Hodge...and now Bill Gatsby just tried to whack Moose Vasko with his stick. And Gordie Howe just threw a left hand at Stan Mikita...and here comes Chico Maki in to help Mikita and referee Bill Friday is ordering Howe off the ice."

Sadly, Lloyd Pettit stepped away from hockey and baseball—and broadcasting in general—as a full-time player far too soon. In 1970, the year after the epic Cubs collapse, Pettit pulled Jack Rosenberg aside late in the season and said, "I've got to tell you something. You've always been good to me and I want you to be the first to know. I'm going to resign from WGN tomorrow."

Lloyd wasn't ill or mentally despondent. He was simply giving in to the wishes of his wife Jane, who had grown tired of Lloyd living out of a suitcase.

Lloyd wasn't over and out. He gravitated to WMAQ to broadcast Hawks home games on radio. Part of Lloyd's package called for him to be given limousine service from his Milwaukee residence to Chicago Stadium with dinner provided in the auto.

What about the tube? Baltimore import Jim West, a wonderful guy, had the next-to-impossible task of trying to replace Lloyd on WGN.

I want to go back to 1969. I flew to Washington on a whim to see the Bears open the preseason against the Redskins and new head coach Vince Lombardi at RFK Stadium. It was also Gale Sayers' first game back from season-ending knee surgery the previous year. I sat to the right of Lloyd Pettit and to the left of Irvin Kupcinet, acting as their spotter. Jack Rosenberg was right behind us. Just watching Lloyd's energy combined with unblemished accuracy and his degree of clarity was a treat I'll never forget.

Lloyd Pettit, you are Blackhawks hockey. And Patrick, when referring to the "Voice of the Blackhawks," please call him Mr. Pettit.

66 The PRICES ARE COOL, the hockey is solid—attend a Chicago WOLVES game

I have a couple of problems getting really revved up about "Today's Message to Live By."

I don't want to suggest the acoustics are bad at Allstate Arena, but the last time I saw Bob Seger work the place, he sounded more like the Pet Shop Boys than the raging, in-your-face Motor City rocker Seger truly is. Years ago, the Arena made ZZ Top sound like the Spice Girls.

Oh, who cares? You're in the house to watch hockey, not Shakespeare's "Shall I compare thee to a summer's day?"

Plus, the Blackhawks factor into the equation. From roughly 1993 to 2007, I spent more time thinking about ice fishing than I did about the NHL or hockey in general. The Hawks' revival has reached a point that I've actually returned to checking NHL standings every other day.

I know this sounds like I'm piling on, but I have to give it a pop. Chicago is a major-league city. So why would I want to attend a minor-league game of shinny?

Answers to follow.

In 1998 and 2000, the Wolves won the International Hockey League's Turner Cup.

This line is so bad, it wouldn't play in the Catskills. Is the Turner Cup named after Ike Turner, Tina Turner, Ivory Joe Turner, Michael "The Burner" Turner, Bulldog Turner, or the Turner Construction Company?

Actually, it's named after Joe Turner, a former goaltender from Windsor, Ontario, who lost his life in Belgium during World War II. Turner was briefly connected with the Detroit Red Wings.

Back to those nasty Wolves. Their head coach is Don Granato, a guy with a dozen years of experience behind the bench. Don's background includes a three-year stop in Titletown, U.S.A., as front man for the Green Bay Gamblers. He also called the shots for the Peoria Rivermen.

Did I mention that he's also Cammi "Ms. Hockey" Granato's older brother? You tell me who carries more weight when they hop into a Downer's Grove gin mill for a little family bonding.

Hey, Don, tell me to shove it. You also captained the 1990 National Champion Wisconsin Badgers.

With the exception of lower-level seats between the blue lines, your best "sight line" tix are in the green-level area. Those tickets are just 19 bucks a game. Hell, a downtown movie at the River East 21 on Illinois Street runs 20 bucks for two tickets.

I know there's no real comparison. But ask yourself this question: When was the last time Brad Pitt dished out a hip check that sent a guy from the Albany River Rats into the dasher?

This does concern me. The Wolves' top scorer in early February 2009 was Joe Motzko, with just 46 points—18th best overall in the AHL. That really makes me wonder if the Wolves have been spending too much time at Halas Hall with Marty Booker and Rashied Davis.

Cash register time. A family of four can take in a Wolves game from the orange section—that's hockey's answer to the 50-yard-line— for just 89 bucks.

To add to your merriment, the Wolves throw in four hot dogs and four medium sodas for no extra charge. Do the math. Hot dogs are what, four bucks a copy? Medium sodas are probably three bills. You're up twenty eight bills before the first two-minute minor.

Here's one move I'd make in under 20 seconds if I run the Wolves. The burgundy-and-gold color scheme has to go. It leaves the fashion designers at Calvin Klein in shock, it leaves customers dazed. The uniforms are dull, sort of lifeless…kind of like any golf event before Augusta.

The Wolves need something new. Maybe blue and orange, silver and black, blue pinstripes, or red and black. Hey, I never claimed I was original.

On the very bright side, in our city of heartbreakers, the Wolves captured the American Hockey League Calder Cup in 2008. And, son of a bitch, they did it without the use of a Greek priest or anybody from the "Billy Goat" Sianis family on hand to eliminate curses or linesmen with agendas.

Quick, head to the bar. Bet the smart aleck next to you a round of sauce that he can't name one player on the Bridgeport Sound Tigers, one of the Wolves' AHL brethren. If the person has more than seven visible tattoos, bet him a double Chivas he can't tell you where Bridgeport is.

Drop the puck. Allstate has some shortcomings, but it does have excellent sight lines. The joint is also parking-friendly. The Rosemont cops do a great job getting people in and out before events.

The Wolves play solid, aggressive hockey. Why blow a hundred and a half at an avant garde restaurant in River East, the West Loop, the South Loop, or—heaven forbid—along Dearborn Street in Chicago when you can see a solid night of hockey?

Make it a family affair. No tipping required.

67 Embrace the legacy of STOSH

"Wayne Gretzky, Mario Lemieux, and Stan Mikita are the greatest stick handlers I've ever seen."
—Troy Murray, former Chicago Blackhawks forward

"You talk about a low-key event. I know; I was there. It was more like a Boy Scout meeting. High end, there must have been 10 media people at the 'Great One's' coming-out party."
—Chet Coppock describing Wayne Gretzky's first press conference as a professional hockey player

No kidding, go back to 1978. Nelson Skalbania, one of many owners of the long-defunct WHA Indianapolis Racers, breathlessly called me to announce that he was bringing the greatest young hockey player in the world to Indy.

I didn't know a damn thing about Wayne Gretzky. Did I feel bad? Why? I guarantee you that there was nobody within 80 miles of Indianapolis who knew a damn thing about this phenomenal talent who closed his career with a record 2,857 points. That's a number, so help me Sidney Crosby, that will never be touched. Along the way, Gretzky won nine Hart Trophies, 10 Art Ross Trophies, and five Lady Byng Awards.

The first time I saw Wayne Gretzky on the ice, I told Al Karlander, the Racers' director of player personnel, "This guy is too small and too slow to ever be a big-time player." Really—I looked at Wayne Gretzky and saw a Zamboni.

I also liked John McCain plus the points versus Barack Obama. McCain didn't cover. I also bet a bundle that the old Soviet Union would never collapse. Would you bet the kid's lunch money on something called "perestroika"?

Let's move to our real subject.

> *"I didn't play with a chip on my shoulder. I played with chips on both shoulders."*
>
> —Stan Mikita

Stosh is a hell of a lot closer to 70 than he is to 60. But when you sit down with this "firebrand on ice," you sit with a guy who's still got more than enough badass in his blood.

Stan isn't rude. He is edgy. He loves to laugh. But he has an aura that says, "Fuck with me and you may wind up with brain damage."

Why the pitch on Gretzky when I'm really writing about Stan Mikita? I just want a younger generation to know a little more about Stan the Man, the game he played, and the legacy he carved.

Yo, you 15 year olds, get to know the Hawks' "Goodwill Ambassador."

By the way, if the Hawks don't lead the NHL in "Goodwill Ambassadors," what team does?

Twenty-nine years after he left the game he loves, Stosh is still number 13 on the NHL's all-time scoring list. And keep in mind, Mikita played when the slot was gang territory, the Mekong Delta with blue lines.

He played before the game went "European" and the unwritten rule became "give the big-time scorers room to breathe in front of the net." That's a "rule" Gretzky pushed for as hard as hard as Hillary Clinton pushed in New Hampshire. NHL referees did more than protect Wayne, they made him the "babe in swaddling clothes."

Calm down. I'm not stupid enough to offer up a suggestion that Mikita would have outscored Gretzky if Stan had had the benefit of a watered-down league with too many defensemen playing on double runners. But this is a lock.

Stan would have at least 500 more points during his career if he'd begun his tenure during the Gretzky era.

A big part of my argument? Mikita's eye-to-hand coordination was every bit as good as the "Great One." You want to argue that point? You're nuts. There is no argument.

Drop a fresh 500 in the Mikita column, and guess what? He's now the NHL's third all-time leading scorer back of Gretzky and Mark Messier...and a notch above Gordie Howe, the larger-than-life Detroit Red Wing.

It didn't take long for a young Stan Mikita to get to know the wrath of Gordie Howe. And Howe was the toughest player I've ever seen play the game. Gordie's elbows were tire irons. Stosh grazed Howe with his stick one night at the old Olympia in Detroit and also taunted Gordie. Our hero was crazy enough to scream at Gordie, "Fuck you, you old bastard!"

Howe didn't forget. Believe me, Gordie never forgot anything. About six weeks later, Howe caught Mikita at mid-ice and left Stan wondering when the league had begun letting players carry handguns. Gordie just creamed Stanley.

"When I finally got to my knees, I crawled to the bench," Stan laughs. "There was only one problem. It was the Detroit bench."

Mikita's greatest accomplishment? This qualifies for Ripley's—a young Stan Mikita had season tickets...to the penalty box. He never missed a chance to cross-check anybody. My guys tell me the first words of English he learned upon arriving in Canada from Czechoslovakia were "tripping" and "game misconduct."

Go back to 1964–65: he logged 158 minutes in the box. Just two years later, he won his first of back-to-back Lady Byngs for sportsmanship....I've always thought Stan might be embarrassed to win an honor for being a gentlemanly player.

How many guys can claim this? Mikita won the Ross and the Hart and the Byng—all three—in '67 and '68. He ranks just behind Howe as the most complete player the NHL produced during the 1960s. So where's Bobby Hull? Let's just say Robert Marvin's the greatest left wing in NHL history and that his slap shot was beyond lethal.

What prompted Mikita to learn that life could be enjoyed without two-minute minors and 10-minute misconduct penalties? It might be Glenn Hall, Mr. Goalie and a Mikita teammate, offering Stan some friendly, down-to-earth advice: "Glenn told me I was gonna get killed if I kept on playing the way I was playing."

Stan now plays the role of "Hawks elder statesman." The team is lucky to have him on the payroll. Mikita is a bona fide link to bygone days when Blackhawks tickets were, no contest, the toughest ticket in town.

The Hawks are fortunate to have the "Uncheckable Czech" for another reason. Stan Mikita does what he damn well pleases—always has, always will.

THE MEMORIES CONTINUE nonstop. There was that night a puck deflected off Doug Mohn's stick and caught Stan on the side of his head. His ear lobe was almost completely ripped off. Blood was all over the joint. The sight was hideous. Mikita just figured, *Hey, this goes with the territory.* He skated off the ice with blood gushing and went down to the trainer's table.

Mikita figured his wife Jill was probably concerned. So while the medics stitched up his lobe, he called Jill to say that everything was fine. Logic says from there he went to Northwestern Hospital. No, Mikita went right back on the ice.

Now, if the NHL would just tack on those extra 500 points…

68 *Teach your children well…teach them to chant* "DETROIT SUCKS… DETROIT SUCKS"

"More than anything, this is a two-word, west-side anthem. Since I can remember, the Blackhawks and Red Wings have been fierce rivals. And the same can be said of the Bulls and Pistons in the late '80s and early '90s."
—"Dangerous" Dan McNeil, Chicago radio broadcaster

"Detroit sucks." It just rolls off the tongue. It has a certain ebb and flow that just seems so completely from the gut. It's like Jack Daniels—no glass, no ice. It's the Stones doing "Sympathy for the Devil."

But before we put the ball in play, let's take a look at father-son responsibilities. A good dad has an obligation to alert his young boy to the realities of a tough, cruel, and unforgiving world. Forget about camping, fishing, or learning which cabin to rent when touring the world-famous Wisconsin Dells. I'm talking here about big-league material.

My old man always told me that the only differences between a car dealer and a loan shark was that a shark generally settled outstanding tabs with a baseball bat. The dealers just grinned and talked in tongues about low mileage and unsurpassed trade-in value. Pop said, "When in doubt, go with the loan guy. When it's 'game over' at least the pain doesn't drag on for 22 more payments."

Dad always preached this football gospel: never bet on Notre Dame in South Bend because "Irish" money always made the number a bookie's dream. Pop was kind enough to warn me that people who doubled down with sevens were the main reason the Flamingo Hotel in Las Vegas was constructed.

Last but not least, and this is sad, Charles Coppock passed away before he could convey to me that Benny the Bull is to be booed not cheered.

Blackhawks nation, I hate to give you the bad news; however, it's time to deal the river card. You guys did not start the chant "Detroit sucks."

The chant belongs to a three-year basketball window of '89 through '91 during which the Bulls were chasing, gasping, and dying before finally throwing a left hook and ending the mini-dynasty of the Detroit Pistons. Think of the big barn. The old Chicago Stadium. Think of the Bulls and Pistons trading punches—literally—during playoff roundball at its best and most excruciating. Have you forgotten just how much Isiah Thomas, Dennis Rodman, Rick Mahorn, and Bill Laimbeer angered our city? Not just basketball fans. Old birds in nursing homes threw soup spoons at TV sets while watching the Pistons cheap-shot M.J., Scottie, and Bill Cartwright.

I don't want to suggest that "Dollar Bill" was soft, but his upper body was made of kitty litter. There was a reason Jordan never wanted the rock in Cartwright's hands in the fourth quarter.

If you didn't hate the Pistons, you were socially unacceptable. You had no chance of earning a ticket to Michael Sneed's column. Kup was out of the question. You probably got turned away at the Burger King drive-thru window.

Laimbeer was the biggest son of a bitch on Earth. This silver-spooned hunk of pig slop from Southern California just reeked of family money and privilege. Bad Bill lived to play the high post and to plant elbows in any guy wearing a Bulls uniform. He could also knock down jump shots and he possessed one quality that endeared him to Pistons' boss Chuck Daly—he knew how to win. That generally will—so history says—cover a multitude of sins.

Laimbeer was New Trier, Highland Park, debutante parties, North Shore Country Club, and Kenilworth. He was all things Republican. With a wardrobe change, he could have been Barry Goldwater. Bill probably carried a four handicap by the time he was nine.

He'd be a perfect MySpace match for Megan Mawike, the TV2 social butterfly. The two should really get hitched. "Do you, William, promise to love, honor, and always allow Megan to shop at Prada? Do you, Megan, promise to honor, cherish, and ensure that William has proper tee times and premium scotch on any and all airline trips? You may now suffer with each other until you absolutely can't stand each other; over-under: two weeks. Don't worry, the pre-nuptial is in the mail."

If you didn't detest William, you had no red blood, no soul.

Don't ask me how it started or why it started. But one given night, the chant began softly. Eventually 20,000 Stadium leather lungs were busting their sternums, screaming "Detroit sucks…Detroit sucks."

Eventually, the chant began to fade. Blame it on the Bulls punching Detroit's lights out in '91 on the way toward winning their first NBA title. Or blame it on the Bulls playing in combat boots the last 10 years.

Hey, Blackhawks fans, we're sorry you didn't win, but no one leaves here empty handed. Take home this handsome Zenith AM/FM clock radio for giving us "Dino Sucks." That was riveting. It was a grand early '80s tribute designed to bend the ears of Dino Cicarelli, the long-gone Minnesota North Star. It was hip, trendy. It remains a vivid reminder of Rick Springfield, Fleetwood Mac when they were relevant, and Tommy Tutone's opus "867-5309…Jenny, Jenny who can I turn to?"

There was just one problem. I always thought Dino loved being jeered. Cicarelli was Jesse "the Body" Ventura with a wrist shot, a terrific player with an eye for the net. But that's just excess baggage. God put him on earth to agitate.

I'd pay an extra three months of alimony just to see him slug it out one more time with Blackhawks tough guy Al Secord. Dino versus Al. It could have been Tyson-Holyfield. Who wouldn't pay scalper's prices to see Al chew off Dino's ear lobe?

> *"The bitterness between the Hawks and Wings—and the fans— brought out the best in the rivalry. Ugly, brawl-filled games were the trademark of the Chicago-Detroit hockey games and they always should be. Fuck Detroit. Fuck their fans.*
>
> —Danny McNeil

We now continue with the Reverend Robert Schuller and this week's edition of *Hour of Power*. Please prepare to empty your wallet as we join hands and chant: "Detroit sucks…Detroit sucks."

69 Screw the big bucks—ENJOY HOCKEY from the NOSEBLEED SECTION

Fifty-yard-line football tickets. A pair of courtside basketball seats. Baseball tix along the third-base line. A deuce on the start-finish line at the Daytona 500.

Those are the bragging-rights boards, the tickets you need if you're trying to hustle the corporate dollars from Allstate Insurance, Taco Bell, or the Bob Rohrman Auto Group. Those are the boards that keep the scalpers busy until the Rolling Stones come to town.

I'll leave out soccer. As I mentioned elsewhere, I can't offer any juice on anything MLS-related until I really know just why the game has midfielders.

But hockey is a different world. If I'm headed to the west side to take in a Blackhawks game, I don't want to sit in the first couple of rows behind either net. Okay, for one, maybe two, periods you feel like you're double-dating with Patrick Sharp or Jonathan Towes. But if you're a hockey nut—and lately, the Blackhawks bandwagon has become high priority for a new breed of hockey nuts—the last place you want to sit is in the first couple of rows at either end line.

Don't ask why; you know the answer. If you're on the west side of the United Center and some guy from the Columbus Blue Jackets fires a slap shot that redirects off Martin Havlat's skate and then caroms off Duncan Keith's elbow and into the Blackhawks cage, you just won't see it. You may as well be watching the game from Hibbing, Minnesota.

Tip time. Always pass on sitting right behind either bench. Unless, of course, you just love to stare at the backs of a coach, his assistants, and the stick boy for two hours and change.

Do you remember the old World Hockey Association Chicago Cougars? I didn't think so. The Cougars didn't have much impact. They were about as thrilling as winter vacations in Rhode Island. Anyway, I did the public address for "The Cougs" during their first two seasons at the old International Amphitheatre.

I sat—ice level—between the benches with no fans and no glass in front of me. In other words, no obstructions. Plus, I got 40 bucks a game, dinner in the press room, and two tickets to every home game. Believe me, when I was 24, that was one hell of a package deal.

You know what I saw? A ton of lousy hockey—when I saw anything. As close as I was to the action, I still had to be told by the scorer from press-box level who should get credit for the second assist on virtually every goal I called.

A Coppock observation: Is it just me or does hockey truly believe if you're ambulatory, can sing the Canadian national anthem, and get teary-eyed thinking about Queen Elizabeth, you should get credit for an assist on any given goal?

Yes, I'm spoiled. Give me a pair eight rows off the ice, between the blue lines, at the U.C. and I feel like I'm at the Kentucky Derby.

But here's some sage advice from Coppock: Think 300 level. If you've never been to a Blackhawks game, go up top. You just get more bang for your buck. Watch the panorama of speed and muscle unfold so rapidly that you may begin to think that college football is played in slow motion.

The "300" will never match the old second balcony at Chicago Stadium. Never will. The "300s" are just too pristine. The second balcony was the morning after a fraternity party—and that was 90 minutes before the opening draw.

The old Stadium rafters were a ticket to Canton on Hall of Fame induction day. It was so special, you didn't mind the layers of smoke drifting upwards that were changing your lung color from pink to various shades of navy blue and burnt orange.

The Blackhawks missed the boat on this whole corporate sponsor thing. Back in 1962, Camels or Lucky Strikes would have been brilliant advertising hook-ups for all parties involved, including the players. In the old days, guys couldn't wait to get off the ice between periods—with their lungs burning—to drag on a Marlboro.

I know. I stood…yes, stood…in the second balcony a bundle of times to watch Blackhawks heavyweights along with out-of-towners "Big M" Frank Mahovolich, Davey Keon, Bobby Baun, Andy Bathgate, and the incomparable Gordie Howe. Did I leave out Bryan "Buggsy" Watson and Eddie "Clear the Track" Shack?

The experience was just unmatched. Ask John McDonough, the Blackhawks savior, about the old second balcony. He probably felt the vibes as many times as I did. I can just hear Mac screaming at referee Franklin Udvari.

Hockey is like football. If you're stuck with season tickets in the first three rows on the east side of Soldier Field, don't feel forlorn. I *do* feel bad for you. You know you'd be better off with seats 30 rows up in the 400 level on the west side of the ballpark.

If you worship the Indian Head and you love your lower-level seats, just don't complain about a linesman's fat ass blocking your view of Duncan Keith or Dustin Byfuglien. Agreed?

But if you want to see hockey at its best, head to the nosebleeds. Watch the game from the 300 level. Besides a fabulous view, you'll have extra dough for beer. And isn't that what our great games are truly all about?

YOU CALL *These* SPORTS?

70 The circus left town, there are no county fairs, and YOU'LL DO ANYTHING to kill time: Attend a CHICAGO FIRE game

Okay, I can't con you. I'm probably not quite as up on soccer as the average mom in Northbrook or Glencoe. In fact, for years I've tried to figure out just exactly what a midfielder is. But let's get started. Let's find a rhythm. Let's do a Q and A to check my knowledge of the game.

Q. When do the Chicago Sting open the new season?

A. Hey, dummy, the Sting folded as an indoor team back in 1988. I should know that for at least one fairly good reason: I was the club's play-by-play man during its final—we're outta here—campaign.

Q. Do you feel guilty about the Sting folding?

A. Hell, no. Lee Stern spent a fortune, millions, to find out he was riding a loser. The poor guy needed a reprieve—or a stretcher. He did, however, wear a really cool, bright yellow Chicago Sting cowboy hat.

Q. Did the MLS Championship game do a 13 or a 14 TV rating this past season?

A. Uh, not quite. The game did an 0.7. In other words, about 285 million Americans and God knows how many Chinese did not consider the game "must see" viewing. ABC is still trying to stop the bleeding. 0.7! You could run the *Best of Kitty Box Cleaning* and do 0.8.

Q. Just how many millions of dollars and new fans has Dave "Bend it like Beckham" generated for the MLS?

A. Who? Let's put it this way. If WWE superstar Triple H walked down the east side of Michigan Avenue and D-Beck walked on the west side, 500 people would congregate around Triple H. One guy would walk over to Beckham and ask, "Aren't you Justin Timberlake?"

Q. Are you aware of the Chicago Fire?

A. Glad you asked. I just checked their website and found out something pretty damn provocative. The club is looking for big things from Cuauhtemoc Blanco.

Enough of the nice-guy act. By now, you can take a wild guess and with some degree of accuracy assume that I don't put soccer in the same league with the NFL, MLB, NHL, NBA, NCAA, or the NRA—and I hate guns.

Here's the issue. For too many years, I've heard soccer fanatics—all 27 of them—declare that their brand of kickball is going to be the Sport of the 1970s, 1980s, and so on and so forth.

Truthfully, here's the extent of my soccer knowledge: I know Rod Stewart loves the game. I know on the big-time World Cup level, I will watch for a half an hour or until I see a yellow card—whichever comes first. I think Brandy Chastain is cool. I saw Pele play in person and I doubt anybody connected with the Chicago Fire gets an automatic booth at Gibson's or Harry Caray's.

NOW WE CHANGE ends. Back in 1981, I thought Lee "Big Bucks" and the Sting were on to something. I recall attending a game at Cubs Park with Jack Brickhouse during the baseball strike and the joint was about 90 percent sold out. That same year, Karl-Heinz Granitza, great player and failed restaurant owner, was named Chicago Athlete of the Year. And this was no soft year, brother. Karl had to bust guys like Noah Jackson, Bob Avellini, and an over-the-hill Artis Gilmore to win the award.

We arrive on January 1982. Bill Buckner, a Cubbie at the time, and I blew a couple of hours at Chicago Stadium watching the Sting play the New York Cosmos. I'm sure Shep Messing had to be in goal for New York. But here's the ticket. The Stadium was in fifth gear. The crowd was raucous. I saw scalpers outside in zero weather hustling tickets above face and actually making some cabbage.

I thought the Sting had a side headlock on Chicago. They didn't.

But don't blame Lee Stern. Lee could be annoying—on his good days. For example, he was so in love with the Sting that on autumn Sundays he'd call after I'd done a show to complain about me leading with the Bears when he had a halftime score on the Sting at Tacoma.

Soccer has never caught on big in this country for a few simple but enormous reasons.

One, have you ever called "your man" to get a bet down on the Kansas City Wizards versus the New England Revolution?

Two, the league has never had a visionary. A Rozelle or Arledge. A Halas. A Selig—yes, dammit, Bud Selig. Or a new-age guy like John McDonough. A take-charge commissioner who could get all the team owners on the same page and con the press into believing that if they aren't giving soccer big play, they're failing their audiences.

Soccer needed Alvin "Pete" Rozelle. I don't even know if the MLS has a commissioner. But, I also have to admit I don't know where Toyota Park, the Fire's stomping grounds, is either. It's either Bridgeport, New York, or Bridgeview, Illinois. I'll get back to you on this one.

(However, call me any time to get a rundown on the sight lines at Pizza Hut Park, home of the famed FC Dallas whatevers. I can also hip you to a gorgeous Great American FC Dallas rock and shot glass set.)

Three, the MLS is mom-and-pop soccer. It's not the red carpet. The World Cup—okay, that's big. But can you think of anybody you know who suffered shortness of breath when the Columbus Crew confirmed "strong rumors" that Robert Warzycha was going to be their new head coach?

So how did I get through my one year as a soccer play-by-play man? Easy, I kept the names in front of me and relied on Mark Simanton, my color guy. He was terrific. I was along for the ride. The gig paid good dough. I would do it again.

Say good night, Beckham. Say good night, Fire. Say good night, soccer. The game is forever frozen in first gear.

Anybody for bocce ball?

71 *Meet the* DUFFER'S DELIGHT—*play Cog Hill No. 4,* DUBSDREAD *golf course*

Welcome to the Cog Hill Golf & Country Club. I understand you're going to play our premiere course. Let's get a few things straight. No gym shoes, no T-shirts, and, in the proud tradition of Mr. Blackwell, please no pink slacks.

I know our venue looks very plain and unassuming. I know we don't offer the palatial splendor of Medinah Country Club. Medinah is so austere and imposing you could be forgiven if you actually thought it was Count Dracula's North Sea summer home.

> *"Rock and roll never forgets."*
> —Bob Seger, bona fide rock 'n' roll icon

> *"Dubsdread never forgives"*
> —Chet Coppock, former pitchman for various weight-loss products

Gather around, you 22 handicappers. Bring patience and your game face. Trust me, by the time we conclude this recital, you may settle for that 6,100-yard-long cow pasture 40 miles northwest of Chicago that you can tour in 81 blows even if you're so hung over, your eyes are holding court with your knee caps.

Let's face it, the 'Dread is mythical. Golfers speak about the track with the same kind of reverence they normally reserve for Bobby Jones or Johnnie Walker Black.

You want a quick snapshot of this wicked golf course I hate to love but love to hate?

Go back to 1997 and visualize a victorious Tiger Woods, decked out in Sunday Nike killer red, marching down the 'Dread's 18th fairway, one of the truly great finishing holes anywhere in golf, as the crowd surged behind him. He was savoring victory in the Western Open. Frankly, it looked like Eldrick was doling out comp tickets to see *Jersey Boys*.

If you're a golfer and you haven't seen that photo, you're conning me. It's in two out of three pro shops in America. Over the years, *Frampton Comes Alive* has received less play than the "Tiger entourage" photo.

Think about that for a second. In '97, Tiger was still a scarecrow-thin 155 pounds. The victory in what was, of course, the Western Open, occurred just a few months after he'd won his first major at Augusta by a mere 12 strokes.

By the way, that 18th hole has been expanded from 448 yards to 494 yards. No, it's not a par five. Your job—my job?—is to try and get up and down in eight blows. Woods would play it with a driver and wedge. After you knock your drive onto an adjacent fairway, I strongly recommend you hit four eight irons to reach the dance floor.

> *"Cog Hill is a multimillion-dollar operation; it's also a family operation. They treat their public golfer special, and the regulars become part of the extended Jemsek family."*
> —Ed Sherman, former *Chicago Tribune* golf writer

Expansion, progress, new concepts—all a big part of the charm and *class* of the Cog Hill Golf & Country Club, which includes three other layouts besides the "Dub." I have no clue what the Jemsek family has spent over the years reshaping its courses, but it's beyond a bundle—more than enough to buy off the Oklahoma football team.

You have to appreciate this. In fall 2007, Dubsdread shut down, full and complete. It didn't reopen until spring 2009. That provided Rees Jones, a global sand trap expert if there ever was one, sufficient time to redesign the existing course.

Let's do a little math. A round of golf on the 'Dread costs 150 bucks and there are no twilight rates. Don't even think about 15 percent off on Mondays. Long-time club pro Jeff Rimsnyder, a likable guy, told me that during an average year about 30,000 rounds of golf are played on the course.

Could you shut down? Could you walk away from that kind of cabbage? Me neither. Is there a twist? Yes, the Jemsek family realized it had to make some "adjustments" in hopes of landing the big fish—the U.S. Open.

> *My favorite Dubsdread moment? I got paired with a guy in from Stuttgart, Germany, back in 1978. This guy was no slouch; he had to play to a four or five handicap. I can still see his putter flying in the parking lot after he holed out on 18. Anybody who plays the game knows a round of 104 by a solid player will cause "unnatural" reactions.*

We already know the 'Dread isn't a free lunch. Here's a suggestion. If you play about 14 rounds of golf a year and think 94 is good for office bragging rights, play the No. 3 course. The tab is $53 with the cart. The number drops to $29.50 after 3:00 PM and—this is just *Ozzie and Harriet* throwback money—22 bucks after 6:00 PM.

Are you looking for an upgrade? Here's the track for the guys who live by the "Nassau" and just can't wait to press when they're down one on the 14th. Test yourself on the No. 2 course—Ravines. The greens fee with the cart is $73. After 3 PM, the ticket will set you back just 53 bucks.

Rules to live by (the tips for palookas who have no business playing Dubsdread):

Bring two extra clubs. Who'll notice?

On the water holes, play the range balls you swiped last week from that course near Libertyville.

Bring enormous patience. Heavy play along with frequent stoppages for guys searching for lost balls can make for a six-hour round.

Don't feel bad if you card a 13 on the 4th hole. And make damn sure you don't go right off the tee, because the water is waiting.

Now, throw the bag in the car and make the drive to Lemont. Every golfer, by law, should be required to experience this magnificent hunk of real estate.

The 'Dread. It's a bigger challenge than sitting through *The Maury Povich Show.*

72 *Become a* MAT WORLD *freak*

This goes back to 1994. I got a call from my pals at the World Wrestling Federation asking me if I wanted to do color on Wrestlemania X with Gorilla Monsoon—Gino Marella—for the Armed Forces Radio Network. I said sure. Have tux, will travel. When I told my homey Bruce Levine that I'd accepted the gig, he served up this warm and loving gift: "You and pro wrestling on the Armed Forces Radio Network? Haven't our people overseas suffered enough?"

This shouldn't require heavy lifting. The task today is to convince all you nonbelievers to become pro wrestling fans, full-blown mat world freaks. I want you locked in to "Raw is War" every Monday night. Your life isn't complete until you understand the step-over-toe-hold legacy of Edward "Bearcat" Wright, BoBo Brazil—real name: Houston Harris—Ricky "The Dragon" Steamboat, "Stone Cold" Steve Austin (he married Mongo McMichael's ex-wife Deborah, a noted full-time gold digger), and the inimitable Yukon Moose Cholak, aka Big Moose Cholak and, from time to time, "The Golden Terror."

Chet in the ring with a gassed Andre the Giant. It's tough trying to keep up with Coppock.

Moose was always billed as hailing from Moosehead, Maine. Not quite. He was a Chicago kid whose family owned a shot-and-a-beer joint at 99th and Ewing.

Blame "Nature Boy" Buddy Rogers for my lifetime addiction. Buddy was a classic strutting peacock in baby-blue trunks with a Hollywood tan and the ability to make 20,000 people boo just by raising his eyebrow. Buddy, uh, Herman Rohde, was a "Heel," a classic bad guy. And young Chet Coppock thought he was even cooler than Chubby Checker.

Check this out. Buddy had his "ducktail" haircut bleached somewhere between blonde and platinum. I don't want to say that I was a enamored by Buddy's locks but let's examine the facts.

When I was about 11 years old, I hustled over to our local pharmacy and spent a couple of bucks to buy "blonde" hair coloring. At this point, a truant officer was really needed in the worst way. I applied it before my mom got home from either a PTA meeting or a bridge game. When my poor ma saw her naturally brown-haired kid with a new top that looked like Kellogg's corn flakes, she immediately graduated from ginger ale to Cutty Sark—no glass, no ice.

I saw Buddy wrestle Pat O'Connor before 38,000 fans at the old Comiskey Park. I saw Buddy blow the roof off the legendary International Amphitheatre and just leave the crowd in "heat" versus Johnny Valentine, Argentina Rocca, Sweet Daddy Siki, and ex-boxer Primo Carnera. Grappling villains are like TV anchors. They were put on Earth to be despised. Be honest, don't you boo Katie Couric?

Primo wasn't much of a "worker." Fact is, he had the wrestling skills of a beanbag. However, Da Preem was the inspiration for *Requiem for a Heavyweight,* a tremendous hunk of cinema noir that should have won Oscars for Anthony Quinn and Jackie Gleason. Simple plot line: Gleason tries to turn Quinn, a punch-drunk heavyweight, into a wrestler.

I miss Handsome Jimmy Valiant, Uncle Elmer, the Missing Link, and George "The Animal" Steele. I really miss good old Haystacks Calhoun, the pride and joy of Morgan's Corner, Arkansas...or so they said. Haystacks was listed as weighing 601 pounds. Naw, that was just a "promoter's" number. My guess is that he didn't weight a nickel over 535.

Hey, I've seen baseball fans leave stadiums looking as happy as folks with crotch infections. Wrestling fans always leave happy. "The boys" always deliver a bang for the buck.

Let's move to 1970. In the category of "making a long story short," I wound up hustling an outdoor show at old Comiskey Park with William Richard "Dick the Bruiser" Afflis, Verne Gagne, and Bob Luce. Bruiser and Gagne had one of the greatest scams in the history of the Western Hemisphere. Most states prohibit wrestlers from being promoters. So Verne and Dick just dodged the bullet by putting the "business" in their wives' names. Hey, wrestling plays by its own rules.

I made the media rounds with Ernie "Big Cat" Ladd, the American Football League legend. I hit the newspapers and radio with Bobby "The Brain" Heenan and Gagne.

Verne pulled off a gem with the "help" of Brent Musburger, who was doing 6 and 10 sports for WBBM TV—before he made the move to the network. Brent really didn't know what Verne was all about. He figured Gagne's "sleeper hold" was a phony. So he told Verne on camera to lock him up.

Gagne had an ego as big as Mount Rushmore, so he snapped the sleeper on "Mus" full and complete. No kidding. This was frightening. Brent's eyes leaped out of his head and you could see his jugular vein sticking about three inches out of his neck before Verne casually said, "Had enough?"

You can look this up: Our Sox Park card drew 27,000 paid. It was the largest crowd for any event in the ballpark that year. Keep in mind, the 1970 White Sox were so bad and so completely lost in the bold shadows of guys like Banks, Santo, Williams, and Jenkins on the north side that they drew 495,000 fans—over their entire home schedule. Jeez, in today's baseball world, if a club hasn't lured 495,000 fans into its mausoleum of overpriced tickets, overpriced beer, and overpriced baby pajamas by May 24, the bean counters are required to increase their intake of Valium.

Gagne and I actually talked about me becoming a wrestling manager. The gimmick: a 6'6", thin guy—at the time—with a pretty good gift for gab makes a living mysteriously conveying to TV audiences that (choose one) The Sheik, The Iron Sheik, Black Jack Lanza, or the Black Orchid is going to make potato salad out of a baby face at next week's card in your home town—and tickets are available.

I said no. I didn't see myself in a spin cycle. I didn't want to spend 28 years in the same spot selling the Ultimate Warrior, Brutus Beefcake, and Kamala the Ugandan Hunter. You get too involved with wrestling and it's like joining the mob. You don't leave…at least by choice.

In 1988, I turned down a gig a lot of guys would kill to get. Vince McMahon offered me his number-one TV job. My partner would have been

Jesse "The Body" Ventura. Jeez, I struggled with that one. My gut says I would have taken it if Vince hadn't been adamant that I had to move to Stamford, Connecticut.

Get my point? I love wrestling. I'm a "mark." Always have been. I still miss ring announcing at the Allstate Arena back in the days when that acoustically miserable joint was the Rosemont Horizon.

Interview Michael Jordan? I'd much rather introduce Hulk Hogan. Hold court with Jerry Manuel? I'd rather change inflections to tell a crowd that in four weeks…by popular demand…"Macho Man" Randy Savage will face…(pause)…Psycho Sid in a steel-cage…loser-leaves-town match.

You edgy? You sick of the economy? Is your wife uptight? Go to a WWE wrestling show. You'll walk in quizzical and walk out wearing a "Triple H" T-shirt.

Trust me, I know. I've been there…and have no plans to leave.

73 Welcome to Chicago, a BOXING GRAVEYARD

I remember the night vividly: September 25, 1962. Heavyweight champion Floyd Patterson defended his title at Comiskey Park versus Charles "Sonny" Liston. We aren't talking about a 15-round brawl that had men whipped into in a frenzy and women screaming, "Stop the fight."

Uh, the "fight" lasted two minutes and six seconds before Patterson, devastated by a left hook, was left prone on the canvas. My father wasn't crazy about the show. He'd paid fifty bucks a board. Pop wanted action, a little blood with a bruised cheek bone. What he got was standing in line at a Best Buy trying to cash out on double-A batteries.

At least Floyd showed improvement. Nine months later in Vegas, he rematched "Sonny" and, historians will tell you, brought his "A" game. Patterson bobbed and weaved and slipped punches like nobody's business. Unfortunately, this was all in the dressing room. Once Floyd stepped in the ring, he lasted two minutes and 10 seconds as Liston retained the title: a truly historic gain of four seconds over fight one.

Back to Chicago. I don't want to hit you with a right cross but this is for real. Liston-Patterson 1 was the last relevant heavyweight title fight in Chicago.

Yes, Floyd Weaver, a guy best defined by words such as dull, listless, laborious, and sleepy—no, I'm not talking about Judd Sirott, the Cubs' broadcast plane crash—defended his WBA title at the Rosemont Horizon in 1981. But that was an alphabet soup championship bout against James "Quick" Tillis. "Quick" had a load of talent. "He coulda been a contenduh…he coulda been somebody." However, Tillis was missing two ingredients that generally determine whether a guy's big time or a tomato can: *heart* and *guts*.

Quick had another problem. His right hand was so pristine, so delicate, I doubt it could've busted a grape.

Does Chicago have a fight history? My god, have you got two weeks? Check this out:

- Dempsey vs. Tunney and the "long count"
- Joe Louis fought 10 of his first 12 pro fights in Chicago
- Sugar Ray Robinson vs. Jake LaMotta
- Sugar Ray vs. Gene Fullmer
- Tony Zale vs. Rocky Graziano
- Who can ever forget Bo Bo Olsen vs. Kid Gavilan?
- Rod Blagojevich vs. Mike Madigan

Here's the drill. Years ago, long before Barack Obama was born, long before the Doobie Brothers, Chicago ranked just a notch below New York and Madison Square Garden on the "hit" list of big-time boxing towns. The Wednesday-night fights were virtually a Chicago fixture. The golden voice of Jack Drees handled the blow-by-blow and the shows always pulled big-time TV numbers.

But times do change, events occur. In March 1962 at the Garden, Emile Griffith beat the living hell out of Benny "Kid" Paret on national television. You can see the carnage on YouTube. In round 12, Griffith caught Paret looking—and unleashed the most savage series of punches you will ever see. Lethal isn't strong enough to describe the whipping. Referee Ruby Goldstein just froze. Ruby's officiating was a complete, world-class disgrace. The fight screamed to be stopped while Bennie was just clobbered.

"The Kid" died nine days later.

This didn't kill boxing in Chicago. But take this to the bank—TV networks, under heavy pressure from Congress, citizens groups, and their own advertisers, couldn't run away from the fight game fast enough.

You think Muhammad Ali wasn't a blessing? Without "The Greatest," boxing might be MLS soccer.

Chicago eventually went in to fistic hibernation. It's never come out.

Think about this. The most talked-about fighter in Chicago over the past quarter century is Andrew Golota. Golata, talkability, that's the end of "Circuit

City." Golata, a living, breathing stiff, is best known for three fights that resulted in total chaos.

Naturally, me being me, I attended all three.

Golota was making pork sausage out of Riddick Bowe in the Garden in '96...the big Pole had the fight won...before he was disqualified for repeated low blows.

A riot with hideous racial overtones followed. I can still see the boxing guru Bert Randolph Sugar talking to CBS Godfather Mike Wallace while chairs were flying five feet away from them. Apparently, both Bert and Mike had been imbibing. I mention that because I don't recall either fellow missing a verbal beat while chairs were zooming past their rib cages.

So, a rematch was a natural, this time in Atlantic City. Andrew was DQd again for low blows after handing Bowe a horrific beating. Bowe's brain is split pea soup today because of the beatings he took against Golata. But the "book" says Bowe won both fights.

Do we have to go on? Okay, in 2000 Golota just quit, walked off after two rounds of fighting an over-the-hill Mike Tyson at the Palace of Auburn Hills. His own trainer wanted to sock him—he should have knocked Golata's head past the international boundary into Windsor, Ontario. By then, I was of the opinion that it was time for Andrew to check out a gig at a Burger King. Maybe in French fries?

Why is Chicago boxing dead? Look at Las Vegas, look at the casinos across the country. Those joints can run a big fight, take a bath at the box office, but more than make it up on the back end with table action, slots, and the impact of "branding." Branding has become the popular word for saying, "So we lose our shirts...guys in Bismark, North Dakota, now know we can compete with Dinty Moore Beef Stew."

Will our beloved Chi-Town ever become a fistic Mecca again?

No dice. We are a club show town...we're about John Collins, Lennie Lapaglia, and "Gator" Bodianowski. I didn't think you'd know those guys.

Jeez, I don't even know if the Golden Gloves is still in business. And frankly, I don't care. Our boxing days have come and gone.

Head to the next place. No mas and then some.

74 You have to SEE IT ONCE, even if you can't stand auto racing— attend the INDIANAPOLIS 500

"Over the years, I've found that drivers with a natural inclination to turn left seem to have success at Indy."

—Coppock

Top off the tank and let's begin the drive from Chicago to Indianapolis. I don't want to suggest that this is a boring tour, but wheeling 140 miles down I-65 is about as empty as an XFL highlight reel or the past 10 years of Whitney Houston's record catalogue.

"Every reporter should cover Indy. It changes your entire perspective on sports."

—Brent Musburger

I covered Indy for six consecutive years, beginning in 1975. In other words, I had the "Golden Era." I saw A.J Foyt become the event's first four-time winner. I saw Tom Sneva become the first driver to run an official 200-mile-per-hour lap. I was in the house when Janet Guthrie became the first woman to qualify for "The Greatest Spectacle in Racing."

The event was already commercialized to the point of absurdity. Trust me, if a guy did a 30-second interview and didn't mention "the Goodyear Tire and Rubber Company" at least twice, he was called on the carpet. Pennzoil also had to be given a blast.

But it was a roguish era. Foyt was perpetually pissed off at the U.S. Auto Club because USAC was the event's governing body. A.J. never has been real keen on authority. Foyt usually referred to USAC as a "popcorn operation." Johnny Rutherford was a nails-tough Texan who didn't mind hopping in anybody's face. Bobby Unser was the kid in high school who figured Biology 101 wasn't nearly as important as offering up tender loving care to the manifold on a 1954 Buick Roadmaster.

Actually, Bobby's a great guy and a great friend. I recall *Sports Illustrated* doing a piece on him that had a rather eye-catching headline: "I will go fast until the day I die."

Death wish? Hardly. Bobby's zest for life is boundless. Hey, he won Indy three times.

Anyway, there is one absolute "must" when you get to Nap Town. Stop by St. Elmo Steak House. The spicy-lung-burning shrimp cocktail sauce, along with unmatched steaks, is beyond fabulous. However, I would suggest you make your reservation about six months in advance. The joint always plays to a full house.

Race day, once you've endured traffic headaches that are in a class by themselves, is an overwhelming experience. You won't believe how big the place is.

Chet interviews his friend and three-time Indy 500 winner Bobby Unser back when Coppock was the sports anchor for Channel 8 in Indianapolis.

You could fit Soldier Field, The Cell, and Cubs Park in the place and still have plenty of room to park about 10,000 cars.

You're on sight, sound, and color overload. Go easy on the scotch the night before the show. You're going to be sitting in blazing Hoosier sunshine. Indy leads the nation in dehydration.

Thirty-three cars, 33 drivers form the grid.

Now, here's what you probably don't know if you're an "Indy virgin." The general notion is that the command, "Ladies and gentleman, start your engines" is the event's most dramatic singular moment. Some might say it's either the first lap or the final lap of the race.

Don't buy any of that stuff. Everybody should witness the moment when a driver kisses his mother, or wife, or girlfriend and squeezes into the cockpit of his racer. It's a sequence that drips with determination, passion, love, and no small degree of fear.

Let's gets real: This isn't a Wiffle ball game at Thillens Stadium. There is always the chance that one of these guys might end the day "dead on arrival" at Methodist Hospital.

The late Dave Nightingale, a terrific writer, once told me the command at the Speedway should be "Gentleman, start your coffins."

Back on the lighter side, don't expect to see the hugs and kisses if you're sitting in turn three. The Speedway is so damn big that turn three may as well be in Louisville, Kentucky.

Indy's popularity has suffered over the past decade. Blame it on the growth of NASCAR and the internal cat-fighting between the Indy Racing League and CART. The rival factions have darn near left the sport a notch below lacrosse. Frankly, once you get past Danica Patrick and Helio Castroneves, there just aren't many drivers who pack star appeal. Or, for that matter, any appeal.

Now, hum a chorus of "O Woe is Chester."

If you're a reporter, Indy isn't fun and games; it's three weeks from hell. One, you need a good two years to learn the place. Two, drivers give you the "once over" about 37 times before they accept you. Three, the size of the 257,000-seat facility is murder. It's damn near a small city.

If you're looking for Danica, bring a crossword puzzle. While you're in the garage area, she may be spending three hours in the second turn "suites" entertaining "money people" from Wellington, New Zealand.

Days are long. The heat from track surface will test an Olympic sprinter's legs.

However, I grew to love the place and the race. My memories are fond. I miss gabbing with Mario Andretti or dealing with a "character"—and I use the term, uh, loosely—like Salt Walther.

You owe it to yourself to see Indy. It's still the Academy Awards of racing despite what the hillbillies at Daytona will tell you. If you have loose scratch, find a scalper and buy seats on the main straightaway. If you want to play it tight, sit in the infield. You won't see a whole hell of a lot of racing, but the human debauchery remains a tribute to Woodstock.

75 Unleash your inner anger: Attend a MIXED MARTIAL ARTS event

"According to my time clock, Kimbo Slice has about 4:30 left on his 15 minutes of fame."

—Coppock

Timeout! My error. I thought Kimbo was with UFC, but he was part of now-defunct EliteXC mixed martial arts family.

Does it really make any difference?

I don't watch very much television. In fact, if stations had to rely on me for ratings, most shows would post a healthy 0.0 number. That's roughly the same figure Comcast SportsNet will draw for one of its late-night sportscasts.

I can proudly tell you that I have never seen *Falcon Crest* or *Grey's Anatomy*. This isn't snobbery, it's just the truth. The last show I really watched on a regular basis was *The Honeymooners* (the classic 39 episodes). Wait, I loved Johnny Carson on *The Tonight Show*. I still dig Letterman's Top 10 list.

Anyway, I was spending a little time in front of the tube when I saw this over-the-top, raging "push" for me to buy a UFC pay-per-view event featuring some guy named B.J. Penn versus the immortal Georges St-Pierre "live from the MGM Grand in Las Vegas."

Don't ask me why, but I did a little homework to see just what all the fuss was about. It left me speechless. Two weeks in front of the Penn–St-Pierre bout, the MGM Grand was completely sold out.

Let's pause for a moment. Whenever I think of the MGM, I think of sitting at ringside watching Mike Tyson reach the zenith of his profession when he chewed off Evander Holyfield's ear lobe. For me, the only "Vegas" moment that compares is the night I had a $400 slot payoff at the Mirage. Of course, I dropped 600 bucks to get there.

Several nights later, I'm back to channel flipping and I catch the tail end of an Elite XC program on Showtime. I didn't know whether to laugh or cry. I'm looking at some kid with cauliflower ears and about four face cuts talking about the match he just won. Won? The poor guy looked like he'd been run over by a pickup truck.

The ringside announcer, clearly trying to take the crowd behind the scenes, posed this question, "Is your best move, the left kick?"

I have bad memories of all this nonsense.

Years ago, I was invited by a small-time local promoter to see kick boxing at the Aragon Ballroom. I can't recall the guy's name, but I do remember that he also wrestled under the name "The Great Scott." I didn't know what the hell "kick" was all about, but it didn't take me long to develop a hatred of the whole package.

I swear, no kidding, I wasn't in my chair five minutes before some guy swung his right leg up toward his opponent's head and caught the poor kid right on the temple with his foot—flush. The sound was excruciating. I thought the guy was dead. I've wondered for years if that one blow left him on Broadway Avenue holding a tin cup.

So here we are in 2009. MTV is 28 years old. The economy, as I write this journal, has gone straight to hell. Generation X has given way to generation lost. Show me a kid who just got a college degree, and I'll show you a kid who wants to live at home.

This is an expensive and frightening world to a helluva lot of people. But there is, obviously, a following that has turned all this ultimate-extreme junk into, arguably, the most unique sports cult in American history.

You think the UFC isn't a major player? It did more than $220 million in pay-per-view revenue in 2006. So don't tell me that we're talking about a concept that appeals only to the mobile home crowd or people missing six teeth.

Mixed martial arts has filled a void for a certain segment of "sports" fans. My gut tells me there is a younger crowd that's grown weary watching the Vince McMahon WWE routine. I mean, how many times can you see "the Undertaker" or Chris Jericho before the act runs stale? These people may love the WWE pyrotechnics and the entrance music, but when the bell rings, they don't want glorified gymnastics. They want blood, they want a real-life sense of danger.

We also live in an angry society. Dick Cheney will do that to you. There is a good-sized chunk of people who want to see somebody suffer worse than they think they're suffering. Get it?

Why is the UFC so damn big? It has some forward-thinking promoters/hustlers running the show. The UFC guys knew they needed exposure. So they emptied their wallets to the tune of 10 million bucks to cover "production costs" to get a regular time slot on Spike TV.

And the gravy? UFC was slotted right after *WWE Monday Night Raw.* The move was genius, pure and simple.

You be the judge. Make your own call. There are plenty of "local' small-time MMA operations. Ironheart Crown runs shows at the Hammond Civic Center. "Crown" has also booked its product into the UIC Pavillion.

You can find an event. Maybe. It will turn you on. Maybe, you'll feel like you need a shower.

Hey, not everybody lives for college basketball.

76 Have you got big-time "clout?" PLAY the RICH HARVEST FARMS golf course in Sugar Grove

"Let me tell you about the very rich. They are different from you and me."

—F. Scott Fitzgerald,
The Great Gatsby

"If I had the bread Tom Rich has, I wouldn't guest on Lifestyles of the Rich and Famous. *I'd host the damn show."*

—F. Scott Fitz-Coppock,
frequently late with MasterCard payments

Just imagine this: A self-made millionaire of enormous proportions inquires about joining the Augusta National Golf Club. He is told politely by an "Augusta snob" to "get lost." Understand that you don't apply at Augusta. You must be invited to join by a membership committee that makes a presidential cabinet look like a bunch of guys who just wandered in from the local Dog 'n Suds in Davenport, Iowa.

I've always bought the time-honored pitch that it's easier to win at Augusta than it is to join Augusta.

Eventually, our man of the hour presides over his own golf course in Sugar Grove. Not just any course, mind you, but a track that screams azaleas, Amen Corner, and the voices of Pat Summerall and Jim Nantz—along with so many other features of the Masters layout.

Do I really have to educate you about Augusta and the Masters? If so, here's the "Official Coppock Your-Dime-Your-Dancefloor Primer on the 'Toonament.'"

CBS broadcasters are forbidden to call the spectators "patrons." Be honest—you'd kill to hear the late Harry Caray during a seventh-inning stretch stand up and shout, "Alright, you PATRONS, let me hear ya now...uh 1...uh 2...uh 3..."

You can bet your life savings on this. Unless Tiger just runs away and hides, the Masters will always define itself when the action moves to Rae's Creek on the back nine during the final round on Sunday.

The Masters has a bullwhip to CBS's back. The network is "permitted" to run about five commercial minutes an hour. That makes the CBS accountants see double. Hey, the "toonament" doesn't want its TV "patrons" to lose focus thinking about Dr. Scholl's foot pads.

Back in 1995, the flamboyant Gary McCord, working the event for CBS from the 17th hole tower, grabbed a one-way ticket to Masters oblivion. Gary must have figured he was doing the Danny Thomas Memphis Gold Classic. He dared to suggest that the Masters greens were so slick, they must have "used bikini wax" on them. It didn't help that Gary also suggested that the bumps in the Augusta turf "looked suspiciously like body bags."

You think the Augusta Brotherhood wasn't sky-high pissed? Half the membership wanted McCord exiled to Peru. The other half wanted to shoot him before the round closed. Gary was never forgiven. The snobs at Augusta never forget a damn thing. If Gary's ever been back to the hallowed joint, he was probably smuggled in through an underground tunnel that somehow leads to Butler Cabin.

But our subject is Tom Rich, a remarkable individual, a full-blown visionary with a passion for, shall we say, "big-time toys." You see, Rich Harvest Farms isn't just about golf. Tom also has an auto museum that features enough Jaguars to fill up Howard Orloff's "Jag" joint just off the Kennedy Expressway.

A little more: Tom's fleet includes a 1935 Duesenberg with, so I'm told, a grand total of 51 miles on the odometer. He has limousines that toted John F. Kennedy, along with a green Rolls-Royce that provided transportation for Princess Diana whenever she happened to be in America.

Get the picture? Our boy is either dealing with "carburetor" fixation or he's carrying an unlimited checkbook. I'd bet the latter.

Rich obviously took his rejection by the old timers at Augusta very personally. Why? Because, after consulting with a flock of architects and tapping the brain of "Slammin' Sammy" Snead (a three-time Masters champ), Tom has achieved his ultimate goal.

He's put together a track that has every right to call itself "Augusta North."

Good Lord, Thomas wanted Augusta and he got Augusta. His caddies even wear white jumpsuits. And consider this: Tom's Masters project began with one hole and a practice range.

Okay, I know you're drooling to get the inside dope. Members pay $33,000 a year for the right to play this splendid track. Throw in food and booze, plus tips, and the average fellow figures to drop around 50Gs.

Maybe this isn't a fair comparison, but who says three-putt greens have a divine right to fall in the category of fairness? I've seen Steve Wynn's "High Rollers Only" Shadow Creek course in Las Vegas. The "Shadow" doesn't have one-tenth the character that Rich Harvest delivers.

Cubs Park rooftop honcho Dave Abrams has lost more than his share of golf balls at the "Rich." Frankly, D.A. doesn't care. "Rich Harvest is a golfer's trip to Disney World without Space Mountain," Abrams says. "The overall feeling when you play the course is 'don't let this day end.'" Abrams isn't a "gym shoe" guy. He's played big-time courses all over the world.

So just how does one become a member of this deluxe country club? No runs, no hits, no applications. Tom invites his players, friends, and business associates, to join this slice of paradise.

Membership is subject to annual review. One insider told me that if Tom doesn't want a member back—a very rare occurrence—he'll just eat the guy's food and booze tabs and tell him "sayonara."

Yes, Michael Jordan is a member. So is Bo Jackson.

Back to the track. I know, this happens to me all the time. I'll hit a shot that finds its way to a bunker and my ball—this just kills me—will get veered off course by a rake. It just drives me nuts. But it's as common as TV dinners.

That just doesn't happen at "The Harvest." Rakes are hidden. They actually pop up out of the turf.

Here's the real keeper—when I wormed my way into the place a few years ago, this just left me doing handsprings. Players can enjoy lunch when they make the turn or, if they want a different approach, they can place a lunch order before tee-off time and the meal will arrive and be placed on the player's golf cart on the hole they request.

Trust me, this isn't some kind of gimmick to speed up play. It's darn near impossible to have a back-up at "Rich." Course traffic, as you can imagine, is very light. On a busy day, seven foursomes might take out the clubs.

Tom Rich, congrats are in order. The best thing that ever happened to you was your rejection by the august Augusta body down south.

In other words, the clowns at Rae's Creek missed out on a keeper. They were nuts not to make you part of their Millionaires Club.

P.S. Yo, Tom, if I promise not to leave divots, can I play your track again?

77 Get off your booty and attend a WINDY CITY ROLLERS flat-track ROLLER DERBY doubleheader

These folks we're going to chat about today obviously have 260 mph imaginations—and that's during their down time. Hell's Belles, one of four Windy City Roller clubs, features "May R. Daley" and the immortal "Athena D. Crime." You're right, you would normally expect to hear those names connected with table dances—not skate keys.

Members of Iron Workers Local Number 122 and honored guests of the Roland Burris Fan Club, please return to your tables.

You need to get the cold, hard facts about "Red Zepplin," "Slamma Montana," "Yvette YourMaker," and a host of other babes that you might or might not choose to take home to meet your 68-year-old mother. If Mom voted for Barry Goldwater or thinks Dick Cheney is just too cool for words, I would strongly suggest you ditch the family theme and take "Mona Lott" or the entire roster of Hell's Belles to Ed Debevic's throw-back restaurant on Ontario Street.

Raffle time—you could be a lucky winner! Take home this handsome leisure suit, courtesy of Goldblatt's, if you can name all four teams that make up the Windy City Rollers flat-track roller derby league. Or, as they're known in Cicero, all babes, all bruises, all butts, all the time…tattoos, hidden or otherwise, recommended and encouraged.

Answer: Hell's Belles, The Fury, the Double Crossers—jeez, those names would be naturals on the fifth floor at City Hall or the Thompson Center—and let's not forget The Manic Attackers.

The Windy City Rollers were founded by "Juanna Rumbel" and "Sister Sledeghammer"…uh, real names Elizabeth Gomez and Kelly Simmons. You tell me what's more likely to "pop" the box office—Simmons or "Sledgehammer"? I can hear the maitre d' barking, "Sledgehammer, party of six, your switch-blade…excuse me, table is ready."

I'm just getting into this new concept. You see, I cut my teeth on Roller Derby, the old-fashioned banked-track "Nightly Skate to Nowhere" back in the early '70s. In the category of "believe it or not," I did telecasts on a makeshift network of 275 stations from coast to coast. I know, all this time you thought *Geraldo* was as bad as TV could get. I made 500 bucks a game. In 1972, that wasn't just good coin, it covered my rent for about 45 days.

I forgive the girls who make up the Windy City Rollers if they're clueless about my "Derby people"—"Blond Amazon" Joanie Weston, bad-girl goddess Anne Calvello (I'll never forget that one-nighter in Philly), Charlie O'Connell, Mike Gammon, or Ronnie Robinson.

I was part of a Derby where I saw big names skate before houses of 18,000 fans but only—you talk about primitive—after watching the same "stars" make an extra 15 bucks before the event to help set up the track. You're right, try and run that one past the NFLPA.

> *Ronnie Robinson's claim to fame was just too easy. His old man was fistic icon "Sugar Ray" Robinson, inch for inch, pound for pound, the greatest fighter in boxing history. If you don't believe me, ask for some private time with Jake La Motta's cheek bones.*

I still miss our Derby tapings at the old Hammond Civic Center. My "usual" job was to pump the daylights out of the Midwest Pioneers, hustle the "marks" that the Pioneers were going to be playing (choose one): Chicago, Kenosha, St. Louis, Dayton, Muncie, Indiana, or some hick town off I-55. This Friday night! This was going to be the biggest game in Roller Derby history! The hatred between these two clubs has never been this fierce. You just have to come up with the cabbage to see the Pioneers challenge the hated New York Chiefs.

The first time I worked Madison Square Garden—Pioneers versus the Chiefs—I was live throughout the New York area via this strange device called

"Cable TV." It was truly a great time to live for a lot of reasons, but mainly because there was no Bill O'Reilly and other Fox News right-wing zealots.

What about the crowd count? The Garden had "gone clean." It was on overload with about 19,500 fans. I don't care if you're doing an NBA game or the Westminster Kennel Club Dog Show, when you do live TV at the Garden, your pulse works overtime.

Most of our old Derby shows closed with "white shirt blow-offs"—that's Derby-speak. In layman's terms, it meant the "baby faces" would win on the game's final "jam" and send the customers out of the building in the mood to buy merchandise and tickets to the next game.

If a red shirt blow-off was the play—and it was only done to hype a rivalry—it meant the "heels" would come up with the win. The skating villains would then jump on mic to scream that, "This was just the warm up." Next week, the villains were going to leave the Pioneers looking like the Spilotro Brothers in their later years.

Just to bring you up to speed, Anthony "Tony the Ant" Spilotro, the pride and joy of Steinmetz High School, and his brother Michael "Micky" Spilotro, were ranking wise guys in Tony Accardo's Chicago mob. They had the misfortune about 25 years ago to tick off the wrong guys. As a result, they were beaten to bits and left in unique open-dirt graves in Morocco, Indiana. It was a shame. Both guys were, reportedly, in line for promotions, including added vacation time.

This is a pretty good marketing twist. The Manic Attackers just don't hop on the track until they hear their fight song, "Raining Blood" by Slayer. You're right, the Beach Boys harmonizing on "California Girls" wouldn't play in this neck of the woods.

Hey, gang, this matters: The old Roller Derby was a con, a play for laughs. The Windy City Rollers, so help me Midge "Toughie" Brashun, are completely on the level. The fact is, they beat the living hell out of each other and then they generally go get loaded.

I know this feels like a Southern Illinois University fraternity party. No, some of these darlings have ear lobes that look like they went through a one-nighter with a pit bull.

Ask yourself this question: Is your life really fulfilled if you haven't tried either Nutri-System or seen the Windy City Rollers in action? The Rollers have a regular series of dates at the UIC Pavilion. They don't need armed guards to protect an overflow at the ticket windows, but they draw around 3,000 people a game. Not bad.

I've seen the girls work, and they give you 125 cents on the dollar. Each card features a round robin—two games for the price of one. If it's October 15, the Fury must be in a hook-up with the Manic Attackers, while Hell's Belles— we just can't get away from those young ladies—are due to tango with the Double Crossers.

How do the Rollers reach the next level? A reality check. They will never be as big as the old Roller Derby was at its peak. Won't happen. There's too much competition for the entertainment buck. But with solid TV exposure, I could see "The Rollers" drawing 7,000, maybe 8,000, fans a show.

I really hope the league jells, if only to pay tribute to retired Fury star "Tall Drinka Slaughter."

Be honest. Don't you just love these names? They remind me of a bygone era when a popular local stripper worked various joints under the name "Princess Sockeetomee."

You think Devo looked a little offbeat? Log on to YouTube and type in "Chet Coppock." You'll get a chance to see a Dan Rather–style Roller Derby interview I did with Joan Weston and Tonette Kademas back in 1973. You can feel the electricity. It's truly a unique journalistic experience—if you don't mind lack of talent.

Meanwhile, you talk about miserable wardrobe selection. I look like an advertisement for just how much bad acid or cheap bourbon fashion designers were downing during the 1970s. I look like I should be a backup singer for Barry White.

> Who says the Windy City Rollers don't keep you cooking well past curfew? They have an official post-bout bar. It's a place called the Bottom Lounge on Lake Street, a block west of Racine. From what I hear, "Ivy Sedation" can drink 92 percent of the joint into the next county.

If Hell's Belles rollers "Athena DeCrime" or "Shocka Conduit" called for reservations at Rosebud on Rush, I wonder what the heck name they'd use. Windy City's Fury features "Carnage Wilson," while my insiders tell me the Manic Attackers just aren't the same club without "Celia Coffin."

You're right, with these kinds of names, does Alfonso Soriano really seem all that relevant?

Time out. My short-term memory has gone south—again. I met several of the Windy City Rollers at a Roller Derby reunion at the Ambassador East Hotel about four years, or three waist sizes, ago.

I can confirm that "Rheina Chaos" made no attempt to take out my legs.

Spend a few bucks. Check out the Windy City Rollers. How can you not embrace the Manic Attackers and the team's adorable captain "Malice in Chains"? During every practice session, the Manics take time out to pay homage to retired star "Ida Ho."

Game, set, and match.

78 Do the right thing! Attend the CHICAGO MARATHON

Put this one in the category of unfulfilled ambitions...ambitions that won't be covered during this lifetime.

I would love to run the Boston Marathon. I'd like to take on the 26-mile, 385-yard grind, spit in defiance when I get to "Heartbreak Hill," and finish in under three hours. In the great scheme of life, that really isn't much to ask. Alright, I understand. At this stage of my life, I should be content to walk up two flights of stairs at the East Bank Club.

The fact is, I have enormous admiration for long-distance runners. You compare the commitment they have to their game to an American League designated hitter and it's almost laughable.

A true-blue runner has an ingrained mindset. You know this whole running racket is really mind over matter. The daily grind—eight, 12, 16 miles—must be met. The American League DH has a somewhat different lifestyle. His primary job is to hide out in the trainer's room after going 0-for-5 until the press gets lost.

Skip Bayless is a terrific example of the runner's mentality.

Time out on the field. Here's a little local media gossip you didn't catch with Stella Foster or Michael Sneed. Don't worry about the clock. You know me. I hate people who are wordy.

Skip, of course, had a brief but ultra-successful run as a columnist with the *Chicago Tribune* before he skipped to the East and a multimedia gig with ESPN. The *Trib* has never replaced him, never had a guy who could nail the vibe like Skip.

When the Skipper left our town, we lost what could have been a tremendous one-round fight. Jay Mariotti, the ex–*Sun-Times* columnist, just detested Bayless for one simple reason: Bayless, also a best-selling author, used to write Mariotti's jock off, just cream him. I mean, Mariotti vs. Bayless was no contest. Mariotti was Bowling Green. Bayless was USC.

Skip's ability to weave the words, paint pictures, and define drama made "Sweet Baby Jay" brutally green with envy. Mariotti resented Bayless' talent so much, he did what punks do. He began "taking on" Bayless in his column.

Skip is a great guy, but he does have a volcanic temper. Plus, he's also a weightlifter and has hands like a young "Sugar Ray" Leonard. It was only a matter of time before Mariotti was going to look at Bayless the wrong way and Skip, in turn, was going to collapse Jay's rib cage and the left side of his brain. High end, Skip would have needed 30 seconds to wipe Mariotti off the planet.

And all this time you thought Ozzie Guillen was the only guy who wanted to leave Mariotti face-down in the Chicago River.

Skip was also a runner, a dedicated runner. If his treadmill didn't own him an hour a day, the treadmill was flagged for illegal procedure.

Imagine this. Skip was in Augusta one year covering the Masters. The *Tribune* wanted him back in Chicago on Monday morning at around 8:00 AM to play in a client golf tourney. Obviously, Skip had to blow off one day of running, right? Are you kidding? Bayless got up at 3:00 in the morning to get his one hour in before he flew back to Chicago for a full day with the clubs.

Did I ever run? Yes, I loved it. Back in the early '80s, I did six miles a day, four times a week. Just me, my Walkman and a buzz about the time I got to mile four. Sometimes, when I was at my weekend home in Michianna Shores, Michigan, I'd push the needle up to 12 or 14 miles.

If you're scoring at home, my career high was 21 miles. When I mention my personal best to guys from Kenya, they do their best to keep from laughing.

I'll never run the Chicago Marathon. But I have covered the race and I caught it during its greatest year, 1984. I was on the press truck about 35 feet in front of Steve Jones, a Welshman, as he staged a great head-to-head battle with Aussie Rob de Castella on a cold and rainy morning.

The two were side by side for roughly 25 miles as they reached the Montrose Avenue on-ramp to Lake Shore Drive. Freeze the moment.

Jones looked at de Castella, appeared to flick his hand in modest disdain, hit a gear he probably didn't know he had, and won the event in world-record time: 2:08:05. It was just riveting to watch, far more dramatic than a walk-off homer in April.

Let me get poetic. Jones was running to win, running for prize money, running for bonus cash for setting a world record, and running with stars in his eyes. Have I covered all bets?

Jones was running because that's what he did. That was his identity, his purpose. The win over de Castella is what's documented. But that's so bland. Distance people run to put themselves through perpetual tests. They really don't have finish lines. They're not allowed that luxury. What was it about the "loneliness of the long-distance runner"?

You make your own determination. I like to believe that Jones went beyond the runner's high. He reached a peak that said, "God can't beat me today. My burning lungs can't beat me. I own this race."

Will the Chicago Marathon ever have another "Jones Performance"? Who knows? But if you have some time, volunteer to work the event. Pass out water to runners at the 14-mile mark. Or just take in Chicago. It's every bit as good as Boston or New York. So it screws up traffic for a few hours. The guys and gals who make the sacrifice, put forth the effort, and run till they scream in pain are more than worth it.

Plus—and this means something to me—you just don't hear about marathon runners holding out or demanding trades or telling slime-king Drew Rosenhaus to call Jerry Angelo a cheapskate.

Runners just do what they love, alone with their passion. Not a bad way to go.

79 Where is PGA golf going once TIGER WOODS waves goodbye?

It's a Monday in February and, frankly, I'm stunned. No, I didn't see naked photos of Jessica Simpson.

Yesterday, Kobe Bryant and the Lakers were in Cleveland and on national TV for a bout with LeBron James and the Cleveland Cavaliers. ABC and ESPN had hyped the game all week to such an extent that, frankly, I thought it had to be the biggest roundball happening since the introduction of the 24-second clock.

Here's why I'd never qualify as a TV executive. I was positive the game would blow the PGA's Buick Invitational out of the water. It didn't. Kobe and LeBron—you know them as Sonny and Cher—did a 4 national rating while The Buick pulled in with a 3.2. In case you were wondering, Tiger Woods was still on the practice tee at his home in Orlando during The Buick, getting ready for his return from knee surgery.

So how long does Tiger Woods play? He's not Tom Kite. He won't be thrilled to "play on Sunday" just to grab the 11th-place money at some track in Nashville before flying back to Orlando. Don't tell me Tiger's competitive juices would be locked in overdrive if he knew the best he could do was make the top 10 at Deutsche Bank Championship.

How will Tiger react when his body begins to betray him? No, I'm not talking about the 2008 knee surgery to repair an injury that made him, basically, the first one-legged player to win the U.S. Open.

Think about the big picture. Tiger can cut a 3-wood out of heavy rough on a dogleg from 260 yards and leave the ball eight feet from the hole. Nobody else on the tour even dreams about that kind of shot. Can he live with himself when the day comes—and this will be miserable for him—that his ball is going to stop dead 20 yards from the fringe?

No—in bold type.

Tiger pull an Arnie? Play forever just to hear the roar of the gallery? It won't happen.

Let's see where Eldrick Woods is in five or six years. My guess is he'll be telling his caddy and buddy, Steve Williams, "Game, set, and match." Meanwhile, when Woods leaves the PGA, some sponsors will bail, purse money will tighten up, and TV numbers will drop.

Let's go back to the Buick Invitational. Why did the Buick pull a 3.2? Why did it steal viewers from Kobe and LeBron?

It's all about the Tiger. The Woods Era, which really got jump-started when he won the 1997 Masters by a staggering 12 strokes, has produced an enormous rub-off effect. That may qualify as the biggest understatement I've made since last Saturday. The Tiger impact has out-Jordaned Jordan.

Tiger galvanized people, so many people, that even when he doesn't play, there are those people—who previously would rather watch VH1 than golf—that will give the sport some viewing time. If Tiger had played The Buick and been within four strokes of the lead when CBS began its Sunday coverage, David Stern and the NBA would have been in the backup car.

Look at the cash numbers. Tiger joined the tour in 1996. Tom Lehman closed that season as the PGA's leading money winner with $1.78 million. By 2004, Vijay Singh became the first pro to top $10 million in single-year earnings. Tiger has since gone on to post a pair of $10 million seasons, along with one near miss—the poor guy had to settle for $9.94 mill in 2006.

This rise in available cash didn't occur because America suddenly became infatuated with 2-irons. It happened because of the excellence and—never overlook this—aggressive charisma and take-no-prisoners mentality of Tiger. Tiger is Rocky Marciano with a pitching wedge.

Check out the field at this year's Buick Invitational. I don't know if these guys are golfers, Northern League baseball players, or overnight desk clerks at the YMCA. When was the last time you carved out extra TV time to watch Nick Watney—he won the sucker—or the quasi-immortal Lucas Glover? He won two-and-a-half million bucks in 2006. Do you believe that? Doing what—is he part of a skeet-shooting league?

Did I leave out Jason Dufner and Rod Pampling? Don't forget guys like Rod. He had the Day 1 lead in the British Open at Carnoustie in 1999. Boy, did this guy capitalize. Rod went out the following day, perhaps a bit distracted by the 47 people who were following him, and carded a somewhat-robust 86.

The Buick's biggest draw? Phil Mickelson, but Lefty didn't really add to the frolics. He was so far down the leaderboard that his Sunday round, I'm told, ended at roughly 10:36 AM.

I love golf. I just can't play the damn game. My swing looks like a busted Ferris wheel.

But I have packed away some terrific memories. Two, in particular, are really special.

I walked the Old Course at St. Andrews one day after watching the British Open at Troon, Scotland, back in 1989. It would have been a blast to have six-time Open champ Harry Vardon along to tell me how to tackle the ancient monster. Just one problem: Harry kicked the bucket back in 1937.

Round 2 takes me back to Louisville, Kentucky, in 2000. I was at the PGA Championship at Valhalla Country Club doing shows for Sporting News Radio. (Side note: Does Sporting News Radio still have a pulse?) Friday was an open day on my calendar, so I took advantage of a golden opportunity. I followed Tiger Woods and Jack Nicklaus—the whole nine yards—as they completed the event's first 36 holes.

The Golden Bear was working his last PGA and, sadly, he failed to make the cut. Tiger went on to win the tourney with a classic display of Eldrick Woods toughness. Woods went seven under par over the event's final 12 holes. The surge set him up to break Bob May's spirit in overtime. May had to feel like he'd been hit by a truck. He'd drained a 25-foot putt on 18 just to force a playoff.

Tiger Woods is approaching his 34th birthday. Will he still feel like playing when he's 41? Will he pull a Nicklaus and fire a 65 on his way to winning Augusta when he's 46?

The bigger questions are these: Where is the PGA Tour, where is the big-time sponsorship money, where are the galleries once Tiger decides to put the clubs away?

Golf isn't the NFL. It can't rely on gamblers to keep the Madison Avenue TV boys in good spirits or to keep fans glued to the tube on Sunday because they bet Tiger minus-1.

Nobody loses Elvis Presley and has the same act or following. In other words, golf becomes Roger Federer: Great talent—no audience pull.

FACES *and* PLACES

80 *The legacy of the* "BRICK"

Jack Brickhouse loved broadcasting the color and flamboyance of professional wrestling, but he once told me that he had long thoughts when he was first approached about hustling the mat world on good old Channel 9.

"Our general manager came to me and said, 'Hey, we're gonna put you on wrestling,'" Jack told me around 1985. "I started yelling that I couldn't do this nonsense, it would destroy my credibility. So after some thoughtful give-and-take we reached a compromise.

"I did what I was damn well told."

Jack's trademark "Hey-Hey" home-run call was a knockout for several reasons. One, it was completely natural. Two, the tenor of his voice and his youthful enthusiasm for what he was doing could make a loan shark smile.

The Brick's museum piece, his ultimate home run call? That's too easy. Opening Day, April 8, 1969. Willie Smith's 11th inning dinger lifted the Cubs over Don Money and the Phillies 8 to 7. I swear Jack's energy level and vocal thrust were so guttural that I was convinced his larynx was gong to require major surgery. If the medics could find it.

This could only happen to Jack. In 1945, the Cubs actually won a pennant. So you have to assume Brick was there with a bottle of cheap champagne, right? Not quite. Jack was in uniform as a member of the U.S. Marines.

Jack may have been the world's worst gin player. He also had a temper that could make a legion of pit bulls melt. But John Beasley Brickhouse also had a heart of gold, a remarkable sense of generosity, and a soft spot for anybody who was down and out.

Brickhouse, a baseball announcer? Much too limited. That's like suggesting Donald Trump builds mobile homes.

The Brick, without question, is the most versatile and complete broadcaster in Chicago history. Forget about a backup choice. No one is even close.

Let's just cover some of the tabs. J.B. did the Cubs, the White Sox, the Bears, college football, the Bulls, soccer, boxing, the Brickouse-Hubbard talk show, barn dances, and he emceed live bands at the Edgewater Beach Hotel. He also anchored sports on evening newscasts. If a banquet or charity needed a full house, it dialed up Brickhouse.

Jack thrived on rain delays. Lived for them. He saw the tarp on the infield as a chance to converse—not interview, but chat living-room style—with a writer, a broadcaster, a ballplayer, or some guy in town hustling a book.

Round two. For years, Jack also was WGN's point man on the station's coverage of political conventions. Trust me. I could list another three dozen forms

Jack Brickhouse (center) with two other Chicago broadcasting legends, Lloyd Pettit (left) and Jack Rosenberg.

of entertainmment that carried the Brickhouse touch, but it's time to get down to the point.

Chicago has never been a racially comfortable town. Would anybody dare suggest that there still aren't areas where minorities just don't want to walk during the daylight hours...let alone after dusk?

So we go back to my growing-up years: I'm in a society with Ozzie and Harriet, *Leave it to Beaver, American Bandstand,* and John Fitzgerald Kennedy. Chicago was a racially cruel environment for "negroes" and it was no great shakes for Latinos.

This is where Jack Brickhouse truly earned his entree to so many different Halls of Fame. As he broadcast sports over WGN TV and radio, Jack's respect and empathy for the minority athlete convinced at least a full generation of Chicagoans that Ernie Banks, Gene Baker, George Altman, Billy Williams, Al Smith, Chico Carrasquel, Luis Aparicio, and Adolfo Phillips were to be just as welcome in our living rooms as our next-door neighbors. No, Jack did not talk down to these athletes or try to play the role of Father Flanagan. Brick talked to these players with just as much respect and appreciation as he talked to white players.

I made this point during a commentary I did on Fox Sports Nets TV when Jack passed away back in 1998: The truly special aspect of the Brickhouse legacy is that he did more than any Chicagoan to promote racial and ethnic harmony during the 1950s and 1960s.

Some people saw this as an insult to Dr. Martin Luther King. Those people missed the point. Yes, I know that Dr. King was struck by a bottle thrown by some racially steamed idiot during a march in Chicago in 1966. I know that King once suggested that Chicago was more racially mean-spirited than Mississippi.

However, King, a man I deeply admired, was working on a national platform. Jack was a day-by-day fixture in Chicago. When Brickhouse spoke, people listened...and people were sold by his sincerity

Why was Jack so uncommonly decent? Perhaps, he recalled his own growing-up years—challenging, Depression years—in Peoria. Jack's own father died when he was just two. He was raised by a mother who was frequently an absentee parent. He knew what it was like to feel uncertain and, perhaps, unwanted.

Jack Brickhouse. He was a father figure, a mentor, a friend, and a critic.

And his pedigree was loyalty.

81 *Ditch the Chuck Taylors, Get some real running shoes and* JOG *Chicago's* SPECTACULAR LAKEFRONT

I'll argue this to the point of violence. Who the hell needs the California coast? It's just so Beach Boys, so Jan and Dean.

A summertime jog along the Lake Michigan shore offers such a panorama of natural beauty, architectural brilliance, and chicks with major-league cleavage that it's somewhere between breathtaking and overwhelming.

> *"Avoid running at all costs."*
>
> —Satchell Paige

Like it or not, I qualify for Team Paige. I haven't jogged since Fritz Mondale and Geraldine Ferraro tried to tag-team their way past Ronald Reagan. Get the timeline? I got wrapped up in the craze about 28 years and 40 pounds ago. In fact, it was a rare day when you wouldn't see Young Coppock out for his daily jog—average pace: 14 minutes a mile—with Olivia Newton John, as flat as plywood, belting out "Let's Get Physical." Who can ever forget Olivia opposite John Travolta in *Grease*? What says fun like a bunch of 26-year-olds playing high school seniors?

Today's adventure requires that I give you the rundown on what has to be one of the most spectacular jogging tours west of the Rhine River.

Note: I have no idea where the hell the Rhine River is, but you have to admit, it does sound "flavorful."

Let's get rockin'. We open the cruise at the south end of Soldier Field. As you begin your series of stretches, think about how cool it would be if Chicago had a second NFL franchise. You know, a team that every 10 to 12 years developed a quarterback or had one wide receiver that scared the hell out of rival defensive coordinators.

Begin to pace east before turning toward the north. Note the gorgeous colonnades that have been reduced to slum status by the god-awful renovation of a ballpark that once hosted 260,000 fans for a religious ceremony in 1954. Soldier Field also drew about 60,000 for James Brown in 1967.

Continue to pace north. Just follow the signs. Eventually, you'll go east toward the Adler Planetarium. Trust me, it's one hell of a joint. Don't be surprised if you see Rod Blagojevich doing the hang at the Adler. "Honest Rod" has been known to show up in the wee hours to exchange text messages with David Letterman, Whoopi Goldberg, and Barbara Walters.

This doesn't relate to jogging, but it's worth a pop. Ever take an early evening boat ride on Lake Michigan? No? Book it.

Watching the sun drift its way down over the high-rise complexes is just flat-out fantastic. If you watch the occurrence after two or three belts of scotch you'll know exactly how Jim Morrison felt every time the Doors appeared in concert. Or how Mickey Rourke felt daily during the 15 years before he turned in the performance of a lifetime in *The Wrestler*.

Back to the run. From the Adler, we head west past the Shedd Aquarium (please observe the sign: Don't feed the people) and the Field Museum. Note the beauty of the South Loop. The area used to be industrial no-man's land. Now realtors often request new buyers to avoid purging when they sign up to buy these trendy, overpriced condos.

This part of the run should thrill you. Or at least make you damn glad you don't live in Casper, Wyoming. You get the full panoramic feel of our world-class city. It's amazing to me just how small the Hilton Hotel looks. Of course, the Hilton is dwarfed by the Sears Tower. The "Sears" was the tallest building in the word from 1974 to 1978. Now it's dropped to four on the All Big Boy list.

Begin to gaze at Lake Michigan. On a cloudless day, the water is as elegantly blue as Liz Taylor's eyeliner or Cubs pinstripes. You're right. What the hell does Kosuke Fukodome have to do with a 77-year-old actress who leads the nation in facelifts? And hasn't turned out quality cinema since *Who's Afraid of Virginia Woolf?*

By now, as you head north—Lakeshore Drive to your left, the lake to your right—you should be into the runner's "high." If not, immediately call Michael Phelps. If you sweet-talk the human bluegill, he might give you a deal on his marijuana pipe.

This part of the run is just a joy. You'll jog past Buckingham Fountain, Monroe Harbor, and the Columbia Yacht Club. If you wish to pause at the yacht club, gentlemen are advised to wear bow ties and six-year-old Oxfords and act as snooty as possible. At least that's what my bookie told me.

Sneak a peak at the Hancock Building off in the distance. As you exert yourself to a new level, this question begs to be asked: "How many tourists in the Signature Room on 95 are paying 13 bills right now to wolf down the Don

Julio Anejo cocktail—heavy on the tequila? Or how many people from Arcadia, Kansas—playing off a budget—had to settle for the Godiva chocolate martini at just 12 bucks?"

Eventually, you'll run by Lake Point Tower. That place always gives me headaches. I could have bought a condo in that place in 1974 for about $32,000. I'm not sure if that'll buy a parking space now.

Take note of the architectural detail at 680 N. Lake Shore Drive. The old guy is a British wool custom-made suit. In fact, when the sucker was zipped up in 1926, it was the world's largest building.

As you near the 990 building on North Lake Shore, you're into the "S-curve" portion of the journey. You can begin to see the glory of Oak Street Beach. Ironically, you'll be heading west adjacent to East Lake Shore Drive. I don't want to get gooey, but appreciate the fact that the Drake Hotel is still in business. The Drake—still as proud as it can be, still delivering tremendous style and service.

Guys, call timeout at Oak Street Beach. Feel free to gawk at the babes. From here, your mission is all yours. I would suggest you play burn-your-calves until you reach Irving Park Road, make a 180, and take the same path back to Soldier Field.

Upon returning to Soldier, take note. The Bears still need help at about 13 positions.

82 *Dive into a big-time* PORK CHOP, *dig the dynamic* MEMORABILIA, *have lunch or dinner at* MIKE DITKA'S *restaurant*

Let's take care of this right off the top: If you're looking for a three dollar cheeseburger or Italian beef with extra peppers, head to the next place.

Go back to 1963, Bears versus Colts at Wrigley Field. Quarterback Billy Wade throws a slant to flanker Johnny Morris. Ditka, running off a different route, takes out Bobby Boyd, the Colts safety, with a block so ferocious, so vicious that my first reaction was, "The guy won't get up." Honest to gosh, I thought he was dead.

Coppock and Da Coach enjoying their postmeal cigars at Ditka's restaurant.

The pride and joy of Aliquippa, Pennsylvania, has put together not one but three tremendous restaurants, Chestnut Street in Streeterville, Oakbrook Terrace, and for those who want do the road trip thing, 1 Robinson Plaza in Pittsburgh, Pennsylvania.

> *"If you can find a better steak than ours, than go do it. But you will not beat our service."*
>
> —Mike Ditka

What? Don't be silly. You're expecting Michael Keller Ditka to say, "Try the foie gras and we strongly recommend that you and your guest take extra time to savor the pâté?"

Time out for my favorite restaurant tale. This goes back 20 years and it is completely on the square. You just can't sip the Kool-Aid and make this stuff up.

May 7, 1989, the Richfield Coliseum. On a lazy Sunday, Michael Jordan drops "the shot" over Craig Ehlo to lift the Bulls to a 3–2 series win over Lennie Wilkens and the Cavs. Johnny Kerr's larynx ages 15 years describing the moment.

The Bulls follow up with a six-game series win in the Eastern semis versus the New York Knicks. Jordan over Pat Ewing and John Starks. The music stops when the Bulls lose a gut-bust of a six-game series to Chuck Daly and the Pistons.

But the Bulls are suddenly sexy, hot, advertiser-attractive. The club is headed toward a run of sellouts that would make Don King green with envy. Chicago has "arrived" as an NBA city.

So I get a call from a "beef and cheese" man—that's Coppockeese for "money"—about opening a restaurant out near O'Hare Field with Doug Collins. Obviously, you can see how this one plays out. I bring in Collins and I get points in the deal. And the points were going to be BIG.

Collins loved the concept. He was all in, ready to shake hands, kiss babies, and, perhaps, pinch waitresses. His attorney flies to town to meet with our investors and, hell, we're already talking about where we're going to put pictures of Doug when he was playing high school ball for the Benton Rangers.

Crash and burn! This only happens on *The Sopranos.* Collins got fired, whacked, KOd by the Bulls the next day—less than 24 hours after our deal was at 35,000 feet—by Jerry Krause and the Bulls.

Just think, I could have been a "Mini-Mike."

If you're a jock and you're going to open a restaurant, here's my first tip: Bring charisma, fan appeal, and a larger-than-life persona. You tell me how long the "Lovie Smith Railroad Grill" or the "Scott Skiles Pancake House" would last. I'd put the over/under on both joints at 2.3 months.

Back to Ditka's. It's obvious Mike didn't take out a hammer and nails and hang the restaurant photos and artifacts himself. The symmetry of design, illustrating Mike's career—and the careers of countless other athletes, pols, Hollywood types, and local movers and shakers—doesn't detract from the atmosphere. It enhances the place. You're walking into Mike Ditka's for a great shrimp cocktail, but you also want to feel the presence of a guy who could have been All-Pro at about six different positions besides tight end: weak, middle, and strong side linebacker; fullback; defensive end; and strong safety. Maybe right tackle.

Ditka was a physical freak. His body type was about 15 years ahead of its time. His arms were like tire irons. A stiff-arm from Mike Ditka, 240 pounds of twisted steel, was about as much fun as your eye making contact with the sharp edge of a pencil.

January 25, 1986, a hotel suite in New Orleans. This was a thrill and half. Mike Pyle, Ditka's former roommate with the Bears, and I hosted Mike's weekly radio show on WMAQ the night before the Bears left the New England Patriots about 14 feet below the carpet in Super Bowl XX. Ditka, nervous? I'd swear his resting pulse was about 44 beats. I guarantee you there are 80-year-olds in retirement homes in Sarasota playing shuffleboard right now who have greater anxiety than Ditka had the night before the Bears' 46–10 blowout championship win.

Ditka didn't just walk in the back door when he arrived with the Bears. He broke the hinges off the front door. The front door never had a chance. Mike's first regular-season game as a Bear was against the Vikings at old Metropolitan Stadium back on September 15, 1961. If you must know, the Vikings crushed the Bears 37–13 behind a young Fran Tarkenton.

I don't know how many catches Mike had or how many Vikes he clobbered, but this is fact: Ditka got so burned up about the way one guy was playing that he punched him. The one guy just happened to be Ted Karras, one of his teammates. A little bizarre, but all Ditka, all the time.

I do Ditka's downtown about once a month. The pork chop is fabulous, the service is always tremendous. The place, as Mike says, "is always trying to get better."

I don't want some chi-chi joint. I like Gibson's, Harry Caray's, Hugo's Frog Bar, Gennaro's on Taylor Street, and breakfast at the East Bank Club. I love Mike Ditka's restaurant. Class, hand in hand with great food and sports. That ain't all bad. In fact, it makes for one helluva joint. Don't have a Metropolitan. Have a double shot of Crown Royal and then lower the boom on some great red meat.

P.S. You can use your fingers to nibble the bone.

83 *Coppock rates the* BEST *and* WORST TV *sportscasters and* RADIO *talkies in Chicago over the* PAST 25 YEARS

This is really a no-win. Part of me says I'm nuts to write this section since it'll probably move me past the 10,000 mark on my cherished all-enemies list. But what the hell? I've been a TV sports anchor in Chicago, and I get a great kick out of people calling me the godfather of sports-talk radio.

So let's go back to 1983. Let's flip the dials, trot out the players, and come up with a list of the 12 best sportscasters over the past 25 years—and 12 guys or gals who've been skating but have somehow avoided the ax. Why 12? My house, my game.

First, a little background—wow, has the landscaped changed.

Go back to early '80s when I was at Channel 5 with Mark Giangreco. There were no shared "feeds," and the clubs didn't have prison-guard control over reporters' access to ballplayers. Giangreco is a free ride for the brass at WLS. Whatever the station pays Mark to do his routine is chump change compared to the impact he gives their sales team.

> *"[TV sportscasters] are just drive-bys," Giancgreco says in complete candor. "There is no competition. We don't have the chance the writers have to establish relationships with ballplayers and managers. You don't win by breaking stories. You win by how you're able to write and report with the time they give you."*

Mark just hit the ball 450 feet.

Somewhere along the way, the bean counters who run TV stations in Chicago determined that their audiences would much rather hear about barometric pressure and the cold wave outside Athens, Georgia, than a Cubs baseball team drawing 3.3 million fans or the Bulls who probably would draw 20,000 fans a night if they trotted out five drunks from Gibson's.

I recall this vividly. Larry Wert, the front man at Channel 5, told me some years back that if he had it his way, he'd drop sports. Part of Wert's frustration was the arrival and surge of ESPN.

So much for the lecture. Let's start the argument.

Chairman emeritus: Wayne Larrivee, former voice of the Bears and Bulls. Without peer. He should close his career in a minimum of at least six halls of fame.

The top 12 heavyweight list:
1. **HARRY CARAY, THE MAYOR OF RUSH STREET.** Just ask Budweiser and WGN what the hell he was worth.
2. **MARK GIANGRECO, WLS.** Gifted writer. A delivery beyond natural. I loved the days we hustled together at Channel 5.
3. **COREY MCPHERRIN, WFLD.** Underappreciated. Classic regular guy. Just shines on Cubs-Sox postgames after Fox Network telecasts.
4. **HAWK HARRELSON, VOICE OF THE WHITE SOX.** Yes, he tells way too many stories about Rico Petrocelli and Catfish Hunter. Great insight.

Great listen. Will give up on a telecast if the Sox are down 14–4 in the fifth inning.

5. **Len Kasper, WGN.** Can talk about Sammy Sosa or Sammy Haggar. Hasn't scratched the surface. You have to love a guy who tells you on air that he's crazy about the Psychedelic Furs.

6. **Mike North, Comcast SportsNet.** Gifted with the ability to print money. Mike understands the "industry" as well or better than any sportscaster I've ever met. Remarkable ability to determine what the public's thinking before the public knows it.

7. **Ron Santo, WGN color announcer.** Ron and the English language still haven't had that dinner they've been talking about. So what? The guy doesn't take himself seriously and advertisers adore him. Fans can't get enough of him.

8. **Jim Durham, former voice of the Bulls.** Too much talent for his own good. Just a fabulous play-by-play man. Rhythm, tempo—extraordinary. An agent on a power trip, looking for Marv Albert–type money, cost him his gig with the Bulls.

9. **Rich King.** The guy next door. Terribly underrated. If I ran WGN, I'd move Rich into the main event Monday through Friday and put Dan Roan on the taxi squad.

10. **Dan McNeil.** High energy. Will take on anybody. It's a slow year if he hasn't been suspended or pissed off at least three prominent sports execs. Knows how to move beer and cars. Survived working with me at WLUP.

11. **Bruce Wolf.** Earns extra credit for keeping his humor contemporary. Don't know if he's ever seen a locker room. Don't care. He's Henny Youngman/Jerry Seinfeld at 5:00 PM.

12. **Steve Stone.** Stoney knows he talks too much, but he just can't resist the lure of the open mic. There should be a rule that he's only allowed to ad-lib every other pitch and that he doesn't have to inform me every time he sees a guy throw the "cutter." Steve has done something I didn't think he could do: mesh with Hawk Harrelson. The two have tremendous synergy. Last but not least (and this is key), Stoney remains clairvoyant. I don't know if he packs tarot cards or a Ouija board, but his ability to guess right in game situations is unmatched.

Missed the cut: Jim Rose; Mike Adamale

On the rise (get the champagne ready!): Mark Silverman, ESPN 1000; Jonathan Hood; Ryan Chiaverini, WLS TV

The fast track: Carmen De Falco, ESPN 1000. Absolutely born to be a TV sports anchor.

The palooka division...AKA the bottom 12:

1. **GAIL FISHER, COMCAST SPORTSNET.** Should know the phrase "high and outside" by 2011.

2. **PAT TOMASULO.** WGN's answer to Beaver Cleaver.

3. **JEFF BLANZY.** Did you know he spent 11 years at WLS-TV?

4. **MARK MALONE.** Can you say rotten?

5. **BOB HILLMAN, CHANNEL 9.** If you can't recall his days at WGN, consider yourself the luckiest man on the face of the earth.

6. **DAN ROAN, CHANNEL 9.** It's a lock. He will complete his career at WGN having never broken a story.

7. **DAN BERNSTEIN, WSCR.** The kind of guy who can make you question why the human race exists.

8. **MEGAN MAWIKE, WBBM.** Shouldn't she be home doing the laundry?

9. **HUB ARKUSH, WSCR.** Spent years kissing McCaskey family butts.

10. **JOHNNY MORRIS, WBBM.** Retired. Look for him at Hawthorne. If he hadn't played for the Bears, he would have spent 32 years anchoring in Omaha.

11. **RYAN BAKER, WBBM.** Too much jock-sniffing. Too much yelling. The Cubs putting a tenth-rate pitcher on waivers doesn't really require busting one's spleen.

12. **NEIL FUNK.** Voice of the Bulls. Excites me to the point that I'll usually blow him off to watch one of the 14 stations running *Law and Order*.

84 *Think Lombardi, Paterno, DiMaggio, and Andretti—visit the National* ITALIAN AMERICAN *Sports Hall of Fame*

"In recognition of his untiring efforts and belief in our SCHOLARSHIP PROGRAM, we the scholarship committee on this 21st day of March, 1992, establish the Chet Coppock Scholarship to be given annually to a worthy student who is majoring in journalism and broadcasting."

—George Randazzo, president and founder,
the National Italian American Sports Hall of Fame

Jeez, I wonder if Patti Blagojevich ever got that kind of play?

How often do you hear this line? "Don't you miss the good old days when (a place or person of your choice) was easier, less complicated, and there were just no hassles or agendas?" That more or less sums up how I feel about the NIASHF. Over the years, I've had enough laughs, good times, and sincere handshakes at Hall of Fame events to fill the back end of a Yukon.

My most thrilling moment? On paper, it would have to be the opportunity to introduce the "Yankee Clipper," Joseph Paul DiMaggio, in the summer of 1998 during a celebration weekend for the Hall of Fame hero. Joe D. was nearing the end of the rope, and it was the last dinner gala he ever attended.

But DiMaggio doesn't run close to the top on my memory list. Everything you've heard about Joe is sadly true—10 times over. He could be mean-spirited, crotchety, and totally unsociable...and we're only talking about his good days.

Nothing could make DiMaggio happy. Joe was a royal pain in the ass for the Italian American Sports Hall of Fame. But Joe was a con man in pinstripes. He knew the "Hall" was forever on its hands and knees begging for the credibility and flair Joe brought to any gala he deemed worthy of his presence. So Randazzo and the Hall endured Joe. Believe me, it was a test of will—kind of like Marine basic training or dealing with TV and radio executives.

Joe's attorney and wingman, Morris Engleberg, would almost always precede him to any event "The Clipper" attended. Morris, another guy born to scowl, would remind the common folks in attendance that Mr. DiMaggio would not sign autographs or discuss his relationship with Marilyn Monroe. (Gosh, Joe, did you bang Marilyn?)

The Hall of Fame now sits across from the Piazza DiMaggio on Taylor Street in Chicago's Little Italy neighborhood. It occupies a building so architecturally dull, so structurally mundane, you figure the joint should really serve as home to the Winston and Strawn law firm.

Glance quickly, and you might think it's the east branch of Cook County jail.

But give me the good old days when the hall was a "back-pocket" operation. I loved helping induct Ron Santo and golf great Ken Venturi in 1983 and welcoming Mary Lou Retton in '84, the year she achieved Olympic glory. Those people lived in the moment. They dripped with pride over their Italian heritage.

The Hall itself was freelance and festive. Randazzo was running the place out of a simple, old-fashioned storefront in Elmwood Park. And—this is hysterical—the joint had been donated by the late Chicago crime boss Jackie "The Lackey" Cerone.

Chet is joined by Carmen Salvino, Mike Ditka, and Tony La Russa at a National Italian American Sports Hall of Fame event.

The Hall will deny this emphatically, but part of the NIASHF charm has been its association with wise guys. Get used to it. It is a fact of life. People love to rub elbows with mob characters. Look at *The Godfather.* We're far more intrigued by Santino Corleone than we are by the Cover 2. Cerone, Tony "Big Tuna" Accardo, and John "No Nose" DiFranzo are among the subterranean luminaries who've been involved with the Hall over the years. Some, of course, have gone to that last great shakedown in the sky.

I can recall years I brought TV crews to NIASHF functions and was reminded by organizers, "Don't shoot tables 2, 10, 24, and 31." That wasn't coach speak. That was a reminder that "the boys" appreciated not being seen on camera.

My gosh, one year—it had to be 1983—"The Tuna's" grandson Eric Kumerow was named the Hall of Fame's Prep Athlete of the Year. It wasn't a fix, a three dollar bill, or a set up. Eric was a fabulous football player at Fenwick who eventually attended Ohio State. The kid could flat out play. Following his tour with the Buckeyes, he was a first-round pick by the Miami Dolphins. He also had a brief fling with the Bears.

In the late 1980s, the Hall made a near-fatal decision. It jumped Grand Avenue and moved to Arlington Heights. The place occupied a beautiful chunk of land with grass as green as the fairways at Medinah. The location was also about as tourist heavy as the South Pole.

You talk about off the beaten path. If a family or group showed up at the "Hall" in Arlington, you figured they'd blown a couple of left turns looking for the Art Institute. However, there were some good times in Arlington. I recall tag-teaming with ex-Bear Doug Buffone to induct Franco Harris during one ceremony. We tossed the love to Tony Esposito at the same induction.

The Taylor Street move has been, I suppose, beneficial for Team Randazzo. The building is dull on the outside, but dramatic, even dazzling, on the inside.

My beef with the Hall? It's far too political. Jerry Colangelo, the Phoenix sports entrepreneur, hooked up with Randazzo about 10 years ago. Colangelo is a brilliant man. But if you're looking for belly laughs, boy, have you got the wrong guy.

Quite frankly, Jerry's presence makes the Hall feel like a library waiting to collect overdue history books. But there is little doubt Colangelo has kept Randazzo in business.

Stop by the Hall. Sit back and just gaze at Rocky Marciano's boxing gloves, or artifacts from Vince Lombardi and Alan "The Horse" Ameche. Mario and Michael Andretti's race cars are fabulous.

I don't want to give away the whole package.

Just take an hour out and enjoy the phenomenal athletic heritage of Italian Americans. Even Charles Atlas—real name: Angelo Siciliano—is an inductee. Remember Charles? He became a global heavyweight with his famous magazine ads selling young boys on how he could manufacture 98-pound weaklings into longshoremen or nightclub bouncers in just four short weeks.

Quite frankly, the Hall is so filthy rich in trophies, robes, shoulder pads, pictures, posters, plaques, and sweat pants that the place probably has more stuff in the basement or storage than it has on display.

Hey, you'll see a game-worn robe from "Macho Man" Savage, aka Randall Mario Poffo.

Don't worry about long waits to get in. They just don't happen. Trust me, you'll enjoy the Hall. The cover charge is cab-fare money.

85 Call the SUN-TIMES. Tell them to make RICHARD ROEPER a sports columnist

This is going to be short and sweet—a one-foot putt, no break.

Richard Roeper is a very eclectic and gifted writer. Whether he's serving up Angelia Jolie, another Cubs collapse, the Rolling Stones in concert, or some guy in Elgin who set a world record for snow shoveling, Roeper is always a quick, lively read.

I've only questioned Richard once—and this has merit. Years ago, he began a column by talking about a long walk he was taking while listening to Vanilla Ice. Ice, Ice baby? Heaven help us, baby.

So why should Roeper change a thing? Did you know that Rich is a White Sox season ticket holder? Hell, he even authored a book *Sox and the City*, a great read that begins with the south siders' historic 1967 collapse and closes with the Sox winning the bundle in 2005.

Roeper also likes big-time poker. He doesn't need to be schooled on flush draws and bad beats. I'm convinced he'd love to play Matt Damon's "Michael McDermott" character in a sequel to *Rounders*. Think about that—a sequel to *Rounders*. Teddy KGB, played with such hostility by John Malkovich, and McDermott get their long-awaited rematch.

What am I suggesting? I'm not trying to bust anybody's chops, but the *Sun-Times* sports section has become very light. The paper only has one bona fide, in-your-face sports columnist—Rick Telander. Rick's been named Illinois Sportswriter of the Year so many times, the award should be retired. But the fact is, his truly great work was done in the 1980s when he was policing college athletics for *Sports Illustrated*. Telander's 1987 piece on rampant steroid use with the South Carolina football team remains one of the two or three greatest pieces of investigative journalism I've ever seen in any publication.

Now, we can tag team Roeper with Telander. Why? Let me count the ways.

Don't tell me it wouldn't be great to have Richard bring a fresh slant to Halas Hall. I don't know if he knows a damn thing about the "Hawkeye offense," but I do know this: Roeper covers people.

If he can bring Al Pacino to life, maybe, just for the hell of it, he could inject some life into Lovie Smith. If Roeper had heard "Brother Lovie" moan, "Kyle is our quarterback" more than twice, I bet he would have thrown his notepad up in disgust and told Smith to try something different—new material.

He might get Rashied Davis to admit that his hands are made out of Smucker's Jelly. You know, so maybe the lambs who purchase season tickets ever year have some idea what Davis is thinking about when balls go sailing past his numbers.

I'd love to see Roeper chat it up with Tyrus Thomas. He might just ask him this very unusual question: "Don't you feel like you're stealing money?"

Put Roeper on Derrick Rose, professional wrestling, Jerry Reinsdorf, the Blackhawks, Lou Piniella, and Channel 5's Peggy Kusinski. Roeper would bring new "meat" to the local sports landscape.

Rich is a busy man. He's carved out a hugely lucrative niche as a movie reviewer. Good lord, he has to see about 50 films a month and probably 15 of those have subtitles. Let's face it. Nothing says fun like Harvey Keitel in a French-language film. Or Nicolas Cage working another flick with a hopeless script that represents a 118-minute license to sleep.

Rich may welcome the change. Wait till he finds out the green room at the *Tonight Show* is bigger than the Cubs locker room.

Richard, talk to the *Sun-Times* brass. It's not like your paper's circulation is booming. I've grown bone weary watching "Quick Hits" waste a page running photos of Anna Kournikova or the Florida A & M cheerleaders.

Give sports a workout. Not for your sake—for our sake.

86 *Meet the ultimate uninvited guest...* Jerry "THE CRASHER" Berliant

Okay, quiet on the set. Cue the actors. We're "rolling film" at Rod Laver Stadium in Melbourne for the windup of the Australian Open. You notice this well-dressed guy, closer to 70 than he is to 60, with what appears to be a salon-type tan, involved in an animated discussion with security.

Our guy is trying to explain to the gendarmes that, while he doesn't have anything resembling a ticket or a credential, he should be given immediate entry to center court and the high-end seats to have forced conversations with, you know, Ben Affleck, some Australian millionaires, and, maybe, Chrissie Evert or Paul McCartney.

Meet Jerry "the Crasher" Berliant, Chicago's godfather of gate crashing.

You don't know "the Crasher"? What rock have you been hiding under? Trust me. You've seen Jerry—you just don't know it.

For years, with no discernable job or source of income or place to go, Jerry has shown up uninvited at sports events, cocktail parties, grand openings, and charity functions with absolutely nothing resembling an invitation or ticket.

If Jim McMahon is signing autographs at a Kmart in Carbondale, Jerry will likely be in the house. He won't introduce himself to McMahon. That's not Jerry's style. "Berls" will treat Mac as if he went to high school with him and this is their first meeting since they played volleyball last Tuesday.

I'll take a wild guess that Jerry's irritated people in at least 10 different countries. "Crasher" was once busted by the heat in Denver for trying to barge his way into the Pepsi Center with phony credentials to watch an NCAA tournament game.

Here's the CliffsNotes examination on Jerry "the Crasher."

Years ago, he conned his way into the Hubert H. Humphrey Mortuary to watch the Bears play the Vikings. The stands weren't good enough for "Crash." So he just walked down by the visitors' bench. Bears officials, led by P.R. Chief Kenny Valdiserri, saw Jerry from the press box and had him tossed out. End of issue, right?

Oh, please. About seven minutes later, Berliant was back on the scene—sitting in the press box.

Jerry used to work for a living. He was an attorney. But he got in a jam with the Feds back in the '80s and lost his license in the legendary "Greylord" judicial bribery scandal. That's part of Jerry's intrigue.

Nobody knows what the hell Berliant does for a living. How he jets to Super Bowls, the Cannes Film Festival, the Bob Hope Desert Classic, the Final Four, or any prime-time Las Vegas boxing match with no apparent source of income is a mystery.

There are always rumors about Jerry. A bundle of people think he works undercover for the Internal Revenue Service.

Jerry and I haven't spoken in years. He got ticked at me when I was emceeing a charity event honoring Tony La Russa at the Westin Hotel. As the party was nearing its close, I told the crowd that, "We should feel blessed. Jerry Berliant has crashed our dinner. We're on the map."

This is Berliant at his best. Jay Blunk, a great friend and vice president of the Blackhawks, got married at the Art Institute. A gala like that had to have "the Crasher" drooling. You got it. Jerry crashed Blunk's wedding.

Now, go back to 1978. I'm in New Orleans for what turned out to be a lousy fight between Muhammad Ali and Leon Spinks. A few hours before the undercard, I'm spinning Berliant yarns at a joint on Bourbon Street about "the Legend of the Crasher."

Nobody's buying. Everybody says I'm nuts.

I said, "Trust me. I guarantee you will see him at the Dome." Sure enough, as I entered the building, the first guy I saw was Jerry. Somehow, some way he had scored credentials to both the Ali and Spinks dressing rooms.

> *"I knew the Cub convention was a hit when Jerry crashed us during our third year."*
>
> —John McDonough, president of the
> Blackhawks and former Cubs exec

Jerry always turns up on "radio row" at the Super Bowl. He'll just go from table to table, station to station, hoping somebody gives him the time of day.

Dave Abrams runs Skybox on Sheffield. He tossed in this nugget. One night at the Allstate Arena, during a Notre Dame–DePaul basketball game, former Blue Demons A.D. Bill Bradshaw had Jerry bounced from his seat three rows behind the De Paul bench because, well, he just didn't have a ticket. What else is new?

Security put the grip on Jerry and tossed him out of the building. Less than 10 minutes later, Berliant was back in the house—three rows behind the Notre Dame bench. You've got to give Jerry bonus points for consistency.

Berliant turns up on camera all the time. The year War Emblem won the Kentucky Derby, he was waving wildly to the ABC cameras while he stood next to War Emblem's trainer, Bob Baffert.

We go back to the summer of 1976. The last College All-Star Game is being played at Soldier Field. On game day, Chet Forte, who was on board to direct the game for ABC, called a luncheon with a handful of guys who were going to be directly involved in the show.

I was in the house because I was handling public address. There were some real A-list people at this lunch…and some guys who couldn't get arrested at their Elks Club meetings. So Forte suggested that everyone introduced themselves. This is classic. Here we go: Cooper Rollow, *Chicago Tribune*…Lee Grossccup, ABC Sports…Ara Parseghian….Chuck Noll…Jerry Berliant…and so on and so forth.

Nobody said a word. But after the gathering, Forte asked me, "Who the hell was that guy?" I gave Forte the lowdown on Jerry and his response was, "That was Jerry the Crasher? I've hears about that guy for years."

Berliant's museum piece? He crashed Prince Charles' wedding to Princess Diana.

Gate crashing really isn't that tough. It's not an art form. If you're wearing a suit, maybe toting a briefcase, and walk with a stride that says, "Don't fuck with me…I'm here on urgent business," almost any event can be crashed.

Trust me—Jerry is living proof that easing past a couple of 19-year-old ushers doesn't require any particular degree of genius.

87 Coppock's ALL-CHICAGO, All-Star, three-deep roster of GO-TO GUYS designed for would-be TALK SHOWS

This is a lock. At any given time, I'm convinced there are at least 127,000 guys in the Chicago area who would junk their jobs, their security, and their IRAs—and without question, their wives—to become sports talk show hosts.

If you're one of those guys, here's my advice. Learn to work cheap. The big- bread days, which peaked back in the late '80s and early '90s, are darn near gone. Blame it on radio consolidation and general managers who figure that "talent" isn't nearly as important as a good table at Carmine's on Rush Street.

I'll give you my All-Star lineup in just a few minutes. But, first—and this is hardly unusual—I have a little story I want to throw in your lap.

I was the first on-air guy The Score tried to hire before the station launched back in 1992. A nerd named Seth Mason approached me about jumping the remainder of my contract with WMVP to be his number-one guy on what he swore would be the greatest thing to hit radio since the invention of the "cough button."

There were two reasons I didn't buy.

One, I felt a deep sense of loyalty to Larry Wert, the top gun at WMVP and, quite frankly, Mason had the kind of personality that reminded me of a turtle lying on its back. He was so dull, so listless, I had no doubt he'd lose an energy contest head to head against Tutankhamun.

It didn't help that Seth wined and dined me in the palatial luxury of the Golden Nugget Pancake House on Diversey Avenue. My guess was anybody that cheap would be a world-class pain in the ass if I submitted an expense sheet from the Super Bowl that included a dinner receipt that ran over 13 bucks.

But Mason wasn't a dummy. As we talked, he asked me how I was able to book so many guests on my 'MVP show. Being an idiot, I fell for the bait.

I told him you had to have go-to guys, people you can call at the eleventh hour who always deliver solid radio. I reeled off names like Doug Buffone and Brian Hanley along with a "cast of thousands." I told him to hire Tom Shaer and put him in morning drive.

Mason still owes me a consulting fee. He tagged virtually every guy I listed. Shaer, by the way, became his first morning guy.

Anyway, so much for Mason. I hope Seth finally broke down and got that personality transplant. I'm certain it would have done wonders for his golf swing.

Here is the Coppock list of go-to guys based on the last 30 years. Hell, I could go back to the late '60s, but I'm deeply concerned about losing our precious 18-to-34 demo.

FIRST TEAM

Michael Keller Ditka. Absolutely the King of the Hill. I loved hosting his radio show the first four years he coached the Bears. Never used the passive when he could throw a right uppercut. Best quote? On the Monday after Mike and the Bears turned New England into Barbie dolls in Super Bowl XX, Mike said on air, "We could have put up 60 points on those guys, but I wanted to be decent about things."

Kevin Butler, former Bears kicker. Used to call Kevin Matthews and Steve Dahl while the Bears were meeting or practicing. What the hell else is a kicker going to do before a club gives its special teams the time of day? Kevin was outrageous. He never tried to hide his dislike for the McCaskeys. Once told me on air that after Ditka got on him for missing a kick, he looked Mike right in the eye and said, "Go ahead and cut me. You know you can't find anybody better than I am." Loved to negotiate his contracts on-air.

Dallas Green, former Cubs general manager. Loud, obnoxious, lovable, and always direct. All you had to do with Dallas was throw out a line and watch him carry the ball. Green thrived on playing bad cop with his ballclub to the point of brutality. Just couldn't stand his employers at the Tribune Company.

Harry Caray, White Sox and Cubs announcer. Once had the gall to tell me didn't see himself as "controversial." That's the kind of cool that reminds me Harry once called White Sox President Eddie Einhorn a "lyin' bastard." He knew during his WGN years that every time he appeared on my radio show, he was violating the terms of his contract. Harry interpreted that to mean he would do my show, or any fuckin' show in the city, whenever he damn well felt like it.

Larry Bowa, Cubs shortstop. Perpetually angry and pissed off. Just the kind of guy you want to liven up the act. Had a big chunk of Jake LaMotta in his personality. I always figured "Bow" knew my side of the street as well as I did. I wanted heat and Larry always threw fastballs. Just a great guy.

SECOND TEAM

Dave McGinnis, former Bears linebackers coach. I'll go to my grave missing the Friday nights when "Mac" would break down Bears games on my show. He never said anything that ranked with, "Give me liberty or seven additional games with the Detroit Lions," but he offered something that very few guys can: He was totally conversational. Dave gave every listener the impression that he was putting them in the huddle without really saying anything of dramatic substance. McGinnis defines the word "class."

Eddie Einhorn, White Sox honcho. No kidding. This is on the square. Before Ditka caught fire with the Bears, Eddie may have been the most talked-about sports figure in Chicago. He just lived to be on the air. Always had great stories. I remember sitting with Eddie at Wrestlemania IX in Las Vegas back in 1993. Einhorn was a rare bird who felt just as comfortable talking about the "upside" of "Hillbilly Jim" or the "Bushwhackers" as he did about Lamar Hoyt and Juice Cruz.

Lester Munson, legal expert for ESPN. We first hooked up back in '92 when Mike Tyson was on trial for raping beauty contestant Desiree Washington. Munson joined us almost every night during the proceedings. Lester became A-plus material the night he told me that Vincent Fuller, the strutting Washington, D.C., peacock, was doing a miserable job defending Tyson. Lester is unsurpassed when it comes to breaking down sports law. Gives great, concise 35-second answers.

Brian Hanley, *Sun-Times* writer and Score sports talk show host. I began using Brian on *Coppock on Sports* around 1991. I loved his wise-ass approach. He just loved to clobber anybody and everybody. Hated the bullshit aspects of sports. Had one of the greatest lines I've ever heard after the funeral of Princess Diana: "When Elton John was singing about Di, he played 'Good-Bye England's Rose.' When he saw Queen Elizabeth, he played 'The Bitch is Back.'"

Dan Hampton, former Bears defensive end and tackle. "Hamp" was a living, breathing sound bite. He swore allegiance to Buddy Ryan, the ex-Bears defensive coordinator, but everybody else was fair game. Hampton should really occupy the Howie Long chair on Fox Network's NFL coverage. The reasons are simple. Hampton is a trip to the fun house with a shot of Absolut vodka. Howie always looks like he'd much rather be back at his Virginia estate planting tulips.

Jeff Torborg, former White Sox manager. A stand-up guy. His first year on the south side was hell. He just didn't have any players, but we made that our story. We talked with Jeff virtually every day and found him candid and compelling. It's a rarity when you can get a manager to politely say his 25-man roster should really be playing Double A ball out of Chattanooga.

HONORABLE MENTION

Doug Collins, former Bulls coach. I hosted his Monday night show for a couple of years. Forget about wearing emotions on his sleeve—Doug's body was wall-to-wall nerve endings. You want Collins at his best? One night at the Stadium during a ballgame, some nut case wearing purple sunglasses behind the Bulls bench kept on screaming at Doug to "put in a scorer." Later in the game, Doug finally screamed back, "I haven't got a scorer, ya stupid fuck head." You live for guys like that.

DENTISTRY AND PODIATRY have changed over the years, so why should sports radio be stagnant? The principal reason things don't change is that general managers like Jim Pastor at ESPN 1000 won't think out of the box—in fact, they treat the box like it's the Old Testament. Still, I love the game, and let's be realistic: I'm not the kind of guy you want to call when you need a plumber, and I have no clue how to sell life insurance.

88 *The* BEST STEAKS IN CHICAGO *and a peek at the "big names"—welcome to dinner at* GIBSON'S

"Kobe Bryant came in for one dinner one night and lunch the following day. He likes his steaks pink on the inside. Beyonce just loves the grilled shrimp."

—Mohammad Sekhani, waiter deluxe at Gibson's

My last name is Coppock. That tells you the obvious. I'm not big on caviar or escargot. When I go out for a dinner, I want a big-time steak—a 16-ouncer—with great sides and a dessert that's a lock to make me feel guilty as hell the following day.

So what? I have a very forgiving nature.

Gibson's covers all the tabs. It's a steakhouse, a joint. The martinis are a ticket to the NBA Finals. Let me give you a little warm-up on Chicago's premiere see-and-be-seen restaurant.

Sid Luckman could lay claim to be Gibson's godfather. The legendary Chicago Bears quarterback did the bulk of the leg work to throw the doors open. In other words, Sid—a guy with no more than 300,000 pals—raised the majority of the investment capital to get the place rolling.

Luckman also had a big-time taste for desserts. He lobbied his Gibson's sidekick Steve Lombardo to create a post-dinner menu that would generate great taste and—this is key—"talkability."

How, do I explain this? Sid and Steve took the dessert concept to a whole new level. For example, the carrot cake at Gibson's is roughly half the size of a bowling ball. Don't feel bad if you can't get through the sucker solo. I doubt the entire Washington Redskins offensive line could finish off the whole dish.

"Derek Jeter and Billy Joel are like family."

—Cathy O'Malley,
Gibson's managing general partner, 1996–98

Go back to the Bulls' second championship run. Dennis Rodman was in the place all the time. "The Worm" knew that he could always call his pals at Gibson's, at the height of the evening rush, and get his entourage served. Even if the entourage was 35 people with 24 decked out in boas.

"Dennis really helped us a great deal," Cathy recalls. "He was always a perfect gentleman."

One New Year's Eve night, Rodman put in a call to get his buddies fed. New Year's at Gibson's is a tough ticket. There are three servings. All tables must be cleared by 9:30 for the midnight revelers. Cathy told "The Worm" he'd only have 45 minutes to dine. Worm said no problem. He brought his flock in and never tried to bend the rules. Dennis was in and out in 45 minutes.

Table 61 is the main event at Gibson's for a very simple reason. It's where Frank Sinatra used to dine when he stopped by the place. "The Chairman" was easy to handle. He just insisted that Jack Daniels keep flowing through his cocktail glass.

Okay, I know you're curious. This is too easy. Yes, Michael Jordan and Charles Barkley have been in too many times to count. In fact, it's a test to find an NBA player over the past 10 years who hasn't found his way to this Rush Street landmark.

Mohammad, Cathy, and I are sitting at "61" as the stories and memories begin to flow. You learn why Cowboys owner Jerry Jones would love to have a Gibson's in Dallas. You find out just how frequently Billy Joel stops in for a visit. Mohammad tells you that he always advises Tommy Harris, the Bears on-again, off-again defensive tackle on how his steak should be cooked.

If you're scoring at home, Rod Stewart and Johnny Depp are both big on pork chops. Steven Tyler, the ageless Areosmith rocker, has been known to walk in by himself to sample fish dishes.

Joe DiMaggio, the captain of my All-Miserable team, loved Gibson's. Surprisingly, Cathy says, "Joe was never a problem. He was just very quiet."

The 2006 Bears were regulars. They stopped in after virtually every home game. One night, a bunch of Bears and other diners noticed a familiar face at a nearby table. It was Al Davis, the Oakland Raider kingpin.

This is no secret: Gibson's caters to the big names. What restaurant wouldn't love to have Shaquille O'Neal and Jack Nicholson chomping on shrimp cocktail? But the restaurant doesn't take advantage of the big names. In fact, the approach is very low-key.

The wait staff is advised to be polite but not fawn over the celebs. The concept is very simple. Make the jock—or the *entire* cast from *Ocean's Twelve*—feel like normal diners. Respect their privacy.

That means, from time to time, a patron has to be told that no, he can't walk over and ask Terry Bradshaw to relive the "Immaculate Reception." Or it wouldn't be good form to ask Howie Long if he likes the Eagles—plus 7—on Sunday versus the Seattle Seahawks.

"Of course we love the buzz. But we will not allow a so-called star to have his dinner interrupted."

—Cathy "O"

Gibson's never drops items to the press. It just isn't done. If you read that Mel Gibson and Reggie Miller dined at separate tables at Gibson's, the item had to come from some P.R. flack or, from time to time, a customer.

The restaurant lives by an unwritten rule, a rule that's also a way of life at the star-studded East Bank Club. Of course, you can gawk, but no photographs, no autographs. Respect every customer's right to be left alone.

That includes Sandra Bullock. One night, Ms. Bullock discoed her way through a reception in the "42 Club" to get to the establishment's private restroom. My sources tell me she wasn't pinched—or bothered.

If you want to wait outside the restaurant to approach a big name, that's your business. And that's exactly what a bundle of people did not long ago when the Brazilian National Soccer Team was at "Gibby's."

Mention Muhammad Ali to the staff at Gibson's and tears begin to well. The Champ came in one night to celebrate his birthday. One of his family members advised Cathy about Ali's condition, warning her that depending upon his medication, Muhammad could be the life of the party or a $100 parking ticket.

Ali enjoyed his dinner and was then given the same treatment all "celebrating" customers receive: a rousing edition of Gibson's truncated version of "Happy Birthday." Ali broke down and cried. Other customers were so moved by Muhammad's natural display of emotion, they gave him a 10-minute standing ovation.

Sportscaster Kevin Harlan loves the place as does his brother/agent Bryan.

Former NBA Coaches Chuck Daly, Mike Fratello, and and Dick Versace are "family members."

A tip: Don't walk into Gibson's without cash or a credit card. The place has "human" radar that detects the phonies. In fact, Cathy has an elaborate set of hand signals to advise the staff that the guy over there trying to bug the Beach Boys should be thrown out—sooner rather than later.

Crashers get the bum's rush. That's a way of life at Gibson's.

One night, Cathy looked at a barrel-chested guy and said, "Aren't you the Cy Young fellow?" She was on target. It was Roger Clemens.

Gibson's. It is big shoulders and big portions. It's one helluva joint.

Late entry: Did I mention that Hulk Hogan and Jake "The Snake" Roberts have both been in more than once?

Just checking.

89 Bar none, the EAST BANK is the most dynamic HEALTH CLUB in America

History book time—this goes back about 24 or 25 years. I was jogging on the quarter-mile track on the third level of the East Bank Club. No, I was no threat to post a top-10 finish in the New York Marathon, but I could still turn out 8-minute miles.

I was about halfway through my grind when this diminutive blonde pulled up by my side and asked if she could "pace" with me. Damn if it wasn't Madonna Louise Ciccone. As I recall, Madonna was in town to hype her *Like a Virgin* album while playing the UIC Pavilion.

The East Bank Club is a 450,000-square-foot, five-level multidimensional slice of birthday cake that occupies two city blocks. The club is private but also open to anyone who's prepared to pay a $500 entry fee along with $170 a month in dues. Your food and beverage tab will actually determine what kind of workout your wallet gets.

Don't get any wild ideas about walking in the front door and saying, "Hi, guys, I was in the area and thought I might try your masters swim class" unless you're on board as the guest of a member. Simply put, the place is without peer. It makes the Reebok Club in New York look like a grade-school playground.

EBC's features include four swimming pools—two indoor and two outdoor. The cardiovascular area, which at 20,000 square feet is roughly the same size of the Playboy Mansion, features more than 400 pieces of cardiovascular and strength-building equipment. Throw in an indoor driving range and classes in everything from step aerobics to tai chi to hip-hop dance, and you have a place that really hasn't missed any bases.

Going back in time, this wasn't the original game plan. When the club opened in 1980, its "big play," or so it seemed, was tennis. Weights weren't given much attention. Boy, has the the club done a 180.

The Chet Coppock All-Showbiz All-East-Bank Hall of Fame Guest List:
1. *Robert DeNiro*
2. *Al Pacino*
3. *John Travolta*
4. *Bruce Springsteen*
5. *Tony Bennett*

Here is something I've always admired about EBC. The club operates with an unwritten rule about "celebs." You can stare politely to a point at a so-called "star," but, for gosh sakes, don't get any wild ideas about walking up to Oprah Winfrey or Michael Jordan to chat about how much you hate your ComEd bill.

Did I mention there are 35 personal fitness instructors, eight indoor tennis courts, and five restaurants? The Sunday brunch is a legit five stars. I know the restaurants inside and out. One, I've been a member roughly half my life. Two, I eat breakfast at EBC damn near every morning. You know if Coppock breaks bread daily at a certain place, the prices must be reasonable.

EBC did more than create a health spa that also features a hair-styling salon, a spinning studio with 60 bikes, and a full-size basketball court with another half dozen mini half-courts. This club has done what most health facilities just don't do. It gives back. Yes, East Bank takes in a great deal of money, but it has never just sat back and said, "Who cares about the lady who drives in from Deerfield, we got ours?"

EBC continuously puts money back into the facility. There are always new wrinkles. The rehabilitation center on the fourth floor is just tremendous.

No kidding, I think there are East Bank investors who become cramped with anxiety if they find out find out that an elliptical machine or a recumbent bike is two weeks out of date.

> *Barack Obama recently pulled his membership. He loves the place. But for security reasons, the club would almost have to shut down if the Commander in Chief showed up for a quick 45-minute session of hoops. Barack has two great assets as a ballplayer. One, he takes the rock to the hoop with determination. Two, he confuses the average weekend player because he's left-handed.*

Obama dropped into the club for a quickie workout the night he won the Illinois Primary. Nobody bugged him for autographs or cell phone pics. In fact, as he strode through the second floor—my hangout—there was just a mild ripple of applause. Barack sheepishly grinned when one member referred to him as "Mr. President."

DID I MENTION that White Sox General Manager Kenny Williams works out like he's training for a triathalon? Or that Sox hitting coach Greg Walker loves to pound the weights?

Back in the 1980s, ex-Cub Bill Buckner lived at EBC during the off-season. It used to kill me to watch the poor guy run on ankles that were like jelly. Bill would just chew himself up. You think Buck didn't take his workouts seriously? No kidding, if he climbed on a scale after a 90-minute sweat session and weighed an ounce over 180 pounds, he'd go right back and start working out again.

East Bank doesn't run on kindness and class alone. It has to cost a bundle just to turn the lights on; 650 employees are currently on the payroll. That includes 150 in the fitness department alone.

Peter Noone, the pride and joy of Herman's Hermits, turned up at East Bank regularly when he was playing the lead in The Pirates of Penzance *at the Chicago Theatre. Donny Osmond worked out at EBC virtually every morning when he was working the lead in* Joseph and the Amazing Technicolor Dreamcoat *at the Chicago.*

Of course, there's a card-carrying golf pro on hand to help you keep your head down and your left arm straight.

Social and business networking is just off the charts. Seven-figure deals are going down at this club all the time. East Bank just exudes power. The club is also blessed with a staff that is above and beyond courteous. Employees with attitudes just don't cut it.

Yes, that's Curley "Boo" Johnson, the ex-Harlem Globetrotter, playing one-on-one hoops with former Bulls guard Randy Brown up on four.

You know, I have a very simple ambition in life. I don't want to shoot 63 or set a world record in the 200 meters, I just want 10 percent of the action on the club's top-floor summer deck. Between food and exotic cocktails, I could buy a Bentley in about three weeks.

Time to take a deep breath. I'll take a wild guess that I've given you a mild impression that I'm crazy about the East Bank. Good lord, I've had the same locker for 28 years—13 more years than I went to grammar school, high school, and college combined.

In fact, it is "snack" time. I'm headed to the bar in the second-floor grill to knock down a cheeseburger and shoot the breeze with my guy David, the bartender and the self-proclaimed Rockin' Moroccan. I'll follow that up with a little steam and a trip to the whirlpool.

East Bank...second to none, baby.

90 JIM O'DONNELL, *just too gifted for his own damn good*

What say we gab about a truly gifted sports writer? His name is Jim O'Donnell. He turns up about once a month in the *Sun-Times*. The question: Why is his playing time so limited?

> *"O'Donnell is a brilliant journalistic writer with a remarkable ability to take seemingly irrelevant items and make them dramatic."*
> —Lester Munson, legal expert, ESPN

So why isn't James a star? A hapless hack like Steve Rosenbloom at the *Tribune*, on his best day, couldn't compete with O'D. Rosenbloom writes blogs and offers his spin on poker. I just can't wait for my Sunday "reward" when Steve explains to me just how Doyle "Texas Dolly" Brunson won a $10,000 "buy-in" at the Orleans Hotel in Vegas in 1997 by flopping a pair of deuces.

In the early '80s, O'Donnell looked like a guy on the fast track. Jim was working at the *Daily Herald* and turning out a TV-radio sports column that has never been matched by any writer in the so-called metropolitan area. It was a must-read. Every Thursday morning—this was years before either Albert Gore or Albert Belle, whoever, created the internet—I had to get my mitts on O'D's column.

Believe me, I wasn't the only TV-radio guy doing the same thing.

O'D scared the hell out of station general managers and program directors. Jim didn't play with a butter knife. When O'D was hostile about some kind of media injustice or some guy he though was mailing it in, or some clown who just plain sucked on the air, he preferred to use a switchblade—aimed directly at the adam's apple.

O'Donnell was a little Hunter S. Thompson going Gonzo, a little bit Rick Telander, and a ton of Johnny Carson monologues. He was flat-out great.

Later, O'Donnell had a brief run with the long-gone *National Sports Daily*, a newspaper that was top-heavy with "star" writers from around the country. The paper's potential, under the direction of Frank Deford, seemed limitless. There was, however, a minor problem. The *National*'s investment team choked on red ink after about 18 months of publication.

O'Donnell wasn't with the *National* from wire to wire. Legend, make that fact, has it that the *National* drop-kicked Jim when he showed up so late to cover a White Sox game at old Comiskey Park that basically all he really saw was an official scorer say "Time of the game: Two hours and 36 minutes."

Jim was also dealing with some personal issues. Call it too many long nights, if you know what I mean. Eventually, he landed at the *Sun-Times*.

Jim's big on the ponies, a legitimate turf expert. His Kentucky Derby work every May—he usually spends a full week in Louisville—is appointment reading. You can feel the back stretch at Churchill Downs, you can feel the "live money" when O'D's rocking.

O'Donnell's byline will also show up on some college football and basketball and he'll do a few "take-outs," long-form pieces that are—almost inevitably—tremendous.

O'D's imagination is world-class. A few years ago, he was covering an event in St. Louis. It might have been a Missouri Valley Conference ballgame. Whatever.

Anyway, O'D intertwined his advance on the game with Johnnie Johnson, Chuck Berry's longtime piano player. It wasn't just special or unique, it was good enough material to show up in *The New Yorker*. You have to have nimble fingers and an accelerated slab of gray matter to make a Johnnie Johnson concept like that work. Jim can do it in his sleep. He's that good.

O'D should be a columnist. Until further notice, I just don't think he's ever wanted the grind badly enough. Why, I don't know. But for whatever reason, Jim is a staff writer. It is sad.

Maybe O'D doesn't want the pressure. Maybe past mistakes have made editors reluctant to let him play long ball. My gut tells me it's lack of interest on O'Donnell's part. If O'D had Rick Telander's mentality, he'd be dangerous. Telander, a terrific defensive back during his college days at Northwestern, oozes killer instinct. Rick, an O'Donnell teammate at the *Sun-Times*, is Hall of Fame material. Telander is consistently solid and fair.

Let's go back 21 years.

Every 19-year-old would-be journalist should be required to read this piece. In 1988, Telander, writing for *Sports Illustrated*, authored a story that was downright brilliant on rampant steroid use by the South Carolina football team. When you read the piece, you knew Telander had produced historic material.

Rick was working new turf. The article wasn't just special, it moved mountains. The piece outright changed, forever, the approach the sports media took to investigative journalism. Telander wasn't big on writing about cheerleaders. He wanted to touch nerve endings, he wanted to feel sweat, and he did—with remarkable flair.

O'Donnell doesn't have Telander's journalistic instincts or his assertiveness. They just aren't there. Hell, Rick's authored eight books, including the masterpiece *Heaven is a Playground*. He's written enough magazine pieces to fill an Olympic-sized swimming pool.

But O'D can more than turn a phrase going head-to-head with Rick.

Jim O'Donnell, columnist? It sounds like a play. Is he good but not good enough? No, until further notice, I just don't think Jim wants the lead role badly enough. Believe me, I'm not alone on that thought.

Don't ask me why O'D isn't a main eventer. I just know Jim's mug should be appearing in one of the downtown dailies four days a week.

O'D, get a column.

91 *Hot Reads*—SEVEN GUYS *who will be* NEWSMAKERS *over the next three years*

"Carry the battle to them. Don't let them bring it to you. Put them on the defensive."

—Harry S. Truman

Quite frankly, I'm not sure why I tossed that quote in the mix…it just feels right for the assembled cast of characters we're going to chat about this morning. Have faith in the fat kid. These guys are "players."

1. **JAY BLUNK, SENIOR VICE PRESIDENT, CHICAGO BLACKHAWKS** Blunk, gracefully, allows the spotlight to magnify his boss John McDonough. Yet the two are remarkably intertwined. When Mac made his move from Cubs Park to the United Center, you knew it was only a matter of time before he bopped Jay on speed dial to try and bring life to a franchise that had actually drifted past "toe-tag" status.

   The two share great respect and friendship. Hey, McDonough can be a test. I think the world of John, but you don't accomplish what he's achieved by entering the ring with 24-ounce gloves. Behind the scenes, John will use the open verbal fist without hesitation if he sees the slightest degree of stupidity.

   No, Blunk is not a "yes" man. Forget about it. The fact is, these two guys love to play their own in-house game of one-upsmanship.

"Jay is fiercely competitive…neither one of us is patient, nor do we ever settle. We challenge each other every day."

—John McDonough

Blunk counters: "We enjoy trying to one-up each other." John is a Bob Knight–type perfectionist. At the end of the day, your DNA determines whether you can enjoy that style. "We're both driven by that same fear that someday we won't be able to pull off a miracle," explains Blunk.

The betting line: Within 24 months, Blunk will be running his own major sports franchise. That is, of course, unless he succeeds Mac as the man in charge of the Hawks. I've already determined that John should be tapped to replace Bud Selig the instant the MLB boss decides he can live without Michael Weiner and the arrogance of the MLB players.

2. **DAVID HAUGH, *CHICAGO TRIBUNE*** He arrived at the *Trib* via the *South Bend Tribune* in 2003 and was immediately given star treatment. Many are surprised that he's not the paper's lead sports columnist.

Nobody but nobody has covered the Bears with greater determination and guts than Haugh since the glory days of Ed Stone. That goes back a mere 35 years. David has done what few guys can do or dare to do. Haugh's fought like a young Roy Jones Jr. against the McCaskey handcuffs…handcuffs that turn "beat men" into "house men."

WBBM TV would be wise to unload excess baggage and tag-team Haugh with Ryan Baker.

Prediction: Limitless potential. D.H. will be the *Tribune's* marquee writer. Down the road, he will be one of America's premiere dot com writers while co-hosting his own radio show.

3. **MIKE NORTH, HOST, *MONSTERS OF THE MIDWAY*, COMCAST** Keep this in mind: Mike's greatest asset isn't his on-air ability. First and foremost, North is a businessman. He understands the envy, jealousy, and hostility that frequently exists between management and talent as well or better than a young Steve Dahl. He also keeps a running list of guys who owe him favors.

WSCR can never repay North for the "branding" and cash he delivered. Mike loves to test himself.

Next phase: Mike has seen the sports talk future; it is on the Web. You will see North, the entrepreneur, in high gear over the next two years. Webio was a minor glitch and no fault of Mike's.

4. **CARMEN DEFALCO, ESPN RADIO TALK SHOW HOST** Blessed with tremendous presence, great pipes, and world-class likability. People line up to tell him he should be on the tube.

The book: Tell his agent to start warming up in the bullpen. DeFalco is going to be a white-hot commodity. Yes, he will gravitate to TV—but not in Chicago—by 2011.

5. **TED PHILLIPS, PRESIDENT, CHICAGO BEARS** Turns up in public about as often as Greta Garbo or an O.J. Simpson fan club member. Has "Teddy–Notre Dame" been napping since he landed the Bears that sweeter-than-sweet lease deal at Soldier Field?

The future: The cards are about to shuffle. By the end of 2011, Phillips assumes a senior advisory capacity, while Virginia McCaskey hands the keys to the Bears to son Brian. That's a fairly substantial position upgrade. Brian, the rare McCaskey who speaks a seldom-used language called "Common Sense," began his tour with the ballclub as an assistant trainer back in 1982.

6. **PAT FITZGERALD, HEAD FOOTBALL COACH, NORTHWESTERN** The play: Patrick takes flight after the 2010 Big 10 season. I know his love affair with Evanston is overwhelming, but he won't be able to resist the cash or the high-wire challenge of running a Big 12 club.

7. **DERRICK ROSE, POINT GUARD, CHICAGO BULLS** No, he is not the next Magic Johnson, Michael Jordan, Kobe Bryant, or LeBron James. Derrick is a jackrabbit on the floor. Don't you love to watch Rose freeze rival defenses who have to respect his ability to penetrate—what else can they do?—as he stops and pops the eight-foot jumper?

Is there a "charisma" issue? Yes. Rose is just too low-key off the court. His quotes don't resonate. You don't sell the NBA around a Derrick Rose. Can Rose become a national darling? Only if he lands a common annual enemy. Even Jordan needed the Pistons.

The ticket: D-Rose isn't so low-key that he won't eventually be able to buy his own two-seat airplane. By 2010, he's dreaming about max-out NBA money—if he isn't talking out loud about it now.

92 *Damn, I loved* CHICAGO STADIUM

Joni Mitchell was right. They paved paradise and put up a parking lot.

The United Center always reminds me of the Oak Brook mall. It's only a matter of time before the U.C. has a Polo menswear shop.

> *"Do you know the greatest accomplishment in Chicago Stadium history? It has to be the fact that no one ever died of suffocation, pressing flesh on flesh, walking up the tiny stairwells from the Madison Street level to the second balcony."*
>
> —Chet Coppock

This will sound so syrupy, so drippy, you have the go-ahead to slam this book against your 61" flat-screen, surround-sound TV.

Be my guest.

First off, I know you won't believe this. The most special night I ever spent in Chicago Stadium didn't involved football, basketball, boxing, professional wrestling, or the circus. No, we have to crack the archives on this one.

Shortly after Olga Korbut galvanized Munich—and no more than 97 other foreign countries—in the 1972 Olympics, she appeared at the "Big Barn" with the USSR Gymnastics team. Olga, like a little girl running through a field of dandelions, and her teammates were spectacular. Naturally, they were honored with bouquets of roses upon conclusion of their performance.

That's when Olga the promoter took over. This just couldn't have been scripted. Korbut and friends marched around the Stadium for about 15 minutes, waving, smiling, and actually creating international goodwill.

I can still see Mayor Daley—not the new breed, the guy who mattered—clapping rhythmically to the background music as Olga spread her unique brand of joy and happiness. Unofficially, there were 18,500 people crying; another 275 were sobbing with joy.

Madison Square Garden had the "name." Chicago Stadium had the funk, the sweat, and the charm that weren't just part of the bricks and mortar, The fact is, funk, sweat, and charm *were* the bricks and mortar.

I don't dislike the United Center. I just want those fabulous Stadium mezzanine seats, 25 to 30 rows off the ice or the hardwood, that provided unmatched sight lines.

Give me back that Hawks "home dressing room" on the east side of the building. I don't want to suggest it was a tad cramped, but it always struck me as being just about the size of the fruit cellar where Norman Bates was, shall we say, "exposed" in the climactic scene of *Psycho*.

This is age exposure on my part, but what the hell? My AARP card is in good standing. Every time I walk from the press parking lots to the U.C., I always remind myself of at least one great night from my Chicago Stadium memory bank.

Let's go back to the good old days—back before San Francisco gave us Jefferson Airplane and Moby Grape. The arena seats, the low-level, high-end boards at the old "Barn," were special. Call them bragging-rights tickets.

Arthur Wirtz, the enormous and immensely frightening man who ran the place, didn't want any guys wandering in from a long day at the local car wash to occupy his precious deluxe seating. There was signage that prohibited gentlemen from sitting in the "Scout" seats—I don't know what the hell to call them—without a dress jacket. Women were forbidden to wear slacks.

This was obviously before Brooke Shields was hustling her way to commercial fame by telling the TV world that nothing came between her and her Calvin Klein jeans. Christ, do you realize that ad campaign is 28 years old?

The stadium didn't have luxury suites. That would have been like putting the Hope Diamond or a Von Furstenberg evening gown on Amy Winehouse.

You got an over/under up on how long Ms. Winehouse will live?

I want to see Mr. Goalie Glenn Hall stopping Gordie Howe from point-blank range. Eddie "The Eagle" Belfour, with a kick save to stop Wayne Gretzky or maybe the Wings' Steve Yzerman on a two-on-one versus Darren Pang. I want bad boy Al Secord to deck a half-dozen New York Rangers—in the first period.

Frank Sinatra, Elvis Presley, Led Zeppelin—saw them all at the Barn.

Really, can you compare The Matadors to Old Blue Eyes?

I miss the old front court, baseline-to-baseline press row at the Stadium. I used to wait every night for Bob Logan, longtime Bulls beat writer for the *Tribune*, to bring his dessert back from the media room—a 14-foot by 16-foot prison cell—for the second half. "Lefty's" ties generally looked like they'd gone 15 rounds with baking soda.

But, jeez, did the Stadium pressroom have great prime rib.

Fifty-yard-line press seating was eventually clobbered for at least one damn good reason. It gave Bulls investor Burt Ury and his family extra legroom while they sat four feet from the sidelines. I get a great kick out of watching Karen

Ury, Burt's daughter, during Bulls games. She sets world records going out of her way to avoid watching the Luvabulls.

Believe me, the way Grand High Exalted Mystic Ruler Jerry Reinsdorf runs the U.C., he'd be thrilled if the press could be kept captive on Warren Boulevard.

I want to see my guy, the late Norm Van Lier, press an elbow in Dave DeBusschere's rib cage, Darryl Dawkins' sternum, and Tiny Archibald's collarbones.

Give me Michael Jordan, 1984 through 1993, driving on Dennis Rodman during a big Bulls-Piston game when, so help me Chuck Daly, the Stadium would vibrate with energy and splattered emotion.

Only a nut does this. On a Monday in 1974, I accepted a job at WISH-TV in Indianapolis. I was so thrilled about the new opportunity and the chance to work with a young Jane Pauley, I flew into my car, established a land-speed record, and got to the Barn in time to see Crosby, Stills, Nash & Young.

Bulls vs. Knicks, May 13, 1994, subtitled "Scottie Pippen Can Be a World-Class Jerk": That was the last event I attended at my beloved arena. You know the plot line. Game 3 of the Eastern Conference finals. New York came up with a demonic fourth-quarter rally to tie the Bulls with 1.3 seconds left.

Phil Jackson didn't call Pippen's number during the timeout. "No Tippin'" Pippen refuses to go back on the floor. Toni Kucoc drains the game-winning jumper that lifts the Bulls to victory. If I'd been Jackson, I would have crushed Pippen's head against the Mighty Stadium Organ. Phil, being just so Zen, chose instead to give Scottie a copy of *Socrates Live at the House of Blues*.

I've educated my young ones about Harvey Wittenberg, the Hawk's long-time public address announcer. Harvey's nasal twang when he told the house, "Assisted by Chico Maki" was an event that sounded like it had been touched by something ethereal.

Go back to 1992 and think hoops. Tell your young ones how the Bulls, down a bundle in Game 6 of the NBA main event, rallied to knock off Clyde Drexler and Portland to win their second consecutive World Championship— the only title the Bulls ever zipped up in Chicago.

Tell your kids that Jeremy Roenik was a Chicago Stadium player, a goal-scoring kid with a mean streak. Alex Zhamnoff was a United Center player—too dainty for his own good.

Explain this to the young ones. You could always "do business" at the Stadium back in the day. Twenty bucks at a ticket window on a sold out-game night to a "union" ticket vendor would generally cover the tab. Ten bucks at a turnstile leading to the balconies was a better option back in the '60s.

Memo to the United Center: Begin building character. I have several suggestions:

- Don't paint the place for a minimum of 36 years.
- Cut out all advertising in the men's room.
- Turn 14 luxury suites on the second level into individual shrines to the joint that used to be next door.
- Eliminate desserts for suite holders.
- Spread sawdust all over the second-level concourse.
- Put up a 10-foot-by-15-foot picture of Montreal's John Ferguson beating the living hell out of the Hawks' Eric Nesterenko. (Hey, the Canadiens always busted our hearts.)

That will be a start. Let's reconvene in 30 years.

Wait—a late entry. I used to do this all the time. Let fans smuggle in six-packs of beer to any and all games.

93 MR. REINSDORF, *let's settle the tabs. Life is just too damn short*

March 2, 2009. It's a bitterly cold morning in Chicago. The almighty hawk is working overtime. The knife-like wind feels so fierce a tourist would swear that it's actually a hypodermic needle being ripped through his cheekbone.

Fourth Presbyterian Church at Michigan and Chestnut streets is just a magnificent place to worship and be reflective. This current "Fourth Pres" has offered a spiritual haven for almost a century. The place opened in 1914.

It's a glorious cathedral. If you let your imagination free flow, the east, or Lake Michigan, side of the church looks nothing if not like the old west wall at Chicago Stadium. The church has an intimacy that the old barn provided on those majestic Friday nights back in the early '70s when "The Moving Van," Jerry Sloan, "Butter" Love, "Long" Tom Boerwinkle, and Chet "The Jet" Walker would slug it out with "Big O" Robertson, a young Ferdinand Lewis Alcindor, and the Milwaukee Bucks.

"Norm was the Pied Piper. He was the chairman of the board of the NBA's original 'Rat Pack.' Dutch was Mick Jagger with razor-blade

elbows. He was Zeppelin's Robert Plant dribbling across the time-line to square off with Walt Frazier."

—Coppock

Maybe I'm selfish. Maybe I shouldn't jot down a few ad-libs from the eulogy I was asked to deliver for Norman Allan Van Lier III, Basketball's "Father of Funk."

I'll let you decide.

I've begun to walk south on the avenue, the brisk wind at my back. Don't ask me why, but I just cannot get Jerry Reinsdorf off my mind. Jerry and I haven't talked in years. I want to clean off the blackboard or "X" my name off his black list. The Sox and Bulls boss doesn't have the most forgiving nature in the world. Privately, many in his inner sanctum will tell you he is "terribly oversensitive."

Consider this an open letter:

Chet and Jerry Reinsdorf, on the field at Comiskey prior to a 1981 White Sox game.

Dear Jerry,

You probably know this better than I do. To coin the old phraseology, a death really means nothing if it doesn't make you look at what you have standing right before you.

Jerry, admit it, there was a time when you and I considered ourselves friends. I respected you and I felt you reciprocated as a gentleman.

I was in the hotel suite to see you and your pal Eddie Einhorn grab the keys to the White Sox from Bill Veeck out by O'Hare Field back on January 29, 1981. I remember how pissed Veeck was when you and Eddie talked about bringing "class" to Comiskey Park.

I vividly recall telling "Joe Fan" that you guys were the "real deal, home run hitters" when you brought "Pudge" Fisk and, with him, a filet mignon-type credibility to old Comiskey Park.

Jerry, you won't recall this, but I do. I remember how you just beamed, a few weeks later, when you told me about seeing Jackie Robinson break baseball's color line at your beloved Ebbets field.

You're darn right I take credit for nicknaming you and Eddie "The Sunshine Boys."

Reinsdorf attended legendary Erasmus High School in the Flatbush section of Brooklyn, New York. You talk about a big-time guest list. Erasmus is simply the East Coast answer to Winnetka's historic New Trier.

Hall of Fame QB Sid Luckman, fight promoter Bob Arum, Oakland Raider czar Al Davis, Neil Diamond, Barbara Stanwick, and some chick named Barbra Streisand all attended your alma mater. You're right, J.R., I left out Roger Kahn, who authored *The Boys of Summer*, a book that deified Gil Hodges, "Duke" Snyder, Carl Furillo, "Pee Wee," Preacher Roe, and, of course, Jackie. Those were your "bums."

Jerry, we both loved Harry Heller. For years, Harry was the man behind the local B'nai B'rith Sports Lodge. Damn right I was honored to present you with some kind of achievement award at one of Harry's annual events back in '82 or '83.

In 1985, the NBA—this had to be desperation—hired me to emcee the annual Slam Dunk Contest at its All-Star Weekend in Indianapolis. Call it the right place at the right time. Since I was going to work "Rim Wrecker's Ball," WMAQ radio sent me down Friday morning to broadcast my show live from the Hyatt Regency. The Hyatt was the "official" All-Star hotel.

Boy, did I get lucky. Just around the corner that Friday afternoon at the Embassy Suites, you settled up with the Johnathan Kovler group to buy the Bulls. The kindest, sweetest, most-humane words I can use to describe Kovler's reign of terror are, well, hopeless or helpless with an added dose of hapless.

Jerry, I remember you asked me what I thought about the package. This explains why you built the United Center and I disregard calls from American Express. I told you in no uncertain terms you had overpaid at around $15 million to land a franchise, but that "in time, you'll make a few bucks on the back end." I was never good with numbers.

Here's what I'm driving at, Jerry. Check your calendar. We're way overdue to break bread. I know there are things you want to say to me. I know you feel you have justification to think I'm a son of a bitch.

Sorry, pal, you have to stand in line to call me a son of a bitch.

I remember when you gave Jerry Krause the greatest career break of his life. You gave him a second chance to run the Bulls.

Krause was at a crossroads. He was holding a clipboard and a stopwatch while he scouted baseball players in every hick town known to man. This memory has lingered for 30-plus years. I can still see Jerry sitting in old Busch Stadium in Indianapolis on a 93-degree night checking out a left-hander. I swear, Krause was perspiring so badly he looked like he'd just stepped out of a riverbed.

Take note: Krause is also the guy who convinced you and the White Sox to peddle Lamarr Hoyt to San Diego for Oswaldo Jose (Barrios) Guillen, a 155-pound inferno with no big-league experience. Sweet deal. Hoyt had issues. Ozzie gave your club backbone at shortstop and, eventually, World Series rings.

This goes back to the late 1980s. I asked you on a Bulls post-game show if you ever thought you were the victim of anti-Semitism. I wasn't grandstanding. I really felt there was a big chunk of Chicago that was anti-Reinsdorf because of your religious beliefs.

I thought I was giving you a platform, Jerry. Maybe I was wrong. Maybe you thought I was showboating. I don't know. Maybe I never will.

I'll admit this. I've said a bundle of times that you aren't Branch Rickey or Red Auerbach. You aren't a judge of talent. That doesn't mean I think you're a car thief. I'm just telling the truth.

You're a deal maker. You make cash speak your language. It's an art form.

Jerry, don't you get it? Every kid at the University of Chicago Business School would kill to be you!

It is time to close the sermon.

I could go on, Jerry, but I hope you see my point. I've always admired you. When you played tough guy, bad cop, and militant owner during the 1994–95 baseball labor stoppage, I didn't bum rap you, I bum rapped Don Fehr.

You're going to swear this is a hustle. My eyes were more than misty when Paul Konerko handed you that "final out" baseball at your 2005 downtown World Series victory celebration. You see, you really aren't a basketball man. You loved the "Jordan Six," but in your heart of hearts, you prefer the seventh-inning stretch to a fast break with numbers.

Jerry, are you happy? Are you content? Just curious? On the surface, you've lived your life on scholarship. But who knows? Some people got angry with me when I dared to tell them that Norm was fighting depression and felt more than a little "vacant" when he left us.

I have to run, Jerry. Let's meet. Let's joke about the night you busted Jimmy Piersall but had the stones to come on the 10:00 news with me from the camera basket at Comiskey Park.

I'll cover the lunch. You bring the post-game cigars. I have no agenda. I just want to hear what's on your mind. You never know. Maybe we do have common ground. It's worth 45 minutes to find out. Ya can't do any worse with me than you did with Tim Floyd.

—Coppock

94 The food is going to surprise you— visit the ESPN ZONE Chicago

Okay, let's establish the ground rules. Guys, if you're looking for that willowy 5'7" blonde with spiked heels who's on the corporate fast track, head to the Viagra Triangle. Ladies, if you're looking for that 32-year-old stallion who's in line for a major-league family inheritance and wouldn't be caught dead without a $215 Brioni tie, head for the Viagra Triangle. You know the joints, Gibson's, Jilly's, Tavern on Rush, and the Luxe bar, for openers.

> *"We don't serve bar food. People who come into our place expecting second-rate food are going to be surprised. They won't be disappointed by what we serve."*
> —Brian Hanover, regional marketing manager at the Zone

I love to check out films at the AMC Theatre at 600 N. Michigan. My only complaint is the ride from the escalator up to the box office can you leave you dizzy. If you're coming off a bender, the ride can leave you befuddled or thinking, "I'll accept the firing squad instead of the popcorn."

On the way out, I usually choose from one of two immediate options. I love the gumbo and the Cajun food at Heaven on Seven two floors down from the theater, but I have a second location, just across the street, where I like to kick back and tell lies.

That's where the Zone comes into play. I don't know how many times I've sipped a Diet Coke at the main-floor bar while watching my pal Mike Wilbon straight-arm Tony Kornheiser on *Pardon the Interruption.*

> *"Chet, for better or worse...and probably for worse...you are responsible for whatever electronic career I have."*
>
> —Mike Wilbon,
> ESPN and the *Washington Post*

I admit it. I have no shame. In a different world, I'd be a hooker.

Let's get down to the basics. The Zone is not a "sports bar" in the classic sense. In other words, when you walk into the East Ohio Street location, don't expect to overdose on Jim McMahon jerseys or 2,000 pictures of Sammy Sosa—whiffing at a breaking ball low and away.

First and foremost, this is about the ESPN brand. This is about the ESPN image as the network that took a living corpse like Rich Eisen and turned him into a broadcast heavyweight.

The Blackhawks montage is spectacular. The "Bulls eye" lightbox will raise your eyebrows and you have to see the miniature Wrigley Field made with 7,081 Wrigley chewing gum wrappers. Cubs Park, 7,081 chewing gum wrappers? Trust me, the guy who designed this sucker is either a genius or had too much time on his hands or—maybe, just maybe—both.

Girls, who wants a standard, old-fashioned ladies' room? Check out the Zone's ladies' rest stop. It features "lockers" dedicated to, among others Oprah, Bonnie Blair, and, this is sort of cool, Dennis Rodman. Of course, the Worm's locker has a pair of boas.

Sure, there are TV monitors galore, including a 15-foot-wide screen in the plush second-floor mahogany bar and grill. That second floor is where the upscale crowd can get back in the ballgame.

Here's the drill. Mr. Right, after you've talked up your 7-series BMW and the party you attended with Kid Rock's road manager, tell your new female chum that you want to do something a little out of the ordinary.

Cab it over to the Zone and slide into one of the second-floor booths. The leather is just as smooth and cushy as it can be. Your new love of the week (or night) will be all about "infatuation" as the two of you swallow up the private surround sound. Throw in your own TV monitor that can let you slide from the Hawks and Wings to Kobe Bryant versus Carmelo Anthony to ESPN Classic bowling, and you may be 12 hours away from securing a marriage license.

Check out the sirloin steak with a big baked potato and the string beans. After dinner, you go for the kill.

Invite this babe—who no doubt makes more dough than you do—down to the "Dream Seats" to hold hands and sip Drambuie while you catch the second half of North Carolina at Wake Forest. Really, does it get any sexier?

Now it is time for the big play. Gaze lovingly at your filly and ask her the most time-honored business question known to man: "Your place or mine?"

Who says I'm not an incurable romantic?

Moms and dads, we haven't forgotten about you. The Zone prices are very moderate. You aren't going to get gouged when you order the baby back ribs or a cheeseburger for your 12-year-old son. My recommendation: the chicken and avocado wrap.

Things you should know about the Zone:

Let little Tommy and his buddy go up to the game room and play the video machines until their hands give out. The P.T.A. will love this. Your little one isn't going to go leaping into an avalanche of video hostility where he'll be playing the role of a C.I.A agent trying to off a third-world terrorist. Forget about him rattling the knobs on a "Compton, California, Heavyweight Championship" where he's a Blood trying to save his turf from a rival member of the Crips.

Need a meeting room? The Zone has you covered. There's a great 50-seat second-floor area to talk about your third-quarter losses. The room features a mural titled *Tinker to Sayers to Grace*. It's a truly gorgeous tribute to Chicago sports, designed by Stephanie Roberts, that covers three walls. Stephanie earned extra credit on my scorecard by illustrating Red Grange, "The Galloping Ghost," in his trademark raccoon coat. Plus, Stephanie picked up 50 bonus points for creating a visual feel that George Halas' trademark fedora is drifting its way toward heaven.

Is this place big on tourists? Hell, yes. When the Cardinals come to town, the joint becomes the Red Sea. But the Zone couldn't pay the freight to operate just off Michigan Avenue without a huge stream of "regulars." Business is brisk. On weekends, the place will serve as many as 1,500 customers a day.

The ESPN Zone isn't a $150 tab for dinner. It doesn't want to be. Or try to be.

So, Ms. Christian Dior, give Mr. Giorgio Armani a break. Let him have a solid meal, watch a ballgame, and play a few video games. It will be a win.

95 *The hip and the hipless—* OZZIE *vs.* ELLIOTT?

Okay, if I haven't got you totally confused—and by now you damn well should be—this should push you over the top. Years from now, when some biology teacher opens the time capsule and reads this book, his students will, no doubt, say, "Jeez, we thought Bernie Madoff was a fucking mess."

Sound the bell. Let's introduce the combatants in our makeshift mock epic. Oswaldo Guillen is the swaggering, cocksure, "make it funky" manager of the Chicago White Sox. Today, we're going to compare the "Blizzard"—his style and outrageous personality—to Elliott Harris, veteran columnist from the *Chicago Sun-Times*. Elliott, who authors the "Quick Hits" column, has the bold, brassy look of a guy who should be working as a ranger at a public golf course somewhere near Chattanooga, Tennessee.

Who is more engaging on a day-by-day basis? O.G. or E.H?

> *"Ozzie despises Cub culture. Guillen sees Cub fans and the guys who cover the team as a bunch of jilted lovers, especially when the [Cubs] get beat."*
>
> —Mark Gonzales, *Chicago Tribune* White Sox beat writer

Do you actually read "Quick Hits"? If so, you know the obvious. Harris isn't sleeping alone at night. He's shacked up with a life-size Anna Kournikova blow-up doll. Elliott's run so many "waste of time" photos of the little Russian tart, you have to wonder if Kournikova's P.R. people are sending him game-worn panties.

Guillen's theatre of improv has no boundaries. In fact, I'm not sure we know if Oswaldo can spell the word "boundaries." Ozzie's idea of great film-making is *Napoloen Dynamite*, a one hour and twenty-six minute hunk of slop that wouldn't challenge a nine-year-old's intellect.

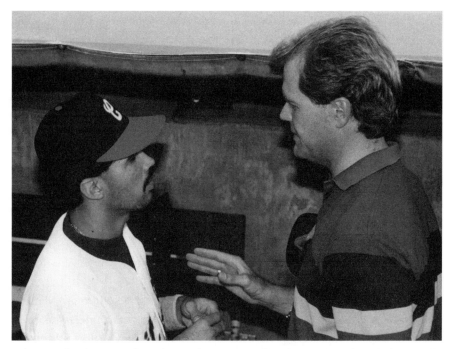

The mouths that roared—Chet and Ozzie Guillen doing what they do best in the Sox dugout.

You think that's dumb? Pal, Major League Baseball clubhouses are culturally a step below sixth grade. This has been diamond gospel for years: "If you can't belch, you can't play."

On March 4, 2009, good old "Quick Hits" left us spellbound when Elliott wrote—no kidding—"Friendly skies? Well, that concept might be tested when the Cubs and White Sox take the same United Airlines flight today to Las Vegas for their exhibition games."

That's the kind of stark journalism that reminds the greats of Truman Capote laboring to turn out *In Cold Blood*.

Ozzie is always on the prowl for the hot button. If the Sox have a couple of bad nights or drop five in a row, you know he'll find a target. As a rule, it's all in the name of taking the heat off his ballclub. Guillen's ability to deflect attention away from a collective slump is almost in a class by itself. His nickname should be "Red Herring."

"In 2005, the year we won it all, our club was ready to spit it up," recalls White Sox preacher/broadcaster "Hawk" Harrelson. "Ozzie took on somebody.

I can't recall who it was, but it shook our ass out of its lethargy. Really the only guy I've ever seen who can work the press like Ozzie was Earl Weaver at Baltimore. Earl had so much control over the media, his guys thought the press was their twenty-sixth man."

"Quick Hits" inspires the same kind of adrenaline rush, the same sense of urgency. Wait, something must be wrong, Elliott hasn't run a photo of himself with a WWE diva for at least three days.

Ozzie could never be a PGA golfer. He'd tell the guy holding the sign reading "Quiet Please" to fuck off.

"Quick Hits" continued its nonstop rush to the Pulitzer Prize on March 4, 2009. Uncle Elliott banging the keyboard—with flames in his eyes and burning passion in his heart—related a line he picked up from the Letterman show off the the show's website.

"It's is so cold that Alex Rodriguez's cousin was injecting Alex with hot cocoa."

You're right. Maybe the *Sun-Times* should rethink the entire Jay Mariotti issue. Mariotti defines the word "prick," but at least he was a prick who, from time to time, was fun to read. That is, until he'd turned out his 1,276th column on "The Jerrys."

On the 4th, Elliott also brightened up his section with his latest photo of the Chicago Shamrox cheerleaders. If Harris isn't on the Shamrox payroll, his agent should be on the phone—yesterday. Who cares if the "Rox" are out of business?

By the way, I just turned the Bulls game off. Anybody, I mean anybody, who wants to deck one of those morons carrying a "Noise" sign, urging millionaires in the 100-level seats to "cheer," don't worry about bail. I'll cover. Praise the Lord.

Maybe March 4 was just a rough day in the office for "Quick Hits." It has to be hell to spend 25 minutes a day researching a column that takes 14 minutes to write.

Hey, smartass, go back to March 3, 2009. Elliott was smoking, just ribald and frisky. He looked like a new-age Frank Deford. The guy was the second coming of Hunter S. Thompson. How about this killer: "The best thing about snow in March is knowing it won't be on the ground the next two or three months. And, if you're lucky, not even two or three days."

Someone want to remind the *Sun-Times*' answer to Amos McCoy that Jerry Reinsdorf and the White Sox lost their first homestand in 1982—full and complete—due to snow?

Go back to 2008. "Quick Hits" and Mark Vancil, a superb writer—with an assist from Grant DePorter, the big cheese at Harry Caray's restaurant—turned out "Hoodoo: Unraveling the 100-year mystery of the Chicago Cubs."

What mystery? Virtually ever year since Rogers Hornsby last worked the lineup card, the team has sucked—out loud. Think Cuno Barregan. Under 22? Think Alfonso Soriano playoff baseball.

If Vancil didn't write 92.5 percent of the book, call your cousin—yeah, that guy who knows the creeper who did the heavy work in the trial of of former *Sun-Times* thug Conrad Black and his tag-team partner, Lady Black.

If Ozzie ever writes a book, I suggest the following working title: *"Quick Hits" and 590 Other Things Less Impactful Than* Napoleon Dynamite. Subtitle: "Coppock Pokes Harris, Strictly Tongue in Cheek, with a Toothpick."

96 Screw the CURSE. Enjoy the cheezborgers, cheezborgers at the BILLY GOAT

Chicago has long been fertile ground for promoters. Think about "Barnum" Bill Veeck, Roller Derby founder Leo Seltzer, Grappling Godfather Bob Luce, Blackhawks President John McDonough, and Blackhawks Baron Arthur M. Wirtz for openers.

Don't think big Arthur wasn't one hell of a hustler. This overwhelming, barrel-chested man, whose personality had all the warmth of the Cook County Morgue, founded the Sonja Henie Ice Show—the forerunner to the Ice Capades and the Ice Follies—back in the 1930s.

Just why did Arthur decided to build a tour, a gimmick, around Sonja? Let me count the ways. One, it gave Sonja, a three-time Olympic champion and six-time European figure skating champ, something to do besides read her scrapbook. Two, it made Arthur, a guy who literally invented ways to make cash, a brand-new stream of revenue. Three, Arthur was nothing if not a visionary. Wirtz dreamed of the day his Ice Shows would screw up the Bulls and Blackhawks schedules during the month of February.

There is one promoter I've left out and, pal, he was a doozy. I would have killed to spend just 30 minutes with the late, great William "Billy Goat" Sianis. Let's do some curse-busting. Here's where I blow all the nonsense you've heard over the years about "The Cub Curse" sky-high.

Bank on this: Sianis wasn't thinking "curse" when he tried to enter Wrigley Field during Game 4 of the 1945 World Series between the Cubs and the Detroit Tigers, a pair of World War II clubs that really weren't very special. (Special? Antonio Alfonseca would have starred on the '45 Cubbies.) William was thinking about the big splash. He was looking for "pub."

Go back one year to 1944. This was really Sianis at his best. Shortly before he died, Jack Brickhouse, my ultimate broadcast hero and the godfather of my daughter Lyndsey, spun this yarn for me. I have no doubt it is on the square. Brick was a master storyteller.

Sianis ran a joint called the Lincoln Tavern right across the street from the old Chicago Stadium. You could almost stick your hand out the "Lincoln" and touch the beloved old barn. The Republican Party conducted its convention—subtitled: "There Isn't a Chance in Hell We Can Beat FDR"—at the Stadium in '44 and Billy welcomed the conservative knuckleheads to town with a sign on his place that read "No Republicans Allowed."

Who cares if Billy Sianis was a Democrat, a Green Party candidate, or if he yearned for the day that we'd all be blessed to have a Libertarian Party? Sianis knew this: His sign was going to create a spark. Republicans—you ever meet a Republican who isn't a tight ass?—demanded to be served. Meanwhile, Sianis walked off with a bundle of ink from the local Chicago dailies.

For the record, here we are at the '45 World Series and, son of a gun, the Cubs lead the frolics two games to one. Sianis arrives with a pair of boards, one for himself and one for his beloved goat, Murphy.

Billy knew what was going to happen. He was a sharpie. Ushers armed with Bronko Nagurski–type game faces and club boss P.K. Wrigley all denied the goat access. Speaking of tight-asses, P.K., in his day, made Alderman Dick Mell look like a young Jerry Lewis.

What about the proclamation? When Sianis screamed, "The Cubs ain't gonna win no more," I'm going to suggest that he just happened to be a good ad-libber—something you just don't see any more on 6 and 10 TV sports.

Anyway, you know the tale…the Tigers beat the Cubs that afternoon and went on to close out the series 4–3.

Hello, CURSE!

Eventually, Sianis's Lincoln Tavern became "The Billy Goat." Yes, I was in the old Madison Street "Goat" back in the early '60s. This was long—almost four decades—before the West Loop renaissance. The Sianis establishment was just a few blocks west of old "skid row," a living deathbed for winos, junkies, longshoremen, whores, bustouts, and, most notably, former sportscasters.

The Stadium itself sat hard in an area where you just didn't walk by yourself after dusk—or, for chrissakes, park in before dusk unless you wanted your tires slashed.

By 1964, "The Goat" had relocated to 435 N. Michigan Avenue. Tip time. Don't look down the avenue for "The Goat" after you've shopped at Nordstrom. The Chicago fixture, now run by ageless Sam Sianis, is downstairs on what most of us refer to as "Lower Wacker Drive."

Have some fun. Do you hate your mother-in-law? Is she a Milwaukee Brewers fan? Tell her next time she visits town to make it a point to visit the "Goat" on Upper Wacker. She'll probably wind up lapping Millennium Park.

Sam Sianis, the proprietor and Bill's nephew, is actually a very sprightly 73 years of age. He still works seven days a week. Sam's joint isn't a tribute to sports. It's a tiny, no-bells, no-whistles monument to what may well be the greatest newspaper town in American history. The walls are lined with photos of Mike Royko, Jack Griffin, Dave Condon, and Ray Sons, all magnificent writers.

Royko is simply the greatest urban columnist of all time.

New-age heavyweights, guys like the *Trib*'s John Kass and *Sun-Times* multimedia millionaire Richard Roeper are regular visitors. A tiny banner pays homage to a Chicago institution, the old City News Bureau, which was journalism finishing school for so many solid Chicago reporters.

> *The bureau broke the story on the St. Valentine's Day massacre back in 1929. The reporter on the scene played the story cautiously. He initially told his office that six people were reported to be seriously injured.*

If you're scoring at home, the Capone gang blew out six members of the rival "Bugs" Moran Army in what CBS-2's Howard Sudberry described as a "strong indication that both teams could land in the NFC playoffs."

Stop in and have a cheeseburger. No fries, "cheeps." Sam will bend your ear about the legendary *Saturday Night Live* routine that gave his place national recognition. He'll tell you that John Belushi and Dan Akroyd made the bit a pop-culture happening, but it was Don Novello, a local ad man, who created the concept.

Yes, the same Don Novello who became the classically funny "Father Guido Sarducci."

Go ahead, believe in the curse. However, if you insist on believing in this delicious myth, you're also under court order to believe Crane Kenny's fairytale that he's a "baseball man."

The "Goat" is no-frills. A six-foot palm plant in Sam's joint would seem as out of place as waiters in the Drake Hotel wearing Spiderman outfits.

I love the "Goat." The "Goat" is Chicago.

97 *Elevate your pulse rate, gaze at the opulence,* JOG *the* NORTH SHORE

Let me level with you. If you have a jealous nature—and who among us really doesn't?—this might not be your play. Chicago's North Shore is a world-class example of power, old money, inheritance, clout, social standing, debutante parties, and upstairs maids banking 65 grand a year.

But, my God, it is beautiful beyond words.

My book, my game. Playing the role of famed explorer Ponce de Leon—he discovered the single-wing—I have decided to show you runners in the house just how special, at times breathless, a jog down Sheridan Road can be.

Where do we start?

I chose Highland Park for a handful of reasons. A big chunk of the magnificent 1980 film *Ordinary People*, with Donald Sutherland as a baffled father, Mary Tyler Moore as a mother who doesn't know her ass from third base, and a young Tim Hutton was shot in this quaint little village.

We're heading south at a casual pace. If you aren't struck dumb by the massive Tudor and Colonial homes, you must be part of the Gates family or in need of a trip to Pearle Vision.

Keep in mind we aren't talking about a straight-line path. A large part of this journey's "expression" is the winding roads that—and this sounds so Dr. Phil—have you wondering what's around the next 400-year-old oak tree. Keep an eye on Rosewood Beach. The "Rose" closes the introductory phase of our journey. At this point, if you can't go any farther, do a 180 and go back to the Walker Brothers pancake joint on Central Avenue. Try the pecan cakes, heavy on the butter.

Vic Walker, one of the Walker Brothers' heirs, was one of my pals during my academically impotent days at New Trier High School. Unofficially, he was the only kid in my graduating class who had two Pontiac muscle cars and a motorcycle.

When I glide (who the hell am I kidding?) through Highland Park, I always have one vivid memory. I saw a young Janis Joplin at Ravinia, the gorgeous outdoor theatre, back in 1967, maybe '68. I love the blues, the delta sound. I love Muddy, B.B., Albert, and Buddy. But you ain't never heard fucking "raw-ass" blues until you've heard Janis belt "I Got Dem Old Kozmic Blues."

"Time keeps movin' on...friends, they turn away."

Alright, back to the ballgame. Shortly after you pass Ravinia, you'll begin to realize something very basic to the run. The over-under on bathrooms per home on Sheridan Road has to be 7. The number moves to 11 if the home has more than 24 rooms.

Soon, Glencoe turns up on path. Glencoe has one emotional issue. It doesn't think its "new" money is as traditional as Highland Park's "old" money. You talk about heavyweight cabbage. A bailout program in Glencoe is a guy in deep thought wondering if he should really buy a new hood ornament for his Bentley.

One of my other high-school chums was Glencoe resident Steve Kulp. His old man Bob was just terrific. Steve went to school somewhere in Arizona for about three good hours before following North Shore tradition: he took over the family cleaning business.

Now you go up and down the magnificent "Ravines." In my younger days—every New Trier kid did this...at least the ones with no brains—I used to go "skitching" in the ravines. Skitching was a quaint little game played on days with heavy snow. It didn't require a degree from Brown. All we did was hold on—by hand—to the back of our buddy's car bumper and enjoyed the ride while he tried to avoid putting his old man's Cadillac, or his own Chevy Camaro, into a ditch.

I really don't like all the "fun" we're having. I was raised in Northfield. In my early years, Northfield, just west of Winnetka, wasn't the North Shore—it was the Washington Senators. Every day I walked into New Trier, I was surprised that nobody told me to "grab a broom and go clean up the technical drawing department." Years of therapy, including time spent with Dick Jauron, still haven't cleaned out my emotional baggage.

As we slide from Glencoe into Winnetka, we slide into another level of opulence. Hollywood "ladies'" man Rock Hudson was a Winnetka resident. Fifties chicks in pedal pushers cooed over Rock. Boy, did his flacks have the audiences conned.

Winnetka is the tradition and elitism of New Trier and it's also the magnificence of the Christ Church, a chapel so Old World elegant, it looks like it was brought to the States by boat from Southport, Lancashire, in England. If you want a local angle, Christ Church would look "admirable and appropriate" in Albemarle County, Virginia.

I still feel blessed to have seen Dr. Martin Luther King speak in Winnetka at Skokie School back in 1965. Winnetka bridges to Kenilworth, a small town where children are required to wear formal attire to the playground. When people in Kenilworth "get down with their bad selves," they generally reach for Perry Como or, after a couple of belts, Jerry Vale. Legend has it that any resident driving a four-wheel vehicle that's more than two years old is generally asked to put up a "For Sale" sign.

At this point, we've gone through four unique villages, four different personalities, all bound by one common bond: phony income tax returns.

We also, no doubt, have seen homes that may "list" as high as $12 million. Heaven help the poor souls on Sheridan Road who have to get by in a four-bedroom house. They must feel like their lot in life is to make do in a mobile home.

Need a shrink anywhere near Sheridan Road? There can't be more than 4,000 of them available.

Eventually, Kenilworth transitions to Wilmette. This just kills me. Besides comic Bill Murray, pro wrestler Barry Horowitz—"The Brooklyn Brawler"—has called Wilmette home.

Slow the pace. Here is America's answer to the Taj Mahal. Gaze at the Bahai Temple, a majestic, vertical, religious masterpiece that is, by the way, open to all faiths. The guys who built the Bahai weren't thinking four-plus-ones in New Town. This ethereal structure, which never seems to gather a speck of dust, let alone dirt, took roughly 40 years, through the Depression and World War II, to construct. To call it one of the "Seven Wonders of Illinois" is an insult. This place is more dazzling than the Eiffel Tower or Camden Yards.

Next stop: Evanston, home, from time to time, to Marlon Brando, ABC's Charles Gibson, Pearl Jam's Eddie Vedder, and Grace Slick, the old "front babe" for 1960s groundbreakers Jefferson Airplane.

Our journey is about to reach the tape. We swing through the campus of Northwestern. Fraternity row sits on the west side of the street, future millionaires struggling with calculus are occasionally seen on the east side of the street. We close with Alice Millar Chapel at the south end of the campus.

Thanks for joining me. Hope you learned something. Now go make the run yourself. I'm visiting my therapist to discuss my overdue East Bank bill.

98 *Attend the Sun-Times Sports* COLLECTIBLES SHOW

"I've got one tip for you about 'autographs.' It's even money or better that any Joe DiMaggio baseball you buy is going to be a phony."

—Coppock

I'm not going to con you. I don't know the card show business backward and forward. In fact, I really don't understand why a guy or girl would want to spend big-time cash to get a signed mini-helmet from a social Bozo like Frank Thomas, or from a guy like Johnny Bench, who's about as friendly as your next-door neighbor's pet rattlesnake.

But I do have a little knowledge about the racket. I actually promoted a show, booked the guests, the whole nine yards at the world-famous Ramada Inn, adjacent to Kennedy Airport in Brooklyn, New York, back in the mid-1990s.

Put a qualifier on the word "promoted." I made one solid move that put the show over the top. I hooked up with Alan Rosen, the sports card legend, to serve as my advisor. I also lined up an investor since I figured it'd be crazy to put up my own dough.

Alan, aka Mr. Mint, aka "the cash machine" is mythical. "Mint" is the Babe Ruth of the card show business. You think he doesn't play long ball? Alan is notorious for carrying as much as two hundred grand in cash to shows in a briefcase. If he sees a deal he likes, he doesn't browse. He flashes the greenbacks.

So Rosen and I put a pretty decent card show together. We had Ron Guidry, "Goose" Gossage, Peter Edward Rose, and the inimitable "Macho Man" Randy Savage. For the record, Rose picked up 10 grand. Gossage and Guidry both fell in the $5,000 range. Savage was the home run. Randy was a pal. We'd done mutual favors for each other previously, so he agreed to fly up from his home in Treasure Island, Florida, for one first-class airline ticket. "Mach" waved all fees.

Warning: Most DiMaggio autographs are about as authentic as the forced smile Chet wears while greeting the Yankee Clipper.

Mr. Mint and I didn't turn the industry upside down, but we walked out in the black. We made some scratch. But I also learned a valuable lesson. If I had to front a card show six times a year, I wouldn't live to see my next birthday. The game is that tough.

> *"I think the biggest payout we ever had was $50,000 to Joe Dimaggio."*
>
> —Joe O'Neil, card show promoter and
> longtime ticket manager for the Chicago Bulls

Joe and his company, Pro Speakers, took over the *Sun-Times* card show in its infancy back in the early '90s. He remembers paying Walter Payton just

$5,000 to be the "go-to guy" at his first show. Over the years, Joe and his part-ner George Johnson built the *Sun-Times* show into spectacles—dotted with lists of athletes extraodinaire.

O'Neil admits he doesn't really know just why people will stand in line for an hour to get a signature from Brook Robinson, but he does have an idea. "People want their five or 10 seconds of fame with an athlete they idolize," Joe says. "It used to amaze me that the same people would turn up at our shows every time we ran."

From his home base in Chestnut Hill, New Jersey, Rosen—with 33 years in the industry—is still trying to figure the whole scenario out. "I have no idea why the people show up," Mint says in his clipped, matter-of-fact style. "I can only guess that people want to feel proximity to Joe Namath, Joe Montana, or Brian Urlacher."

So why do I attend these cards shows? Simple, I love the vendor tables. I shop for the unusual. For example, I bought a huge mounted photo of Philadelphia Eagles Hall of Famer Chuck Bednarik. Not just any photo. A knockout pic of Chuck after he'd flattened the Giants' Frank Gifford at Yankee Stadium back on November 20, 1960. The picture is inscribed with this smarmy message: "Sorry Frank…the fucking game is over. Chuck Bednarick, HOF."

A few years earlier, I bought a gorgeous poster advertising St. Louis Billikens basketball with play-by-play man Harry Caray. I'm also a sucker for vintage pro wrestling magazines. If Nature Boy Buddy Rogers or Killer Kowalski is on the cover, I buy.

Here's the red flag on DiMaggio. When I was doing my New York TV gig back in the mid-'90s, I had lunch with a very prominent New York talent attor-ney. I mean, this guy was the goods. His client list over the years included Robert De Niro and Luther Vandross.

He'd also been a bat boy years earlier when Joe D. was wearing Yankees pinstripes. And he didn't hesitate to tell me that part of his daily routine included signing "Joe DiMaggio" on about four dozen baseballs.

DiMaggio items aren't the only three dollar bills around. You'd have to work overtime to find any big-name athlete whose signature hasn't been forged on either a jersey or an 8 x 10 photo.

Caveat emptor is the bottom line. The *Sun-Times* card shows are tremen-dous. You want a signature from Matt Forte or Scott Fletcher—go for it. My advice, check out the vendor tables. Hang out with Mr. Mint. Simply put: The event is always worth the price of admission.

Just avoid all things DiMaggio, please.

99 WHEN I KICK, *I expect the following to be arranged...*

Jack Brickhouse left me keeled over years ago when he told me this. The Brick said that when he died, he "wanted every son of a bitch who ever hated my guts to have to stand around the funeral parlor and talk about what a great guy I was." Brick could say that with, or without, tongue in cheek for one very simple reason. Just like Harry, Jack knew he'd play to a full house when he left us—and he did.

Me? I want the same Brickhouse drill. That doesn't guarantee that Holy Name Cathedral will be half full, let alone S.R.O. But I'm reasonably sure we should draw enough curiosity seekers and tourists to fill the lobby at Boston Blackies over on Grand Avenue.

In the meantime, since I plan to work until the age of 90, I have a short list of items I'd like to see and do.

I want to ring announce for Vince McMahon, just one more time.

And this is important. I want to do the buildup on James Harris, recognized by millions as "Kamala the Ugandan Head Hunter." James, attended by his handler "Kin Shee," was always the perfect heel to get the crowd buzzed for the arrival of Hulk Hogan. If we can't get Kamala, I'll settle for Koko B. Ware or the unforgettable King Kong Bundy.

I want all members of the Mayor's office and the City Council to wear buttons that read "We're on the take. You know we're on the take. What's the big deal?" That might have to be condensed.

There's not a chance in hell this next request will pass the school board. I want a return of P.R. men like Ben Bentley.

Ben, whose real last name was Goldberg, hyped anybody and everybody from Rocky Marciano to Norm Van Lier. Bennie knew the game and the territory. He set global records for feeding items to columnists.

He understood that press releases were generally a waste of time. Ben was about face-to-face relationships and tipping you that "between us, Ali is gonna take that fight with Ken Norton, and [Dick] Motta's had it with the Kennedy McIntosh kid."

You know what "Media Relations" is today?

It's Lou Hernandez, a decent young guy, working his way up the White Sox P.R. ladder, sitting in on a meeting I had recently with club marketing chief

Brooks Boyer. Lou looked so concerned, so alarmed during our totally non-threatening gab session, I fully expected him to have me strip-searched for "tough questions."

Lou didn't see a guy in for laughs, he saw a 250-pound gorilla with hair restoration. I don't blame the kid. I blame the Republican Party and the fact that baseball's on corporate overload.

I will only mention the Schaumburg Flyers in negative terms. Their pussy-cat owner "Little Richie" Ehrenreich stiffed me on a deal over football tickets about six years ago. Richie was just gung-ho to get our package in place. However, when game day arrived, when his check was due, little Rich was "bye-bye Richie." He left me a voice mail on a Sunday at 3:43 AM telling me he was jumping ship because his wife would be "angry with him." Suppose Ehrenreich had been Douglas MacArthur. You know what happens. America loses World War II to Japan, 5–4.

Book John McDonough, Mark Giangrerco, "Macho Man" Randy Savage, Bert Randolph Sugar, and Mike Ditka to speak. We're going to have to package some star appeal if we expect to do any kind of numbers.

Golden voice time. I want Wayne Larrivee back at ringside for Bulls' telecasts on WGN. Wayne Larrivee? Neil Funk? Oh, please. There's no comparison. It's like suggesting I'm Vin Scully.

I want the Hollywood crowd to reconvene. Kate Winslet didn't deserve an Oscar for her work in *The Reader*. She absolutely should have been given a gold statue for her spot-on role as a frustrated 1950s suburban housewife married to a frustrated husband (Leo DiCaprio) in *Revolutionary Road*. The only cinematic brilliance I saw in *The Reader* was Kate's gorgeous, heart-shaped ass.

Why is the NHL helpless? I'm watching NBC's warm-up for a New York Rangers game and the two talking clowns are standing in front of New York Knicks banners. Tell me that isn't big-time marketing. Don't sell skaters, sell Willis Reed. Plus, what is a "Pierre McGuire"?

Stop the music—White Sox homeboy scorer Bob Rosenberg just made a change. Bob has determined that Alexei Ramirez's third inning "E-5" should now be scored a triple and, what the hell, give Alexei three RBIs.

I'm glad you brought up the Pat Ryan obsession. If Chicago lands the 2016 Olympics, I have the over/under on hookers arriving from Las Vegas and Southern California at 1,237.

I have to appear in another major motion picture. Did you see Dennis Quaid and Rob Brown in *The Express*? Did you see me? My face time lasted about as long as the Chicago Shamrox.

I want to see Tiger Woods miss the cut at the Masters. I love Tiger, I just want to see how the hell CBS will fill air time on Saturday and Sunday without the greatest meal ticket this side of Michael Jordan.

I demand that the dummies in Springfield give racetracks the right to operate slot machines. The ponies aren't dead in this town—they're Jim Oberweis running for office. In case you've been busy every two years, Oberweis blows a bundle of his own "milk" dough running for office only to have voters throw him face-down in a dumpster.

I demand the day arrive—within a week—when AMC Movie Theatres or any goddamn theatre chain, put a "salary cap" on ticket prices.

I want the Cubs to understand that baseball in October is slightly more important than baseball in April.

> *I don't want any traditional music at my funeral. I want Len Kasper and Bob Brenly to tag team on "Gimme Shelter." That shall be followed by Ronnie Wickers chanting "Chet-woo...Chet-woo." After six "woos," tell Ronnie there's a joint just around the corner offering two-for-one popsicles.*

I want Virginia McCaskey to issue a statement telling us which of her kids, if any, work more than four hours a month. The average McCaskey kid has perfected the 40-hour year.

That's enough for now. I'll get back with you when I begin book two. Working title: *Clueless: The Life and Times of Todd Stroger*. Subtitle: "Always Say Yes to Daddy."

100

Film noir...cinema verite...the Coppock guide to **SPORTS MOVIES** *you must* **AVOID** *at all costs*

"What's the worst fight film of all time? Probably any film I've done."

—Bert Randolph Sugar, friend and boxing historian

All right, I'm dying to take the gloves off. Here's the assignment. Just how do we determine a list of absolutely miserable sports films? Pictures that are so bad they rank with busted plumbing like *Vanilla Sky* and *Eyes Wide Shut*.

Eyes, directed by the late, great Stanley Kubrick was especially galling. In fact, one shrink friend of my mind said he thought the flick "was Stanley's cinemagraphic wet dream." Despite all the naked broads, *Eyes* was about as sexy as visiting Home Depot. Maybe it was blessing that Stanley dropped dead before *Eyes* actually went into release.

Anyway, let's get to all-time cinematic sports clunkers.

10. **GRIDIRON GANG.** Just one more reason why The Rock should bail on Hollywood and rejoin the WWE Follies. Wait. Sorry, our hero now wishes to be referred to as Dwayne Johnson. This 2006 "Hindenburg over New Jersey" also features rapper Xzbit.

Go back to 2008. Vince McMahon almost knocked me out when he told me he could "see a day coming when The Rock will win an Oscar." My tote board has a different career path. I see The Rock doing infomercials for garage-door openers sometime before his fortieth birthday.

9. **JERRY MCGWIRE.** Boy, did I get the wrong messaage. I was anticipating a riveting film about the ugly world of Drew Rosenhaus. I had to settle for Cuba Gooding Jr.—what happened to him?—and "show me the money."

The nonpareil. The elixir. The single-greatest sports movie quote of all time:

"Who am I kidding? I ain't even in the guy's league...if I can go the distance, ya see, and that bell rings, ya know, and I'm still

standing, I'm gonna know for the first time in my life, ya see, that
I weren't just another bum from the neighborhood."
—Sly Stallone to Talia Shire in *Rocky*, the 1976 box office monster

Honorable mention:

"You lay off that pet shop dame. Women weaken legs."
—Burgess Meredith to Sly Stallone in *Rocky*

8. **ROCKY IV.** Subtitled: "Rocky, the Ghost of Mickey, and Paulie Spend Quality Time in Siberia before Rocky Fights Ivan Drago." Dolph Lundgren turns in a seismic performance, make that hopeless effort, as Drago, the commie heavyweight who looks like a billboard for steroids.

Brigitte Nielsen (there's a name from the outer limits) also had a role in the film as Drago's advisor; her only asset was her butt. Legend has it that Nielsen earned her role in grand Hollywood tradition. She was banging Stallone.

7. **ONE ON ONE.** Robby Benson looks so rail-thin and undernourished that he couldn't post up your seven-year-old daughter. "Lil Rob" plays a naïve basketball player at a college "factory." Benson also co-wrote this piece of swill.

6. **THE WATERBOY.** Skip the dominatrix. If you really feel the need to get whipped and verbally abused, try and sit through this Southern-friend hunk of garbage. Killer line: Ex-San Diego Chargers quarterback Dan Fouts exclaiming, "Bobby Boucher sure knocked the poop out of him." A movie designed to increase your level of Prozac.

5. **FIELD OF DREAMS.** Hello, research department? I walked out of the film and threw my Dots down in disgust when I saw "Shoeless" Joe Jackson, one of the greatest left-handed batters in baseball history, hitting right-handed.

Nuuummmbbbeeerrr two. The second-greatest quote in sports-flick history:

"He is great. Geez, that old fat man. Look at the way he moves, like
a dancer...and those fingers, them chubby fingers. And that stroke,
it's like he's, uh, like he's playing the violin."
—Paul Newman raving over Jackie Gleason
as "Minnesota Fats" in *The Hustler*

4. **TWO MINUTE WARNING.** Director John Frankenheimer won the "Lifetime Humiliation Award" for this Motel 6. A group of terrorists decide to hijack the Goodyear blimp and land it in the Los Angeles Coliseum during the Super Bowl.

Sideline man Jay Glazer says the blimp's arrival is a strong indication Dick Jauron will not be rehired by the Buffalo Bills. Glazer, as warm and fuzzy as a Phillips screwdriver, goes on to spend 12 minutes telling us how thrilled he is to have Terrell Owens' cell phone number.

3. **1978 CHICAGO BEARS HIGHLIGHT FILM.** Bob Avellini in his greatest role. Number 7 quarterbacks the Halasmen to a 7–9 season.

2. **THE FISH THAT SAVED PITTSBURGH.** Figure this one out. Following a player "walkout," the club owner conducts open tryouts for new talent. Here's where the plot reaches the Alfred Hitchcock level. All players must be Pisces for a very logical reason: the team's star player is a Pisces. Julius Erving was somehow talked into doing this impossible piece of crud.

1. **SEMI-PRO.** Will Ferrell at his absolute worst, joined by Woody Harrelson. Frankly, *Natural Born Killers* had more laughs.

All my love for the dear old red-white-and-blue ABA was absolutely shattered in a picture that should not be viewed by anyone under—or over the age—of 11.

Dishonorable Mention: *The Babe Ruth Story*. William Bendix makes the Babe look like he should be a doorman at a drag queen joint.

The Babe. Another disservice to George Herman Ruth. Babe, why does Hollywood fuck with you? You're the man who saved baseball after the 1919 "Black Sox Scandal." John Goodman plays the lead. I know Ruth was fat, but Goodman's gut is bigger than the Ferris wheel on Navy Pier.

THE WRAP

Over and out. Call the home and tell them to send the car for Coppock.

I'd like to thank the Academy, Clint Eastwood, and the wonderful people at MGM for making this all possible. Timeout. That's next year's speech.

It's time to lower the curtain, so I figured, what the hell, I'd ask myself about what's gone down since Mitch Rogatz and the guys at Triumph stuck their necks out and decided to have me write a book.

C.C.: What do you find most exciting about closing the book?

Coppock: Easy. Collecting the second half of my advance and making plans for my first appearance at Borders on State Street. Is Borders aware of that?

C.C.: Why didn't you dedicate the book to Jay Mariotti?

Coppock: It was a toss-up between Jay and former Governor Ryan. Frankly, if I were stuck in a foxhole with one bullet left, I'd rather have Ryan than Mariotti. Lonesome George, currently unavailable for dinner at Gibson's, has more credibility and far more honesty.

C.C.: Do you think you were too rough on Cubs Hall of Fame executive Crane Kenny?

Coppock: Crane will be fine. He'll just keep reminding us that after he invented baseball, he also created the safety razor and windshield wipers and was the driving force behind Led Zeppelin.

C.C.: Did the book cut into your workout time at the East Bank Club?

Coppock: Frankly, anybody who works out at EBC is losing valuable time that could be spent in the second-floor bar and grill.

C.C.: Do you hate the New York Yankees?

Coppock: No more than I dislike the Republican Party or paying valet parking rates at downtown restaurants. Twelve bucks to park at Ballo? That's armaggeddon.

C.C.: What's the biggest single disappointment of your career?

Coppock: The settlement I got from the bums at Channel 5 when they cut my legs off back in 1983. No kidding. They owed me about $800,000. The best we could do was 50 Gs. They had a pretty strong answer for all of our requests, "Fuck you. Take us to court."

C.C.: Didn't you work with Mark Giangreco during your Channel 5 days?

Coppock: Yes, he was a blast. The guy laughs like nobody else. I wish we could have worked together for 30 years instead of about 18 months. Did I mention that he also replaced me?

Warner Saunders was also part of our sports team at that time. Warner's grasp of minor sports—gum chewing and Monopoly—along with helpless writing skills was truly inspirational. Don't ask me how Warner achieved such remarkable success. I don't know, and I'll guarantee you Warner doesn't know either. Warner wrote the book on establishing cozy relationships with the people who hire and fire. If in danger, he's not the first guy you call.

C.C.: Do you have plans for another book?

Coppock: Yes. I don't want to give away the ranch, but the working title will probably be, *Is That You Out There, Matt Murton?*

C.C.: What's your all-time favorite interview?

Coppock: This goes back to the Stone Age. I interviewed Muhammad Ali a day or two before he left for Zaire to meet George Foreman. I'll never forget Ali telling me, "White America fears Elijah Muhammad."

C.C.: If you ran the Bears and decided to fire Lovie Smith, who would you hire?

Coppock: Anybody with a pulse and lips that actually move.

C.C.: Anything you want to say in conclusion?

Coppock: Three things. One, I had no idea what the phrase "word count" really meant until Don Gulbrandsen from Triumph told me I was at 78,000 words. Two, I set a modern Triumph record for illegal use of adverbs. Three, they just don't make sportscasting giants like WGN old-timers Bob Hillman or Sid Garcia anymore.

Over and out, I have an aerobics class to attend with Megan Mawike.

What was it Hendrix said? "I'll meet ya on the next [world] and don't be late."

ABOUT THE AUTHOR

Is there anybody out there more qualified to write the ultimate, intimate guide to the Chicago sports scene than Chet Coppock? He's been an integral part of the city's sporting fraternity since his schoolboy days. Through his father, Chet had the good fortune of meeting legends such as George Halas, Red Grange, Sid Luckman, along with the man who may have had more influence on Chet's future path than anybody else—Jack Brickhouse. It was no surprise that by age 17 Chet was broadcasting New Trier football and basketball games on the high school's radio station, WNTH, or that by age 22 he was hired as producer for the Milwaukee Bucks radio network. Soon, Chet was sharing the mic with, and getting to know, everybody who mattered in Chicago sports. Along the way, he won a large and loyal following—as well as an Emmy Award for his efforts.

Chet's resume is a litany of one highlight after another. Sports director for WISH-TV in Indianapolis; lead sportscaster for Chicago NBC affiliate WMAQ-TV; host of Cablevision's *NewSportsTalk*; and sports director at WMAQ radio were among his many high-profile gigs. It was at WMAQ that, in the 1980s, Chet revolutionized sports radio by launching *Coppock on Sports*, an in-depth, interview-driven vehicle that captivated listeners and spawned countless imitators. *Coppock on Sports* later moved to WLUP and after a few years in hiatus was revived for a six-year run on the Sporting News Radio Network.

One of the hardest-working people in broadcasting, Chet has lent his talent to a fascinating mix of endeavors. Among his exploits: national TV voice for Roller Derby; public address announcer for the Bears; ring announcer for World Wrestling Federation; co-host of talk shows featuring coaches Mike Ditka, Phil Jackson, and Doug Collins; Sunday columnist for the *Chicago Sun-Times*; and commercial announcer for numerous clients, most notably Wheaties (including national TV spots with the late Walter Payton) and Chevrolet—Chet and Michael Jordan were the longtime co-pitchmen for the Chicagoland and Northwest Indiana Chevrolet Dealers.

Chet has raised funds for numerous charities and served as state chairman for Indiana March of Dimes, Indiana Easter Seals, and the Illinois Smiles for Little City campaign.